The Great American
Depression Book of Fun

TEXT BY

John O'Dell

The Great American Depression Book of Fun

ART BY

Richard Loehle

1817

HARPER & ROW, PUBLISHERS, New York

Cambridge, Philadelphia, San Francisco, London, Mexico City, São Paulo, Sydney

Grateful acknowledgment is made for permission to reprint:

"Dust Can't Kill Me," words and music by Woody Guthrie. TRO—© Copyright 1960 & 1963 Ludlow Music, Inc., New York, N.Y. Used by permission.

"Jack Armstrong's Secret Whistle Code" reprinted by permission of General Mills, Inc. JACK ARMSTRONG is a trademark of General Mills, Inc.

"Ralston Straight Shooter Pledge of Allegiance" reprinted by permission of Ralston Purina Company.

"Shoot-Out at the Red-Horse Barn" originally appeared in The Reader's Digest.

FIRST EDITION

Designer: Helene Berinsky

Library of Congress Cataloging in Publication Data

O'Dell, John, 1924-
   The great American depression book of fun.
   (Harper colophon books ; CN/898)
   1. Toys. 2. Games. 3. United States—Social condi-
tions—1933–1945. I. Loehle, Richard. II. Title.
GV1218.5.O33 1981   649′.5′0973   81-47408
ISBN 0-06-090898-X (pbk.)   AACR2

81 82 83 84 85 10 9 8 7 6 5 4 3 2 1

I dedicate this book to all the young at heart regardless of age, especially Killer—the best villain a kid ever had.

—JOHN O'DELL

To Mr. Yarbrough, who showed me how to build a bateau.

—RICHARD LOEHLE

Contents

A Word from the Author

Hard times? Not for us kids. During the Great American Depression, we romped through an unending string of wondrous, carefree days which flowed like honey from one magical season into another. Fort Gibson, the small farming community in east-central Oklahoma where we lived, was still a bright, gleaming world for most of us, teeming with fun, excitement, and adventure.

The so-called business section of our town, hardly more than a wide spot in the road, had a bank, general store, drugstore, post office, one-pump gas station, and two streetlights. These downtown buildings, along with the church and the school, were ultramodern too, having both indoor plumbing and electricity. Most of the homes, though, scattered throughout the community, could not boast of such extravagant conveniences as yet.

We were a long way from being wealthy, but my friends and I thought we lived in castles—and far better than kings. Kitchen tables provided adequate food, warm fires crackled in stoves and fireplaces, presentable clothing adorned our backs, and a new pair of back-to-school shoes (which we hated) came our way each fall.

A child's weekly allowance (if we got one at all) was about a nickel, sometimes a dime. So instead of buying toys (outside of an occasional bag of marbles, a ball of kite string, or a top), we made our own, and spent this hard-to-come-by money for more luxurious things: candy, ice cream, and an occasional Saturday matinee movie over in the big city of Muskogee. Most of our homemade toys weren't nearly as good as the manufactured ones, but we pretended that they were. And by using our lively imaginations in playing with them, we were provided with countless hours of entertainment.

We cordially invite you now to step back a few years to spend the summer of 1934 with us. Come back to the time of smoky coal-oil lamps that burned night into delicious, shivering shadows; to a day when the wind was music, and people took time to hear its beautiful, ever-changing chords strumming over a field of corn or a persimmon grove, around the corner of a deserted shack, or through an old barn loft. Close your eyes. Listen to that wind sweep up the steep banks of a river, down a cold chimney. Come back to that moment, just before electricity, an expanding population, asphalt paving, and electronic toys transfigured rustic America forever. Look out the window. It's almost daylight. Hurry. Jump out of bed and hop into your playclothes, your overalls and flour-sack shirt. Run outdoors where you can actually smell a June morning. And it smells *good*. Kick off your shoes and squish the grass, wet with dew, between your toes. Doesn't that feel great?

Now ask your mother if you can come over and play with us. We'll show you how we made old-time toys, played fascinating games, and had thrilling adventures—and maybe you will experience (or happily remember) the best time of your life.

—John O'Dell

Acknowledgments

Many assisted in the writing of this book. Some of the contributions came from people I have never met and probably never will. I am grateful, nonetheless, to the readers of *The Reader's Digest* who responded so amiably to my article about Oklahoma kids and their rubber guns, and to Jeremy Dole whose acceptance of the article made this book possible.

Numerous others helped, too, and of these, I want especially to thank:

My wife Jean, the most encouraging and loving live-in typist any author could have; Paul Spera, friend and fellow ex-worker who can still whittle the best whimmy-diddle around; Relda Hale, Elizabeth Tucker and the staff of the Millington Public Library (Tennessee) whose research know-how was invaluable.

Warm appreciation to Carol Cohen, my understanding and fast-penciled editor who made my best effort even better; and Helen Moore, her capable assistant.

Also, I am indebted to Nach Waxman, the first to recognize this book might be a lot of fun. And, then, there is Keith Korman—who didn't have any fun at all.

Gratitude beyond measure goes to relatives, old friends and new acquaintances in Oklahoma, Tennessee and Arkansas who gave their time so willingly to help jog my memory.

—J. O'D.

To my wife who endured my reports of progress or setbacks in the making of this book, and to the friends who encouraged me with their enthusiasm and contributed ideas of their own—thanks.

—R. L.

Foreword

During the Great American Depression, most homemade toys were fairly easy to construct. But finding the materials was no simple chore. Once in a while you might have to search a whole day to come up with a suitable board to fashion a toy rubber gun that wouldn't take thirty minutes to make. A reasonably straight board, as long as your arm and free of knotholes, dry rot, or termite damage, was worth its weight in gold to a youthful Depression-era toy maker. To buy lumber from the lumberyard to make toys was unheard of. A person would have to be either rich or crazy or both to spend a dime on a 2-by-4 pine stud just to use for toys, when bread cost a nickel a loaf and hundreds of men in CCC camps considered themselves fortunate to be working for wages of a dollar a day.

Tin cans, too, were in short supply as all soft drinks and beer came in bottles. (FDR had repealed prohibition.) The empties were worth a penny when returned. The major proportion of vegetables and fruits were home-canned in Mason jars. Needless to say, a litter problem did not exist in most rural communities. A tin can just lying there alongside the road, shining in the sun, was a real find, better than buried treasure. And to stumble upon an old discarded broom- or mopstick, or a piece of leather harness, was a truly remarkably lucky discovery. A bonanza!

This scarcity in toy-building materials frequently resulted in adults being confronted with mysteries so baffling they would put Agatha Christie to shame:

• "I can't for the life of me figure out what happened to those tin cans I was saving for begonia pots. . . ."

• "I'd swear I left some clothespins out here on the line yesterday. . . ."

• "You know those old brogans I was gonna give to Grandpa? Well, somebody cut out the tongues!"

• "I went out to fix that loose board on the back gate, and the danged thing was gone. . . . No, not the gate! The danged board!"

Fortunately, though, some free (or nearly free) materials were usually in ample supply for young toy makers. There was plenty of baling wire, rusty nails, hog rings, and wind-ripped shingles. Buttons and sewing-thread spools were readily available, as most mothers made the bulk of family clothing. If you just chanced to drop in on a big, bustling, gossipy quilting bee, you could have a pocketful of spools in nothing flat. The rubber market (located in the tall weeds behind the gas station) was virtually saturated with old multipatched inner tubes and ruptured tires. The ungraded roads were deep-rutted and potholed and took their toll on the older automobiles' rubber, which wasn't particularly durable even when new. It was almost impossible to drive 20 miles without having at least one flat.

Today, of course, inner tubes are made of long-lasting synthetic materials, not real rubber. And bands cut from them will not stretch sufficiently to use for slingshots or rubber-gun ammunition. They are totally unsuitable for toy making. Many of the toys described in this book cannot be made the way they were then, as the materials are no longer available. For example, sewing-thread spools are now made of plastic (the wooden ones are becoming collectors' items). Cork-lined bottle caps have vanished from the scene, and tin cans are being replaced with those made of aluminum or plastic. Most buttons and beads are plastic, not glass. And boxwood yardsticks, wood shingles, cotton string, wood barrels, and wagon wheels have gone the way of glass milk bottles and white-oak butter churns.

Five decades ago most people did not assume there was such a thing as a safe toy. Parents did not rely on toy manufacturers to warn them about the dangers, misuse, or for what age group a certain toy was designed, as toys then did not come packaged with this information. Realizing that children simply did not always play with a toy the way it was intended to be played with, responsible adults used common sense, supervision, and old-fashioned discipline (sometimes referred to as "a dose of peach-tree tea" or "hickory-stick learning") to teach youngsters the righteous ways of playing safely.

Some of the homemade toys described in this book that children played with in the '30s were dangerous without proper care and adequate supervision. Therefore, it is not recommended by author, artist, or publishers that children today make the toys or play the games the way it was done nearly a half century ago. The sole objective of this book is to elicit nostalgia and fun. No other purpose is intended.

A Word from the Artist

John O'Dell and I shared a childhood, though we never met and lived miles apart. I grew up in Georgia, he in Oklahoma, but we shared the toys and games, stories and myths, and attitudes and do-it-yourself skills that were a universal of that period.

Now the world has shrunk and Atlanta is a few hours or an electronically assisted voice from Chicago or New York, Tennessee is just over the hill, and way back then seems to be only yesterday. And so we are neighbors and it is possible to rebuild that past together, the past of Oklahoma and Georgia childhoods and all points between.

As the child is the father to the man, we are well led, and it is a fine, fine adventure.

—RICHARD LOEHLE

The Great American
Depression Book of Fun

1

Rubber Guns and Cowboys

Toy Guns in America

It is reasonable to assume that toy guns in America have been in existence practically as long as the real ones. Children have always emulated their elders, and replicas of adult objects have always been popular toys. Children are taught that the Pilgrim Fathers used a blunderbuss to put their very first Thanksgiving turkey on the table, that muskets in the hands of revolutionaries won our independence, and that the West was tamed with a Colt six-shooter. Historical luminaries such as Davy Crockett, Bat Masterson, Wyatt Earp, Daniel Boone, William Cody, Annie Oakley, and Melvin Purvis are closely linked with guns in the public mind. So there is little wonder that young Americans have always loved playing with toy ones.

Until the late nineteenth century, toy guns were manufactured from wood or lead and wouldn't make a realistic firing noise. The cap pistol became popular in the late 1920s, however, giving a child a toy that not only had the weight and feel of a real gun but made a loud bang as well. The small percussion caps, spaced on rolls of pink paper, added even more realism to the "bang" by giving off smoke and the smell of gunpowder.

During the '30s, cap pistols became so popular that some midwestern theater owners were forced to make the young gunslingers check theirs at the door before being admitted to the Saturday matinee if a cowboy movie was playing. This policy was put into effect because the enthusiastic gun-toting audience was inclined to give the good guys a helping hand against the "baddies," filling the theater not only with noise but with so much cap-pistol smoke that it became difficult to see the screen.

Toy rubber guns were so named because they shot rubber bands cut from automobile-tire inner tubes for ammunition. Also known as "rubber-band guns" they were, undoubtedly, the most popular homemade toys during the Depression. There was little or no anti-gun sentiment in our society then. This was, after all, the heyday of the cowboy movie, and western novels, pulp magazines, and even western comic books were at their peak. Because the heroes of these were totally good, the villains totally bad, and the heroes always won, it was acceptable for children to take up their toy rubber guns and to re-enact the fatalities of good versus evil; we kids played "dead-and-out" rubber-gun games without our parents' giving it a second thought.

Rubber guns were ideal toy guns for a number of reasons: They were easy to make and reasonably accurate at close range, the ammunition was cheap and reusable, and adults knew they were relatively safe. Unlike BB guns, they wouldn't inflict serious injuries on a person—or kill birds or small animals. This did not mean, however, that children never got hurt playing with rubber guns. (Some kids were so accident-prone, they could get hurt just shelling black-eyed peas.) Mostly, though, we could square off and shoot one another all day with rubber bands and, come sundown, have only a few red welts to show for it— unless, of course, the villain got the hero up a tree and out onto a skinny limb that wouldn't support his weight.

To make rubber-gun pistols, a saw and pocketknife were the only tools needed. Of course, using sandpaper or a wood rasp added a nice smooth finish to the wood. Softwood such as pine or fir was easier to saw and sandpaper. But hardwood—oak, elm, hickory, maple—made a gun that was both durable and attractive.

Before the start of rubber-gun season, my ten-year-old friends and I would start our search in earnest for wood appropriate for making rubber guns. We'd hop a ride in the back of the ice truck and chomp on ice all the way over to Mr. Buford's place. He was constantly repairing his dilapidated old outbuildings, especially in the spring when he was feeling spry. If we caught him in a generous mood, he was usually good for a couple of scrap boards—if he had any left over. It really wasn't all that far over to his place. One could walk it in twenty minutes from downtown, but the ice truck took the long way round.

Shoot-Out at the Red-Horse Barn

As far as Forrest Youngblood and I knew, the barn had always been there, leaning precariously against a large sweet-gum tree in the pasture that separated my house from the railroad tracks. The weathered, silvery gray, board-and-batten siding sagged and warped in petrified-wood protest against the elements and time. The pitifully small clusters of hand-split cedar shingles remaining on the skeletal roof pointed brittle fingers at the Oklahoma sky. On the gable above the loft door, a faded red-painted image of a prancing horse was vaguely perceptible:

My best friend, Frosty (for Forrest), frequently boasted he could repaint the horse, but we never could find a ladder tall enough. When I offered to hold him by the heels from the roof (accessible from the tree), he suggested that hanging upside down caused his nose to run and would hinder him from doing his best work. Frosty was an accomplished fifth-grade artist, no doubt about it. He could draw the profiles of Mickey Mouse and Dick Tracy—where you could really tell it was Mickey Mouse and Dick Tracy—always in that order, and always the same size.

One of the barn's massive black-locust doors was weather-welded shut; the other swayed on rusty hinges. When the persistent southwest wind of summer swept over the Grand River bluff and caught the door just right, we kids in Fort Gibson would swear that folks could hear the screeching hinges all the way over in Muskogee, twelve miles away. Sometimes in the middle of the night I would hear my father tell my mother, "If those kids don't oil those hinges, I'll kill 'em!"

We promised to but never did, because on stormy days when we played haunted house in our barn, the eerie, tooth-on-edge squeals would put goose bumps on us something awful.

The barn also was our fortress, castle, or pirate ship, our Last Chance Saloon—or whatever our ten-year-old imaginations desired.

Frosty was my nearest neighbor and my idol. A foot taller and eight months older than I, he could run and jump like a deer and do an earsplitting war whoop like the Cherokee Indian he was. Adoringly, I hung on his every word and deed; secretly, I wished we were brothers. On Fridays, I ate supper at Frosty's house, or he at mine. He loved my mother's chicken and dumplings, and Mrs. Youngblood's chili was so good and peppery hot, it made my eyes water.

During the school year Frosty and I had the barn pretty much to ourselves, but

Cowboy Heroes

When he galloped onto the screen astride a spirited horse, his fancy six-shooters flashing in the sunlight, he was identified immediately by millions of American kids. He was the cowboy hero!

His credentials did not include superhuman strength, extrasensory perception, or telekinetic powers. And his head—which he protected from the elements by wearing a peaked white ten-gallon hat—did not harbor an intellect equivalent to that of superior beings from outer space. His heroic status was in no way inhibited or complicated by any psychological scars, or by economic or social pressures. He was simply a hard-riding, fast-drawing, straight-shooting cowboy, who championed the cause of the downtrodden poor, or the honest rich, against the contemptible evildoers of the world.

For two hours or more on Saturday afternoon in practically every movie theater from coast to coast, the cowboy hero waged his battle of good over evil. Oblivious to the roars and excited screams of popcorn-munching, candy-chewing kids, he would either whip the despicable villain, shoot him, or throw him in jail, depending on his degree of criminal wickedness. But, alas, this does not mean that the hero always came out unscathed. Victorious, yes, but not unharmed. He paid for his good deeds with lacerations, bruises, concussions, gunshot wounds, knife stabs, and assorted fractures. But you never had any doubt about the kind of stuff this guy was made of. He'd always say, "Ain't nothin'... just a scratch. Lemme up. . . . I gotta see to my horse."

Though the lines of his face showed hardened determination, and his metallic eyes glinted menacingly like twin bores on a shotgun, he was the epitome of homespun gallantry: polite, congenial, quick to display a warm smile. Never a naughty word passed his lips, and he chivalrously tipped his hat to ladies and said, "Ma'am." He didn't chew, smoke, or drink anything stronger than sarsaparilla. Old folks cherished his heartfelt respect. His affection for his horse was irrefutable, and not once in over a decade did he ever kick at a dog.

Through it all, reel after reel of bedlam and mayhem, the kid down in the front row knew the violence was only make-believe. The wounds were "playlike"; the knife blades that inflicted them were rubber; the bullets were blanks—all phony. The kid's cowboy hero, however, was real enough, for sure, and in a week's time would return to the screen, old wounds healed good as new. And the very villains who had gone to their just rewards time and again were back in the same saloon, drinking the same red-eye, hissing in the same voice, "You and Bart cover me from the balcony. When he comes through them doors, we'll give him a taste o' lead. . . ."

Perhaps the greatest cowboy hero of them all was Tom Mix. He and his Wonder Horse Tony (five horses in twenty-five years) held young moviegoers captivated through 180 feature films for more than two decades. According to Fox Studio press releases during the silent-film days of the '20s, Tom Mix was the most authentic cowboy hero ever to hit the movie industry. He had fought in the Philippines during the Spanish-American War, the Boxer Rebellion in China, and the Boer War in Africa. Between wars he worked as a Texas Ranger, a sheriff, a U.S. Deputy Marshal, and a champion rodeo star.

Unlike William S. Hart and other silent-film stars who portrayed the cowboy hero as a humorless, hard-drinking loner, Mix created the first clean-cut cowboy—the sometimes funny, carefree teetotaler, who would only go into a saloon for one purpose: to flush out the baddies. "I want my pictures to be clean and wholesome," Tom explained earnestly, "so parents won't object to letting their children see me on the screen." And all his loyal fans believed his every word. What they didn't know, however, was that offscreen each of his luxurious automobiles (equipped with large steer horns on the radiator caps) contained a lavish, well-stocked bar that would equal any popular "waterin' hole" in Los Angeles.

In public life he wore glamorous white or pastel-colored hand-tailored western outfits, magnificent hand-tooled boots, belts and holsters studded with

when summer recess started, our ownership was constantly threatened. At least once a week, during the peak of rubber-gun season, we had to defend it against takeover by a gang of owlhooters who called themselves the Red River Renegades. Ofttimes we were outnumbered, and even though we fought valiantly, the barn would fall into their dastardly hands. But, chances were, the following week would find us the victorious occupants once again.

The Renegades were nicknamed Sticker, Kong, Whetstone, and Killer. Killer (Carl Peterson) was the leader of this bunch of cutthroats, and we were half afraid of him. Killer wasn't any bigger than Frosty, but he had a tough reputation. Without even flinching, he could crack open scaly-bark nuts with his back teeth—and pop all the knuckles on his right hand three times in a row before they stopped making any noise. Miss Bowen, our teacher, was hard of hearing and always thought the cracking sounds were coming from the lumber mill down at the river.

In our eyes, the Renegades were "rich kids." They lived in the big stone houses on the hill, part of the fort complex used as federal officers' quarters during the Civil War. Flaunting his wealth, Killer sported an expensive cream-colored Hopalong Cas-

HOW DO YOU LOAD A RUBBER-GUN? VERY CAREFULLY

sidy hat and wore, low on his hips, a brace of the most beautiful rubber guns you've ever seen—made of bowdarc wood, hand carved and handsomely checkered.

My guns were sawed from pine and so warped they would practically shoot around corners. Frosty's weren't much better, except he'd rubbed them with black Shinola to create a menacing appearance.

Killer's guns were truly grand, but his Hopalong Cassidy hat was something else. I wanted one in the worst way, but they were out of my financial reach ($1.25 at Kress's). Such a hat, I figured, would do much to improve my image, because an earlier bout with polio had earned me the nickname "Hoppy." I had a sensational name and a limp just like my favorite western hero, Hopalong Cassidy. One day at recess, in a weak moment, I offered Killer a swap of my superb collection of buckeyes for his hat. I discovered that he was not a connoisseur of *really* fine things because he just glared at me from underneath his magnificent tawny brim and cracked another scaly-bark.

The first big shoot-out in the summer of 1934 took place on the second Saturday of school vacation. On the preceding Friday afternoon, the war clouds had gathered. Elated with the feeling that summer would be a million years long, Frosty and I were playing in the barn when Killer and Kong entered. The short fat Kong tried to look mean while he sucked on a candy cigarette. The tall slim Killer, with hat pulled down low on his forehead, *did* look mean. He patted the checkered handles on his guns and said, "We aim to take over the Red-Horse come daybreak."

Frosty pigeon-toed over to look Killer square in the face. He squinted his coal-black eyes and said calmly, "Make it after sunrise. It's against Indian religion to fight at night." Translated, this meant he had to do all his chores before he could leave the house Saturday morning.

The war lance was set and broken.

After supper at Frosty's house we planned our strategy. Frosty said he didn't like the odds of four against two, and maybe we should hire a couple of mercenaries. Actually, those weren't his words. What he said was, "Let's see if we can bribe Waldo."

Waldo, who lived up the dirt road from my house, was about two years older than we were. Sometimes he helped his father at the lumber mill; therefore he had real muscles, not just stringy calf ropes like ours. He was a good man to have on your side. With only two hours of recruiting time remaining before dark (parent law de-

diamonds, and silver-plated pistols with inlaid pearl grips. He lived in one of the most elegant mansions in Hollywood. His young followers loved his public image as much as his screen image. It was odd, indeed, that during the decade when the country was going to the poorhouse, Mix could appear so much the spendthrift dandy and still draw the respect and awe of cowboy fans.

Throughout his film career, Tom Mix went out of his way to include spectacular riding sequences and rope-twirling episodes in his adventures, whereas rival Bill Hart's films avoided stunt work and fancy tricks. Tom's superb handling of horse and rope had little or nothing to do with the plots and added not a whit to the story. He reasoned, though, that his movies appealed mostly to kids, and they preferred action over logic. Also, he felt that audiences were bored, as he was, with slow-moving, realistic films. They came to movies for entertainment, to escape the hard realism of everyday life.

In 1933, Tom Mix movie fans were joined by millions of radio listeners who could now hear his "Code-of-the-West" credo of victory: "Reach for the sky! Lawbreakers always lose! Straight Shooters always win! It pays to shoot straight!"

Young cowboys thrilled to hear their favorite hero's voice coming into their living room. Naturally, when he recommended that Straight Shooters eat Ralston cereal because it was good for them, they hastened to do just that. And when Tom said that a few Ralston box tops could bring treasures like Straight Shooter whistle rings, spurs, pocketknives, flashlights, or a genuine Tom Mix six-shooter, even a branding iron (an ink pad with a stamp that printed TM), what real Straight Shooter kid in America could resist?

When Tom Mix departed for that "big ranch in the sky" in 1940, he left behind an international following of loyal fans that numbered in the millions. In Lisbon, Portugal, the Tom Mix Fan Club gave up all movies for two weeks as a sign of mourning. Throughout America, kids sadly and solemnly remembered the Ralston Straight Shooter Pledge of Allegiance:

To take the pledge, give the Straight Shooter's salute and in the presence of your mother or father read it out loud. Then sign your name at the bottom. Be sure to read the pledge carefully and thoroughly—understand it before you take it.

"As a loyal and faithful follower of Tom Mix, I pledge allegiance to his Ralston Straight Shooters and promise to obey, to the best of my ability, the following rules:

"1. I promise to shoot straight with my parents by obeying my father and mother and by eating the food they want me to eat.

"2. I promise to shoot straight with my friends by telling the truth always, by being fair and square at work and play, by trying always to win, and by being a good loser if I lose.

"3. I promise to shoot straight with myself, by always striving to beat my best, by keeping my mind keen and alert, and my body strong and healthy.

"4. I promise to shoot straight with Tom Mix by eating at least three bowls of Ralston every week,

manded we be in our own yards by then), I hung sidesaddle on the bar of Frosty's ancient bike while he pumped us furiously up the rutted road to Waldo's house. But Waldo, it turned out, had to help his dad at the mill all day Saturday.

A stop at Kenneth Parker's house proved futile, too. He was going to Muskogee. We hurried off to see Laughing Pete Fulbright. (He was called Laughing Pete because he laughed all the time—even when he was getting paddled at school.) In his part of town we had better luck. We hired on Pete and two others: Eskimo, Pete's cousin, who spent his 10-cents-a-week allowance on Eskimo Pies; and Bluegill Turner, the only kid I've ever known brave enough to bait his own hook with live catalpa worms.

Our mercenaries' double guarantee to show up at the barn early, armed to the teeth, cost us dearly: twenty unchipped marbles, two Big Little Books, and a cross-our-heart promise of one Eskimo Pie the next time we went down to the drugstore, where my father worked as a pharmacist.

Later, in Mr. Youngblood's toolshed, satisfied that our well-paid army would be a match for Killer's Renegades, we prepared fresh ammunition. Frosty cut bands from old multipatched inner tubes while I knotted them into figure-eight-shaped double zingers.

We were worried, knowing that Killer would cheat, as always, especially on Rule 1. The three rules for rubber guns, Oklahoma style, were as follows:

1. When a fighter receives a torso or head shot from the rubber-band ammunition, he is "dead-and-out" on the spot. After a few moans, he is to lie still and not utter a word, either of warning or encouragement.

2. A hand/arm or foot/leg hit constitutes a "winging," and the fighter may continue the battle. But he is on scout's honor not to use the wounded limb for walking, running, loading, or shooting.

3. No one may be granted "King's X." This age-old finger-crossed appeal for a temporary time out is definitely waived. The *only* exception to this rule is the parent command, "If you don't come home this instant, I'll skin you alive!"

While we worked, Frosty came up with a diabolical scheme that would prove when Killer was *really* dead-and-out. He dipped a double zinger into a can of creosote, then wrapped it in a piece of oilcloth to preserve its tarlike potency. "This one's got Killer's name on it," he said. Delicious shivers started up my backbone and played there right till bedtime. Born gunslinger that I was, I slept like a log.

Day broke quietly over the Red-Horse Barn. But not for long. Suddenly the serenity of Muskogee County was rent with war whoops, and the screams of the wounded and near-dead pierced the air.

On the opening skirmish, the battle went decidedly against us: Eskimo was dead-and-out, and I was winged on the kneecap. I managed to drag and barricade myself into the corner behind the poker table (an oak barrel with two staves missing), and was holding my own. Because I couldn't run as fast as the others, I was nearly always the first casualty. For one to survive any time at all in a rubber-gun fight, he had to be able to outdistance the opponents in order to reload his guns.

The tide turned in our favor when Frosty nailed both Whetstone and Sticker with his fantastic "act-like-you're-running-away, then-fall-to-the-ground, roll-over-three-times, and-let-'em-have-it-right-in-the-belly" shot.

I got off two remarkably fast shots at Killer when he came tearing through the front doors and out again. But my guns had warped some more during the night, or Killer was cheating again, because he yelled, "Yah! You just creased me!"

Good old Laughing Pete took care of Kong with the simple "act-like-you're-loadin'-when-it's-already-loaded" trick; then he took two fatal hits in the back from above—bushwhacked by Killer, who had sneaked up the tree and down into the loft.

Taking a steady uphill bead on the coward, I was squeezing off the shot when his scorching double zinger caught me square between the eyes. While they watered (like eating Mrs. Youngblood's chili), I saw a blurry Bluegill bite the dust. He rolled around and took on something terrible for five minutes—Bluegill always could die real good. I counted bodies. It was now one on one: Killer versus Frosty.

A graveyard silence fell over the barn. You could have heard a wheat straw drop. Killer moved slowly down the ladder, approached the front door, and reloaded his guns. Cautiously, he peeked outside, then whirled around as Frosty jumped catlike from the loft to land a foot or two from my body. His hands were smeared with creosote. He was loaded for bear!

The antagonists inched toward each other.

"This barn ain't big enough for both of us," Killer snarled. Then, moving faster than the eye could follow, his carved guns came up—and like the sound of the whisper of death, they belched a pair of double zingers at Frosty.

But Frosty wasn't there. At the last split second he rolled to his left and fired from

because I know that Ralston, the straight shooter's cereal, will keep me strong and healthy and make me a better Straight Shooter all around."

(Signature)

Through the Depression years Tom Mix and other cowboy heroes kindled and fulfilled the American dream. Whenever they rode off into the sunset, they left behind a feeling of all's well. In the hearts and imaginations of the nation, the cowboy hero would never vanish entirely. He would survive to return, again, and again . . . forever.

Rubber-Gun Safety

Even though rubber guns ordinarily didn't shoot hard enough to hurt anyone, we played with caution. *The first rule of safety*, of course, was never to shoot anyone deliberately in the face. Only the most villainous kids did this. The long-barreled guns such as rifles, machine guns, and cannons which are described in Section 4 naturally shot harder than pistols. This first rule of safety went *double* for *them*.

Another important precautionary measure was to be sure the gun was loaded properly. (If the rubber-band load isn't fitted securely into the scoop-shaped notch on the muzzle end of the barrel, it can slip off while you're aiming and slap you in the face.)

It's wise, in any event, to wear eye protection while playing with rubber guns. Back in the days when rubber-gun battles were the favorite sport of young cowboys, the parents of professional rubber-gun gunslingers like us knew we could handle ourselves in a skirmish without getting hurt. So they didn't insist that we wear eye protectors. But, when amateurs (little kids or girls) participated in a shoot-out, they

BATTLE VISOR

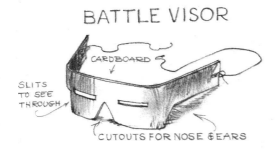

CARDBOARD

SLITS TO SEE THROUGH

CUTOUTS FOR NOSE & EARS

sometimes wore homemade cardboard battle visors or some other form of eye protection.

One of my playmates, a nine-year-old semi-professional, wore his Jack Oakie aviator cap for protection. The celluloid goggles made his eyes look big and scary. In fact, he wore his aviator cap just about everywhere—even to bed. His mother made him take it off, though, in Sunday school and church.

For Halloween, some of the kids would turn their battle visors into grotesque masks by painting or pasting on evil-looking eyes and adding soda-straw fangs.

My best friend, Frosty Youngblood, would punch holes above the eye slits of his visor and insert either marshmallows or stuffed olives to give it a wild-eyed look. This way he figured he had an "ace-in-the-hole." If he didn't get any trick-or-treat candy, he could always eat the eyes.

his famous prone position. Killer's cream-colored hat spun off his head and fell at his feet. He looked at it, unbelieving. A black smudge of creosote desecrated the crown—proof of a fatal hit.

"You're dead-and-out, Killer," Frosty said softly and grinned at me.

"The barn is ours, Frosty," I said proudly and grinned back. But inside I knew that one battle doesn't win the war.

Many shoot-outs lay ahead.

BASIC PISTOL

From the old boards Mr. Buford gave us, we'd pick out one at least ½ inch thick, 5 inches wide, and from 6 to 18 inches long, depending on the length of barrel we wanted. Never mind if it contained a knothole or two. We'd use it anyhow and tell everyone the gun had once belonged to a member of the Hole-in-the-Wall Gang, which had a knothole as its trademark.

After selecting a board, we'd cut a pistol-shape pattern out of paper, place it on

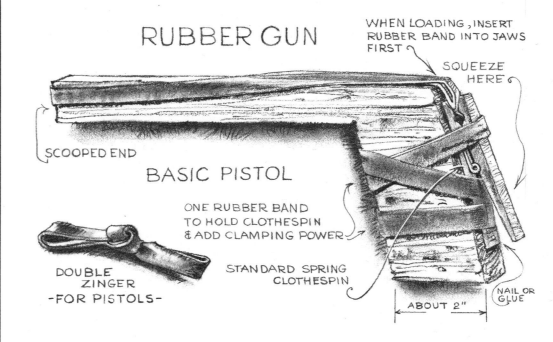

RUBBER GUN

WHEN LOADING, INSERT RUBBER BAND INTO JAWS FIRST

SQUEEZE HERE

SCOOPED END

BASIC PISTOL

ONE RUBBER BAND TO HOLD CLOTHESPIN & ADD CLAMPING POWER

STANDARD SPRING CLOTHESPIN

DOUBLE ZINGER -FOR PISTOLS-

NAIL OR GLUE

ABOUT 2"

the board, and draw around it with a pencil. Then we'd saw it out with a coping saw, taking it easy so as not to break our one-and-only blade. (This could cause a major setback in construction plans and also result in a financial catastrophe, as a coping-saw blade cost 8 cents.)

After the pistol was cut from the board, a scoop-shaped notch was cut or filed horizontally across the end of the barrel. It was important to do this on all rubber guns because it prevented the rubber-band ammunition, when loaded, from slipping off the end of the barrel. Then, if we could find some sandpaper, we'd sand off all rough edges and splinters. (A sharp splinter in the hand could slow down a fast draw quicker than anything.) Some kids would paint, shellac, or varnish their pistols, but mostly they were left unfinished.

Attaching the clothespin trigger to the pistol was always the last step of construction. It was glued or nailed against the rear end of the gun butt, jaws up, and wrapped in place with a rubber band cut from an inner tube. It was wrapped tightly with heavy tension over the jaws, catching the underneath portion of the clothespin too. The tension on the clothespin trigger had to be heavy enough to hold the rubber band in place when loaded but light enough so it could be squeezed with just one hand to fire.

The pistol was loaded by first inserting the rubber band into the clothespin's jaws, then stretching it out to and over the end of the barrel. The pistol was fired by squeezing the lower portion of the clothespin to open the jaws. All rubber-gun pistols, rifles, and shotguns that had clothespin triggers were loaded and fired in this manner. The maximum range of a basic pistol with a foot-long barrel was about 12 feet. The striking force was like the slap of a cow's tail. Cost? About one cent, if your mother wouldn't give you a clothespin.

FANCY PISTOL

In the mind of the young rubber-gun cowboy, fancy pistols were synonymous with fast-drawing, straight-shooting heroes. In books, comics, and films, the bigger the hero, the fancier his guns. If a guy packed a plain, ordinary-looking old gun, he was tagged a minor character—a ranch hand, a sidekick (the hero's best friend), or even a villain. Therefore, in make-believe Old West adventures, a kid's fancy gun was a symbol. It warned, "Walk easy, stranger. I'm a keen, lean hombre who's faster than greased lightning!"

Rubber-Gun Games

ANYTHING-GOES SHOOT-OUT
The greatest rubber-gun game of all. Any number could play, but the more the better. We played it whenever a lot of folks got together for a holiday picnic, cookout, or family reunion. We kids would even let the grown-ups participate if they'd promise to abide by the rules.

Unlike some of the other shoot-out games where only a single-shot pistol was used, in this game you could arm yourself to the teeth: two- and three-shooters, rifles, shotguns, machine guns, and sometimes even cannons.

First, we'd choose up sides, making them as even and fair as possible. Little kids, girls, and grown-ups were naturally classed as amateur rubber-gun gunslingers by ten-year-old expert shoot-out cowboys like us. It took about three of them to equal one professional. Using this three-to-one ratio, the talent on both sides was distributed equally. Of course, there was always the possibility that some sneaky girl or adult was a top gun but had kept it a well-guarded secret.

Next, we drew straws to decide which side would be the ambush*ers* and which one the ambush*ees*. When this was determined, the ambushers ran (on the count of *one*), hell-bent-for-leather, to establish their hideout (ambush) positions within the boundaries established beforehand.

They had exactly one minute (to the count of sixty) to dig in.

With the minute elapsed, the ambushees—who knew they were going to be ambushed—yelled, "Here we come, ready or not!" The shoot-out was on—and Lord help any unsuspecting dogs, cats, chickens, or innocent strangers that happened to get in the way.

As the game progressed, the three basic rules of rubber guns, Oklahoma style, as explained in "Shoot-Out at the Red-Horse Barn", were staunchly observed. The side with the most survivors was the winner. But the losing side didn't mind. This was a game where losing was equally as much fun as winning.

Rubber-gun shooting, like guitar playing or whittling, requires constant practice and true devotion if one is to excel in the art. Skilled professionals in any walk of life are made, not born. To be picked out in a crowd, one must first diligently work one's fingers to the bone. Rubber-gun cowboys who hungered for fame at their game practiced target shooting at least ten minutes a day (unless, of course, they were lured away to greener pastures—to play something else).

For a target we'd use anything that would go *clink*, *clank*, or *clunk*—or produce any manner of noise when hit. Our favorite target, however, was a spinning one that was simple to make from sticks and tin-can lids.

NOTE: *Sharp edges of tin-can lids were filed smooth and covered with tape. A cut finger could impair a cowboy's marksmanship.*

On the other hand, if a person was a compulsive gambler who couldn't control the urge to bet a few chipped marbles on the outcome of a target shoot, the lard-can target was our choice. It eliminated any arguments over whether or not the bull's-eye was hit. If the rubber band hit the target, it remained inside.

SPINNING TARGET

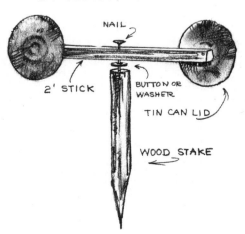

NAIL

2' STICK BUTTON OR WASHER

TIN CAN LID

WOOD STAKE

SPOOL OR BROOMSTICK CYLINDER SAWED IN HALF & NAILED OR GLUED INTO PLACE

FANCY PISTOL

ROUNDED BARREL

While our homemade toy guns may not have looked quite as fancy as Tom Mix's, Hopalong Cassidy's, or Ken Maynard's six-shooters, we put forth a pretty good effort. Carving initials in the butt was a start. A spool or a piece of broomstick (sawed in half and glued or nailed in place) made an authentic-looking cylinder. And a dowel stick glued to one side underneath the barrel hinted at a frontier Colt .45 look. Or a dummy piston ramrod underneath the barrel simulated a cap-and-ball Colt Dragoon—a fancy gun just like Buffalo Bill's. Fancy guns could evoke all sorts of praises, but the standard one was, "That's a fine-looking hogleg you got there, pardner."

TWO-SHOOTER

When a basic pistol was sawed out to have two barrels (over and under), with the lower barrel shortened about ½ inch, a two-shooter was in the works. Attaching a second clothespin trigger underneath for the short barrel finished it off. Rubber bands were wrapped around the clothespins' jaws for tension, the same as with the basic pistol.

THREE-SHOOTER

A three-shooter took a little more time to make, but it wasn't all that difficult. The two extra barrels nailed or screwed to each side of the basic pistol's barrel were about ½ inch shorter, and the scoop-shaped notches in the ends were cut vertically instead of horizontally. The clothespin triggers were positioned just about where the barrel and the butt joined.

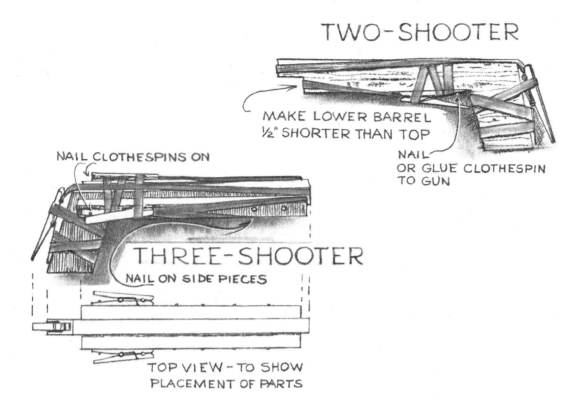

TWO-SHOOTER

MAKE LOWER BARREL
½" SHORTER THAN TOP

NAIL
OR GLUE CLOTHESPIN
TO GUN

NAIL CLOTHESPINS ON

THREE-SHOOTER

NAIL ON SIDE PIECES

TOP VIEW – TO SHOW
PLACEMENT OF PARTS

Two- and three-shooters were popular among kids who were not dexterous or swift enough to reload a single-shot pistol in the heat of a shoot-out. Or when hunting imaginary big game they came in mighty handy against a charging elephant or an enraged rhinoceros. For target practice a three-shooter couldn't be beat for seeing who could keep a spinning target spinning the longest.

BELT AND HOLSTER

An old pair of jeans or overalls was perfect for making a belt and holster. The waist-band was used for the belt, and the back pocket for the holster. To make them fancy to match their guns, kids (or their mothers) sewed on beads or buttons. A few hog rings attached close together not only served as a splendid decoration, but they would

MOCK DUEL

It takes two to have a duel. And common knowledge tells us that it is usually instigated when one person insults another by casting aspersions on his intellect, courage, or choice of companions (not necessarily just female ones). This verbal insult will inevitably contain an adjective pertaining to one of the primary colors— primarily *yellow*.

Back in the '30s if you felt like drumming up a rubber-gun duel, you'd try to pick a day that would lend the right atmosphere for it. Bright, warm days were out.

A good duel day was one that was gloomy, overcast, storm-threatening, and windy, and started out with your father saying, "Sure, I'll give you a nickel for a ball of kite string. Just as soon as you finish cleaning out the garage—the job you've been putting off for six weeks now!"

A garage job hanging over your head all morning like a dark wraith really puts you in a dueling mood. Consequently, to the first trigger-happy sidekick who crosses your path packing a gun with a barrel shorter than yours, you say, "Hey, didn't I see you playing jack rocks with some girls yesterday?"

While he glares at you openmouthed, you deliver the *coup de Jarnac:*

"Anybody who plays jacks—especially with *girls*— is a yellow-bellied sissy!"

That does it! He challenges you to a duel.

After the place and time is agreed on, you both rush off to find a second. (This is a buddy who will serve as a witness and give advice.) Finding a second is no easy task. Most kids had rather fight a duel than second it.

Finally, the stage is set. Seconds have been procured, and a crowd of your playmates have gathered (all three of them). Your second has offered his expert advice: "Take your sweet easy time. This guy couldn't hit the side of a barn with the door closed!"

Now you and your opponent stand back to back. The rules are read aloud: "Take five paces. On the count of five, turn and fire. Each dueler gets only one

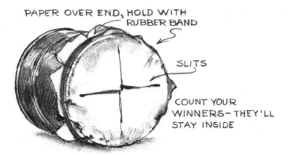

PAPER OVER END, HOLD WITH RUBBER BAND

SLITS

COUNT YOUR WINNERS—THEY'LL STAY INSIDE

LARD-CAN TARGET

shot, If the first one to shoot misses, he must stand and take his medicine. No dodging around in circles is allowed. And no running into the bushes over there."

With rubber gun in hand, held at shoulder level, pointing skyward, you take the final steps. The count of *five!* comes much sooner than you'd like. You turn.

Zap! A red double zinger hits you squarely in the armpit. The onlookers roar. Your opponent whoops with delight.

Your gun goes off and hits you on the big toe.

You muster your courage to show you're a good loser and say to your victorious pal:

"Hey, pardner! You yellow-bellied sissy! Wanna make it best two out of three?"

FAST DRAW

This was a game of progression. Each year it began on the opening day of rubber-gun season in June and continued until school commenced in the fall.

It started like this: All the young cowboys in town congregated to show off their newly made hardware. Fancy guns and holsters always grabbed the limelight of this show-and-tell gabfest, and invariably the bragging got hot and heavy as to who was the fastest fancy gun around.

"I'm so fast I can outdraw Tom Mix," one would say, going into a crouch.

"I can outdraw myself in the mirror," piped another. "Best two out of three."

"Pshaw! You ain't seen nothin' until you see me

clink together when you were running and jingle like cowboy spurs. We also adorned our holster sets with pop-bottle cap *conchas*. A bottle cap was attached to fabric by first prying out the cork liner of the cap. Then, holding the liner on the inside of the material with the bottle cap on the outside, the liner was pressed back into place, catching the cloth between the liner and the cap so that it would stick there. Bottle caps also made dandy badges. You could press one onto your shirt, draw on points with a piece of chalk, and have yourself a sheriff's star.

Using scraps of denim or canvas, one could design twin holsters with shoestring leg ties, a shoulder holster, or even a small hide-out holster for a derringer. It could be taped or tied to your calf under your pants leg for rubber-gun skirmishes. No one but you would know it was there.

BELT & HOLSTER

BUTTONS OR BOTTLE CAPS

WAISTBAND FROM OLD JEANS

BACK POCKET

HOG RINGS. —THEY JINGLE

CUT HOLE

SHOESTRING LEG TIE

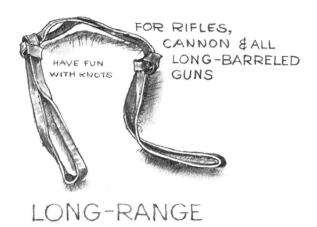

FOR RIFLES, CANNON & ALL LONG-BARRELED GUNS

HAVE FUN WITH KNOTS

LONG-RANGE STRINGER

AMMUNITION

DOUBLE ZINGERS. Rubber-gun ammunition cut from old inner tubes came in different calibers and velocities. For normal plinking, a standard rubber band was used. However, to give it more zing and accuracy the band was shortened by tying a loop knot in the center, giving the zinger a figure-eight shape.

LONG-RANGE STRINGERS. For long-barreled guns (rifles, machine guns, and cannons), two or more rubber bands were loop-knotted together so they would stretch from the trigger to the end of the barrel easily. Rubber guns that used long-range stringers naturally would shoot much farther than standard ones.

slap leather," another cowboy would boast. "Up against me, Tim McCoy looks slower than a girl with bursitis!"

"Oh, yeah? Well, let's see you outdraw me. Ready? . . . *Fill your hand!*"

Throughout these fast-draw square-offs, a lot of minor not-planned-for incidents would occur. Several holsters would be rendered unserviceable with rips or snags, or by being stomped to shreds ("The danged thing ain't made right to fit my gun!"). Some hair-trigger guns would discharge prematurely while still holstered, winging the owners with a stinging rubber band. Legs and bare feet suffered the most. And, unfortunately, terrorized bystanders received the brunt of any wild shots that happened to clear leather.

Nevertheless, on this day before the sun had set behind the barn, one jubilant cowboy emerged victorious. By "slick or trick" he had established himself as the fastest gun in town. He swaggered home confident, elated, full of the stuff top guns are full of. But the summer was young, and worse lay ahead.

He was a marked man.

From daylight to dark, weekdays or Sunday, he was the target for every rubber-gun-happy kid from Main Street to Sudden Canyon. Wherever he went his reputation followed, and a dozen times a day he was called out to defend it . . . which he did, magnificently. Sooner or later, though, along would come a kid a little bit younger, with reflexes not slowed by age, with eyes that had not grown dim from seeing too much. So, alas, the title changed hands, as it would do many times throughout the summer, until in the fall on the first day of school a steely-eyed, square-jawed kid would come a-saunterin' across the playground, feeling half naked without his rubber gun and holster (rubber guns were forbidden at school).

"That's the fastest gun in town," someone would whisper.

"Maybe," replied the new kid in school. "Maybe not."

2

Downhill Fun

Summer or winter, during the '30s, a hill attracted children the way a sweet-potato patch attracts hogs. Whenever a boy found himself on top of a hill, a powerful, uncontrollable urge came over him. An inner voice echoed, an impelling force commanded, "Fling something off this hill!"—which he invariably did with great exuberance. Oh, the sheer joy of seeing how far it would fly, sail, whiz, or drop! The object to be thrown could be any old thing: a stick, a rock, a piece of paper—or the raw turnip he was saving for an afternoon snack. The mysterious impulse that compelled a kid to throw something off a hill is close kin to the force that prompted him to kick a can, poke a finger into a freshly iced cake, slam a door, race with the moon—or look down into a dark well and holler, "Hello, anyone down there?"

The King of Standpipe Hill

We had the greatest hill to play on you've ever seen anywhere. Occupying nearly half of Mr. Buford's cow pasture, it was shaped like a plump, inverted ice-cream cone with the tip bit off, and it was so high that from the top you could see every house in town. On the flat quarter-acre summit stood the crumbling remains of a stone building with a concrete standpipe about 50 feet tall. None of us kids knew what the structure had been used for in the past, but nine-year-old See-Thru Thompson (his playclothes had more holes in them than Swiss cheese) said he bet the Indians used it to barbecue Oklahoma cowboys. Frosty bragged he was going to climb the pipe someday and tie an American flag on top so that airplanes wouldn't crash into it if any ever flew over Muskogee County.

The thing that made Standpipe Hill exceptionally great was the spiral red-clay road that wound around it, reminding us of a stripe on a barber pole. It wasn't a road, exactly; a goat trail would be more like it, cut precariously into the hillside, fairly wide in some places but narrow in others where it was washed out. During the ice and snow of winter, our homemade sleds and ski stools would fly like the wind down the winding trail. And in the summertime, when the red clay was sun-baked brick hard, the hill was marvelous for scootmobile racing. With the area isolated from pedestrians and what few cars there were in town, the only thing we had to worry about when we skidded off the road and over the side of the hill was crashing into Mr. Buford's hen house located at the bottom of the south side.

The reason Kong McAfee stayed the scootmobile-race king of the hill most of every summer was because he was so fat. Kong was the only 150-pound ten-year-old kid I've ever seen outside a carnival side show, and the bottom board of his scootmobile had to be a piece of hardwood instead of pine like ours. He could snap a pine bottom board like it was a toothpick. Also, he would wear out two sets of old skate wheels on his scootmobile before the summer was half over.

Kong remained scootmobile king sometimes weeks in a row, for he would invariably cheat at the starting gun. This sneaky move put him out front at the very top of the hill, enabling him to finish first, because he was so broad no one could pass him on the narrow road. One time Pete Fulbright, a real courageous kid, tried to get around Kong on Dead Man's Curve, which was the widest stretch. His scootmobile's left headlight hooked horns with Kong's rear bumper, flipped over on its side, and dragged poor Pete halfway down the road.

Pete's mom gave him the devil for bloodying up a brand-new pair of overalls. Also the scrapes on his elbow got infected later, so he sported a dandy iodine-soaked bandage for two weeks.

Kong's winning so many races was one thing; his winning all the valuable marbles we wagered on them was another. Our folks, had they known we bet for keepsies, would have boiled us in lard, or worse. In fact, I worried so much about their finding out that during church, whenever my Uncle Eura preached a sermon on "The Evils of Gambling," I'd swear he was looking directly at me the whole time. When I scrooched down in the pew and sneaked a look at Frosty, he'd be scrooched down too. Nevertheless, when my mother poked me sharply in the ribs to sit up straight, all I could think about was that Kong still had the fullest sugar sack of marbles in town. And about twenty-five of them were mine.

One afternoon, Pete, See-Thru, Eskimo, and I were shooting Ringtaw with what few doughies we had left when Frosty sauntered into the yard with a big grin on his face. He told us to round up all the betting marbles we could lay our hands on before race time Saturday afternoon because he had a foolproof plan that would remove the precious swirlies, glassies, aggies, milkies, and clearbells from Kong's sugar sack and return them to the previous owners. Actually, what he said was, "Somebody might get killed, but we're gonna get our marbles back!"

1934 PRICE LIST
(For living "high on the hog" in hard times)

TOYS

Scooter (two-wheel metal)	$2.50
Roller skates	1.50
Bicycle	10.95
Tricycle	3.98
Little red wagon	2.50
Sled	1.45
Cap pistol	.25
Caps (roll)	.02
Holster and belt (leather)	.75
BB air rifle	.79
Top (wood)	.05
Yo-yo (small)	.10
Kite (two-stick)	.10
Kite (box)	.15
Kite string (large ball)	.05
Model airplane kit (rubber-band powered)	.15
Glider (balsa wood)	.05
Basketball	1.00
Rubber ball	.03
Jacks and ball	.10
Fielder's glove and ball	1.25
Catcher's mitt	1.19
Bow and two arrows (suction cup)	.39
Paper doll cutout book	.25
Doll (china face)	1.50
Doll carriage	4.98

ENTERTAINMENT

Movie ticket (adult)	.25
(child under thirteen)	.10
Radio (cathedral model)	29.95
Comic book	.10
Big Little Book	.10
Magazine (slick)	.20
Magazine (pulp)	.10

EATING OUT

Plate lunch (meat, three vegetables, coffee/tea/milk, biscuits/corn bread, dessert)	.35
Hamburger	.10
Hot dog	.05
Soft drinks (12-oz. bottle)	.05
Candy (jumbo bar)	.05
Candy (bulk per lb.)	.10
Ice cream (double-dip cone)	.05
Ice cream soda (three scoops)	.10
Banana split (four scoops)	.15

GROCERIES

Sirloin steak (per lb.)	.29
Round steak (per lb.)	.26
Rib roast (per lb.)	.22
Bacon (per lb.)	.22
Ham (per lb.)	.31
Leg of lamb (per lb.)	.22
Chicken (per lb.)	.22
Pork chops (per lb.)	.20
Salmon (16-oz. can)	.19
Milk (per qt.)	.10
Butter (per lb.)	.28
Margarine (per lb.)	.13
Eggs (per doz.)	.29
Cheese (per lb.)	.24

My enthusiasm for Frosty's plan subsided a notch or two when I discovered the somebody he had referred to was me. His ingenious scheme for maybe getting me killed in order to get a few old marbles back was this: My scootmobile would be modified by highly skilled mechanics (Frosty and Eskimo) so that the hood, the widest part of the scooter, could be jettisoned on command. "We'll fix it so it'll fall off when you give it a good hard kick," Frosty said. "Then, with that big thing out of the way, all you'll have to do is stand sideways."

"And with you being so skinny," Eskimo piped, "you'll have room to squeeze right past old Kong on Dead Man's Curve!"

"Slick as a whistle," added See-Thru.

With bravery being on the very tail end of my long, many-attributes list, I told the guys that any other time I would be happy to oblige them, but come Saturday I would be occupied all day, as I had contracted with my father to deweed our vegetable garden, for which he would pay me the staggering sum of one nickel. This fib held up satisfactorily until shortly after supper, when Eskimo's dad sent him over to borrow our wheelbarrow. When Eskimo went out back to fetch it from the shed, he saw that our garden was as weed free as the church cemetery.

Most of the day Friday was spent in the secrecy of Frosty's garage, under tight security. While See-Thru stood lookout, Frosty and Eskimo disassembled my beautiful scootmobile into a million pieces. I wasn't asked to help, but I took it on myself to keep track of all the parts that hadn't been easy to come by, to make sure none turned up missing. These valuable accessories included: two No. 2 tomato-can headlights, polished mirror bright with Old Dutch Cleanser; one Washington State apple-box hood with the colorful labels still attached (I had picked up this beauty by sweeping out Mr. Boatwright's store); one red-painted chicken-wire grille; one broomstick handlebar with black rubber-band-wrapped grips; and one of the fanciest front bumpers in town, made from half of a slick-treaded Model-T Ford tire.

By the time we broke for lunch, the fifteen six-penny nails, with which I had so laboriously nailed the hood to the bottom board, had been pulled, their heads damaged beyond repair. That afternoon the hood was jury-rigged back into place with two flimsy baling-wire clamps. By 3 P.M. my altered scootmobile was ready for a trial run, so See-Thru let Mrs. Youngblood pass through the security net with a pitcher of pink lemonade.

After supper, under the protective blanket of dusk, we pushed my trick scootmobile down the road to the church sidewalk, the only stretch of concrete in town outside the business district. With the mechanics chirping instructions at me right along with the tree frogs, I pushed off down the gentle slope. I don't like to brag, but I could ride a scootmobile with the best of them, as long as I didn't try to push it with my limping leg. My good leg was just as good as anybody's. By the time I reached the dip in front of Uncle Eura's house, I was moving at a pretty good clip, with Eskimo and Frosty hard put to keep up. As preinstructed, I rared back to kick off the hood, when it suddenly fell off on its own. This unexpected maneuver leaving me handlebarless unnerved me for a moment, but I regained my fabulous balance immediately. Then, with all the grace and expertise of a ballet dancer, I turned sideways on the bottom board, extended my arms parallel to the ground, spread-eagled my legs just so—and hit a raised crack in the concrete.

I kept on going, but my scootmobile had never come to a more abrupt stop, not even when slamming into Mr. Buford's hen house. I'd never seen so many stars in my whole life.

"Perfect!", Frosty whooped, admiring the knot on my forehead that felt bigger than a cantaloupe. "Our marbles are in the bag!"

"Sensational!" said Eskimo, retrieving my scootmobile's hood, which now had one headlight bent something awful. "You should be in the circus!"

"Unbelievable!" See-Thru gasped in admiration.

During our feeble efforts to get home before the real stars came out, I told them that I frankly was not too pleased with the trial run. And seeing as how ideal conditions had contributed to such disastrous results, I didn't even dare think about trying the same thing coming down Standpipe Hill, much less actually doing it. What I honestly said was, "You're crazy as bedbugs if you think I'll ever try that stunt again!"

That night while waiting for my forehead to stop thumping so I could sleep, I imagined there was a yellow stripe down my back that lye soap wouldn't wash off.

Saturday afternoon, Standpipe Hill was crawling alive with kids. Even half the girls in town were there, sailing their whizzers, paper gliders, and whirligigs. There were so many objects flying around in the air, it looked like the sky was falling. Some of the younger kids kept trying to roll their roller hoops down the steep road. But the hoops would speed ahead of them and go clanging down the hillside and out into the cow pasture.

The pit crews sweated nervously in the scant shade of the standpipe where we readied our scootmobiles for the big race. Killer and the Renegades had painted a

Bread (20-oz. loaf)	.05
Coffee (per lb.)	.26
Sugar (per lb.)	.05
Rice (per lb.)	.06
Potatoes (per lb.)	.02
Tomatoes (16-oz. can)	.09
Oranges (per doz.)	.27
Bananas (per lb.)	.07
Onions (per lb.)	.03
Cornflakes (8-oz. package)	.08
Oatmeal (lb. box)	.05

CLOTHING (*Children*)

Overalls	.49
Shirt	.25
Pants (dress, cotton)	.78
Cowboy outfit	3.00
Sailor suit and hat	1.75
Dress (cotton)	.75
Shoes (leather)	2.00

CLOTHING (*Women*)

Cloth coat	6.98
Silk stockings	.69
Shoes (leather)	1.79

CLOTHING (*Men*)

Wool suit	10.50
Trousers	2.00
Shirt	.47
Shoes (leather)	3.85
Necktie	.25

SERVICES

Office visit to physician	1.50
Filling in tooth	1.00
Extraction of tooth	.50
Man's haircut	.20
Shave with bay rum	.10
Lady's hairbob	.30
Child's Buster Brown haircut	.30

$49⁹⁵ Cash Price

THE IMPROVED "WASH KLEAN"

APPLIANCES

Electric coffee percolator	1.39
Vacuum cleaner	18.75
Electric washing machine	49.95
Electric portable sewing machine	24.95

AUTOMOBILES

Ford sedan	605.00
Pontiac coupé	585.00
Chrysler sedan	995.00
Dodge	595.00
Studebaker	840.00
Packard	2,150.00
Truck, half-ton pickup (Ford/Chevrolet)	650.00

TRAVEL

Oklahoma City to L.A. (round trip) Air	205.00
Rail	78.50
Bus	49.00

Travel by sea:
Tour of Europe (2
months, 11
countries)   500.00
Around the world
(85 days, 14
countries)   750.00

MISCELLANEOUS

Double-bed sheets   .67
Bath towel   .24
Soap (hand bar)   .02
Wool blanket   1.00
Linen tablecloth   1.00
Wool rug (9′ by 12′)   5.85

Razor blades (10)   .49
Alarm clock   2.00
Fountain pen   1.00
Desk typewriter   19.75
Kodak box brownie   2.50
Automobile tire   6.20
Gasoline (per gal.)   .18
Oak firewood (per
cord)   .50

REAL ESTATE

Average modern house in
city, six rooms, two-car
garage   2,800.00

mean-looking red skull and crossbones on Kong's machine that looked exactly like the poison warning on iodine bottles. In addition to this foreboding sign, I could swear Kong had put on another twenty pounds in three days. And it all seemed to be in the horizontal direction.

Along with us professionals, two girls had entered the race: Bobby Ann Smith and my red-haired cousin, Norma. Norma was tougher than a boot, but like most other eleven-year-old girls, she couldn't scootmobile worth a hoot. Also, she and Bobby Ann were too sissy to bet any marbles on the outcome. They just raced for the glory and to get in everyone else's way. They had their silly, pastel-painted scootmobiles all geegawed up, with flower cutouts stuck all over them.

Earlier, we high rollers had placed our bets. If I won (which I sorely doubted), Kong's sugar sack would be 85 marbles lighter. If I lost (which was a near certainty), our remaining combined doughie collection would add up to three rusty steelies and seven chippies.

Tension mounted as Chris Carson, an eleven-year-old ordnance genius, fired his homemade carbide cannon a couple of times to make sure the starting gun was in good working condition. As we lined up for the start, Frosty assured me that he had wired my hood on so it wouldn't fall off again without being kicked. I wanted to tell him that if it did, something else was going to be kicked, but I was too scared to talk.

I figured all along Kong had supersensitive ears; he could hear when the carbide gas had built up peak pressure in the cannon, thereby enabling him to scoot off a split second before the cork popped. Hoping to confuse him, I started banging around on my scootmobile, making all the noise I could legally get by with, but I stopped when Killer cracked a scaly-bark nut with his teeth and gave me a look that threatened to put me in the hospital. Kong scooted, the cannon boomed, the spectators roared, and we were off and running!

The track was dry and fast. Kong, in front as always, leaned over his hood like a big performing bear as Frosty ate dust in his ample shadow. I was a close third, behind Frosty, but didn't know who was fourth. I was too petrified to care.

Like the well-oiled machine it was, my scootmobile overtook Frosty easily. He hugged the inside lane and waved me around, grinning confidently. I zoomed past him to see that up ahead Kong, his tortured skate wheels plowing furrows in the hard clay up to their axles, was kicking up a cloud of red dust that would put a herd of stampeding cattle to shame.

When we hit the narrow approach to Dead Man's Curve, I put on my famous three-pump-spurt and came up so close behind Kong I could see the stitching in his sweaty overalls. The curve widened; the time had come. I kicked my hood; it didn't budge! I kicked it again . . . *hard*. It only moved over to one side—but to the *outward* side. There was still a chance, because Kong always stayed to the inside as close to the hill as possible. We careened into Dead Man's Curve. It was now or never!

With a final unbelievable burst of speed, I held my breath and went into my death-defying tightwire position. Facing Kong, I came alongside. I caught the startled look on his face when he saw me, just before the speeding blur of a pink-and-white scootmobile and streaming red hair shot between us.

Kong lost control, slammed into the side of the hill, ricocheted over, and hit me broadside. Off the road and down the hillside we went.

Kong and I finished in a dead heat against Mr. Buford's hen house.

All bets were null and void.

Sunday afternoon, down at my father's drugstore, Frosty, Pete, Eskimo, See-Thru, and I treated Norma to a double-dip ice-cream cone and a box of Cracker Jack. While we had her in a good mood, we told her we'd gladly give her 10 percent of all the marbles that she could win back for us from old Kong in next Saturday's scootmobile race. Norma said it wasn't nice to gamble, and she was thinking seriously about quitting racing, thus retiring her title of "The Queen of Standpipe Hill."

WHIRLIGIGS AND WHIZZERS

Children have come up with some utterly sensational toys for throwing off hilltops. A lard-can lid whizzer would sail like you couldn't imagine. The lids (the largest about 14 inches in diameter) were similar to canister lids and had no sharp edges or rims; however, the rims were sometimes stomped down to alleviate wind resistance. In the days before vegetable shortening became prevalent, cans of lard could be found in most rural kitchen pantries. Since the lard rendered from "hog killing" each fall seldom lasted a full year, additional lard had to be store-bought. It came in tin containers of several sizes; the largest, called a "lard stand," held 50 pounds. When not being whizzed off hilltops, the lids were sometimes used as cookie sheets and serving trays.

A whirligig was another flying toy. One made from a wooden prop and a sucker stick would go up, out, and away!—if the prop had been whittled to the same pitch on both ends and was balanced properly. It was airborne by twirling the stick fast between the palms and releasing it. Another type of whirligig was made by sticking chicken wing feathers into the end of a corncob. The cob was thrown high into the

WHIZZER

LARD-CAN LID

air, and as it fell downward the feathers acted like fletching on an arrow, making it spiral faster and faster. This fun game soon ended, however, for although it was simple, the toy wasn't terribly durable. After a few flights the cob lost most of its feathers, making it look as scraggly as the plucked chicken that had reluctantly provided them.

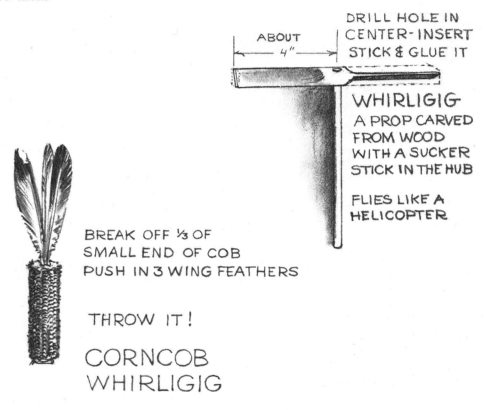

ABOUT
— 4" —

DRILL HOLE IN
CENTER-INSERT
STICK & GLUE IT

WHIRLIGIG
A PROP CARVED
FROM WOOD
WITH A SUCKER
STICK IN THE HUB

FLIES LIKE A
HELICOPTER

BREAK OFF ⅓ OF
SMALL END OF COB
PUSH IN 3 WING FEATHERS

THROW IT!

CORNCOB
WHIRLIGIG

PAPER AIRPLANES

Of course, folded paper airplanes were the best to fling off a hillside—and the least expensive. Each kid had his favorite and boasted that his design could fly higher and farther than anything with wings, even Wiley Post's airplane.

TAKE PA'S OLD
FELT HAT (ASK FIRST)

PUSH OUT
CROWN

CUT OFF BRIM

SCALLOP
BOTTOM

TURN UP,
ADD BUTTONS

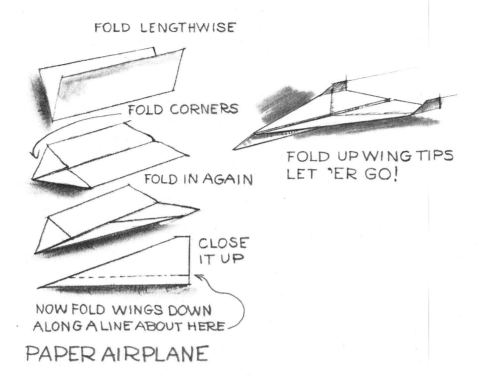

FOLD LENGTHWISE

FOLD CORNERS

FOLD IN AGAIN

FOLD UP WING TIPS
LET 'ER GO!

CLOSE
IT UP

NOW FOLD WINGS DOWN
ALONG A LINE ABOUT HERE

PAPER AIRPLANE

NOTE: *Observers on the ground watched whizzers, whirligigs, paper airplanes, and other flying toys with an eagle eye. Flying toys were always given ample space in which to fly and land.*

CARBIDE CANNON

A carbide cannon was a hilltop toy too. Somehow, it seemed to emit a louder boom when fired from a lofty position high up in the thinner atmosphere. Later, trying to find all the corks the cannon shot off the hill was much like an Easter-egg hunt. Calcium carbide, when mixed with water, formed the gas that produced our cannon's marvelous boom. If there was a hunter in the family, a kid could probably find a can of calcium carbide crystals on the storage shelf alongside the jug of coal oil. Calcium carbide gas was burned as fuel in the carbide lanterns (also used by miners) carried at night by possum and coon hunters.

CARBIDE CANNON

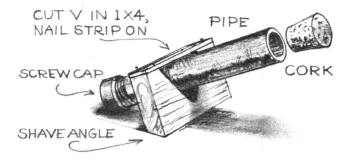

The barrel of the cannon was made from a length of ½-inch pipe about 12 inches long, threaded and capped on one end. Actually, a pipe of any diameter would work as long as one had a cork that fit snugly in the other end. The cannon was loaded by placing ½ teaspoon carbide crystals in the barrel and adding about 1 tablespoon water. Then the cork was pushed quickly and tightly in place. Stand back! In a few moments the gas pressure would blow the cork with a pop that sounded like a thundercrack to a kid's ears.

NOTE: *It was always a good idea for children to have adult supervision while playing with carbide-gas-operated toys. As carbide gas is highly inflammable, our parents cautioned us to be careful never to play with these toys around open fire or flame, to heed all the warnings on the carbide container, and to follow them unerringly.*

RAINMAKER

A wooden shingle's beveled shape was perfect for making a rainmaker, another toy which seemed to produce more racket when twirled from the top of a hill, and seemed to be more effective at heights. Frosty Youngblood's grandmother, who was reverently respected by all for her age and wisdom, avowed that the closer one could get to the clouds of heaven, the better the rainmaker would work. Children believed her; if they intermittently twirled it "fast and furious" over an extended period of time, sooner or later the hurricane noise it made would undoubtedly induce rain. Grandmother Youngblood was a very sage person. She also said, "If you can make it

Roller-Hoop Hockey

Five or six players on each side made this a highly competitive contest. Boys' matches rarely needed a referee. If there were any disagreements, the players just fought it out among themselves. But, if the match-up happened to be girls versus boys, for some reason the pace fiercened dramatically, and at least one forceful referee with a notably loud green-willow whistle was absolutely necessary.

For our hockey field we used the side lawn of the church because it contained only two trees for players to contend with, and the grass was mowed at least twice a month. The sidewalk in front of the church established the southern goal line; Mrs. Watkins's clothesline, the northern one. If a game was scheduled to fall on Mrs. Watkins's washday, the northern goal line would become an imaginary line, moved in a few feet. (Mrs. Watkins seemed especially grumpy on washdays and had a morbid aversion to hockey players, besides.)

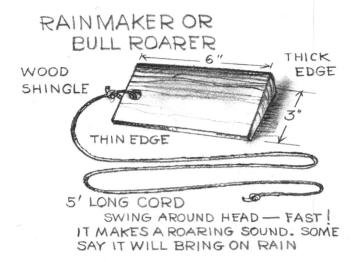

rain on the first day of the month, it will rain—or at least sprinkle a shower—fourteen more days during the same month."

NOTE: *Rainmaker strings can break and cause injuries. Bystanders always gave a kid who was trying to make it rain plenty of room to operate.*

ROLLER HOOPS

Hoops have been rolling down hills since ancient times, Lord knows—probably even before the wheel was invented. However, the American roller hoop, the small one widely favored by Depression-era kids, did come from wheels, or more precisely from wagon-wheel hubs. A discarded farm wagon wheel might provide as many as five metal hoops: one from the rim and four from the hub. The rim hoop was generally from 3 to 5 feet in diameter and ordinarily worn paper-thin. But the four bands ranging from 6 to 11 inches in diameter encircling the wooden hub were usually good as new. Constructed of heavy steel, these hub bands had a high degree of maneuverability—and the durability of a schoolmarm's paddle.

These hoops were rolled along by means of a "pusher." Hoop "pushers" or "rollers" varied according to the individual's taste or skill. A bent coat-hanger wire was the most commonly used pusher. Next in popularity came a stick with a short piece of wood nailed on the end to form a T. The deluxe pusher consisted of a stick with a half cylinder cut from a tin can nailed on the end of it. The deluxe pusher gave the hoop operator maximum control.

Metal bands from kegs and barrels, though somewhat flimsy, could be put into service as hoops too. These larger hoops, like the wagon-wheel rim, were propelled by slapping with hands or kicking with feet.

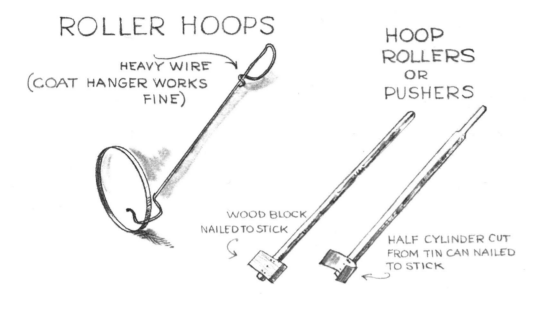

ROLLER HOOPS

HEAVY WIRE
(COAT HANGER WORKS
FINE)

HOOP
ROLLERS
OR
PUSHERS

WOOD BLOCK
NAILED TO STICK

HALF CYLINDER CUT
FROM TIN CAN NAILED
TO STICK

In rural America when insects sang their final summer song and plunging nocturnal temperatures withered the leaves on the pumpkin vines, children knew that old man winter was on the way—and they rejoiced! Colors splashed the trees, birds began to migrate, squirrels frantically stored nuts, and woolly bears were on the prowl. Chances seemed good that before long the world would be transformed into a sparkling kingdom of snow and ice. Adults did not always welcome this change of seasons so ecstatically, for severe weather could make the hard times even harder.

To start the game, the two opposing sides lined up facing each other in the center of the field with their backs to their respective goal lines. Blowing his whistle loudly three times, the referee would roll the hoop into play—and shout, "How come I always get stuck with being the referee? I wanna play too!"

The hoop, one from an old wagon-wheel hub, was pushed along as it rolled by contrivances called "pushers," made out of coat hangers or sticks. The crux of roller-hoop hockey, of course, was to try to roll the hoop across the other side's goal line while striving to prevent them from rolling it across yours. The side scoring 27 goals first won the match. Official rules were many and complex, and subject to change during the course of the game. But three of them were ironclad:

1. A player cannot curse the referee, cast aspersions on his or her vision or judgment, or tell him or her what he or she can do with his or her green-willow whistle.

2. If a player becomes irate or overzealous during the heat of a game, he cannot use his pusher as a weapon to strike an opponent whose back is turned.

3. A player cannot, after rolling the hoop across the opponents' goal line, keep on rolling it—taking off faster than a summer grass fire—in order to turn a simple hockey game into a prolonged cross-country anything-goes chase.

Sleds and Sliding

When the frigid north wind blows, if there is a hill, a slope, or even a slight incline within a five-mile radius of his house, a kid will find it. The first snowflake of winter brings one thought to mind—*Slide!* He will set out on the coldest morning, into the worst blizzard in forty years, in search of a slope, or just any surface that isn't flat, to slide down over and over again. And whether or not these perpetual downhill trips are made on sleds, skis, cardboard boxes, or plain old derrieres doesn't matter. It might take fifteen minutes of tremendous exertion to reach the summit of a hill that even a mountain goat couldn't climb in order to experience a downward plunge that won't take five seconds. No problem. The steeper the incline and the rougher the ride, the greater the fun.

Sleds, of course, came long before wheels and have remained in use for carrying loads because they can go places wheeled vehicles cannot. From the beginning, though, if you ever saw a sled, no matter what its cargo, that didn't have at least one kid riding on top of it, chances are it wasn't moving. A moving sled attracts kids like molasses draws flies.

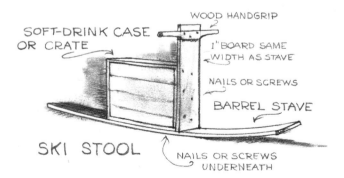

SOFT-DRINK CASE OR CRATE

WOOD HANDGRIP

1" BOARD SAME WIDTH AS STAVE

NAILS OR SCREWS

BARREL STAVE

SKI STOOL

NAILS OR SCREWS UNDERNEATH

"I don't like the looks of the sky. Sure hope we have enough hay in the barn to feed the stock all winter."

"Dad, do you think it will snow?"

"More than likely there's plenty of meat in the smokehouse and canned goods to see us through. Hope the roads don't get too bad for us to get into town if anyone gets sick."

"When do you think the snow will start, Dad?"

"Firewood's getting low. I better lay in another cord or two and check the patches on our old rubber boots. Seems like this winter's gonna be a punkin-buster."

"Oh, boy! It's really gonna snow!"

Heavy snowfalls in our area were scarce as hens' teeth—a lamentable fact for Oklahoma children. How we envied those living in northern climates. Imagine thick, slick, mysterious, delirious snow to play in all winter long!

Once in a while, however, a mixture of snow and sleet would blow in, the kind the old folks referred to as a "northern" or an "ice doozy." For snow-starved kids it was a blessing from heaven. Sometimes, after one of these storms, the temperature would stay below freezing around the clock and keep the hard icy crust for a week or longer. What elation it brought! Hearts beat faster with excitement, and young voices shouted with glee.

When an ice doozy hit, the homemade sleds and ski stools came out of storage. With loose boards renailed in place and a fresh coat of candle wax applied to the runners, they were ready for the hilltop winter sports. From sun to sun, Fort Gibson echoed with screams and laughter of sledding, slide-crazy kids, and the wintry air hummed with flying snowballs.

At least once each year before the glazed earth thawed, Mr. Buford would hitch his mule, Leroy, to his ancient handmade wooden sledge and take the children for an invigorating night ride. Whether or not the Christmas season was near, we would sing "Jingle Bells" with raucous holiday gaiety and pretend that Leroy was one of Santa's reindeer. Leroy had no sleigh bells, but the two goat bells adorning his harness produced sufficient tones of enchantment as he pulled the loaded sled around the sleepy town and countryside. Not very fast, though;

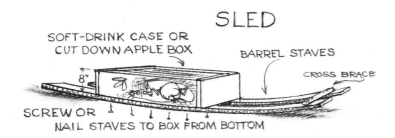

SLED

SOFT-DRINK CASE OR
CUT DOWN APPLE BOX

BARREL STAVES

CROSS BRACE

8"

SCREW OR
NAIL STAVES TO BOX FROM BOTTOM

Leroy never enjoyed a winter wonderland sleigh ride as much as we thought a mule should.

Home again, we welcomed the warmth from the fireplace. The temperature inside the house would sometimes drop so low after the fire was banked that the cedar water bucket would freeze right up, trapping the gourd dipper in a solid block of ice. Needless to say, there would be no getting up to go into the kitchen for a drink of water during the night.

At bedtime, red runny noses, sore throats, and near-frostbitten fingers were soothed with home-remedies—cups of steamy, pungent sassafras tea and hot mustard plasters—accepted without a solitary whine. Then to bed we'd go, covered by so many heavy patchwork quilts it was difficult to turn over. With hot bricks preheated on the hearth toasting our feet, we'd drift off to sleep wishing that the night would pass quick as a wink, and that morning would bring "just one more day" of glorious snow.

SCOOTMOBILE

Whatever the season, store-bought toys that kids could ride in, or on, were as rare in our small country town as calves in an unfenced pasture. Even on a clear day you couldn't count more than half a dozen bicycles, including Frosty's old warped-framed Montgomery Ward, four tricycles (toddler size), two scooters (one with a wheel missing), one pedal car (in fair operating condition), and maybe five little red wagons still sturdy enough to haul a half bushel of potatoes in.

But that didn't mean we had no wheels, because every kid worth his salt owned a

Scootmobile Follow-the-Leader

Next to downhill racing, follow-the-leader was the grandest scootmobile game of all. Contestants were not limited in number, and speed was of little importance. To be a successful follow-the-leader participant, one needed only stamina and a devil-may-care attitude. A good sturdy scootmobile helped too.

On follow-the-leader day, the scootmobilers would gather in the schoolyard (the start and finishing point) and from there go wherever the leader led. The leader, selected by drawing straws, had a free rein to take the pack anywhere he had the intestinal fortitude to go—except downtown, of course. The business

district was permanently off limits to any type of caravan exceptionally noisy in nature, especially one that left in its wake a boiling, choking cloud of dust.

To get the line of scootmobilers warmed up and into the proper spirit of the game, the leader would take them around the schoolhouse a couple of times before heading toward the old fort grounds. After fifteen minutes of horn-tooting, bell-ringing, and riding around and through—and between—the deserted fort buildings, the leader would suddenly pick up speed while cutting across Claude Thompson's yard, then shoot through the hole in Buster Ross's fence, skirting his vegetable garden, to come whirring out onto the Gilliams' driveway next door.

By this time the game was only about twenty minutes old but had already managed to attract a pack of dogs, enthusiastically yapping to join in the festivity: Lillian Thompson's cocker spaniel, Mona Ross's Boston bull, Euell and Cleo Porter's part beagle, Orin and Lorraine Gilliam's pointer, Bill and Mary Howland's English setter, and, of course, my Airedale, Nicky. Mr. Buford's twelve-year-old coon hound, Rosemary, would bark approvingly at the procession when it sped by his place later.

The primary objective of the leader was to make the trail as difficult as possible to follow. He wasn't supposed to draw his followers into hitting pedestrians, destroying property, disturbing the ill, or overly encouraging the wrath of the cranky. (We usually stayed clear of my Grandmother Porter's house.) The leader remained leader throughout the game, unless he got into a situation he could not convince his followers was a purposeful one. In other words, if he

homemade scootmobile (or skatemobile, as it was sometimes called). Never in the history of child transportation has there ever been a riding toy to compare with this wonderful old-time scooter. Made from discarded roller skates and a little scrap lumber, it cost absolutely *nothing* and had more speed and maneuverability than manufactured scooters priced $2.50 or more. For many years in every American city, town, or hamlet, pedestrians kept a wary eye peeled, ears alert, for these *clack-clack-clack*ing, freewheeling, kid-riding projectiles that would suddenly come from out of nowhere, bearing down at something near the speed of sound.

THE BASIC SCOOTMOBILE

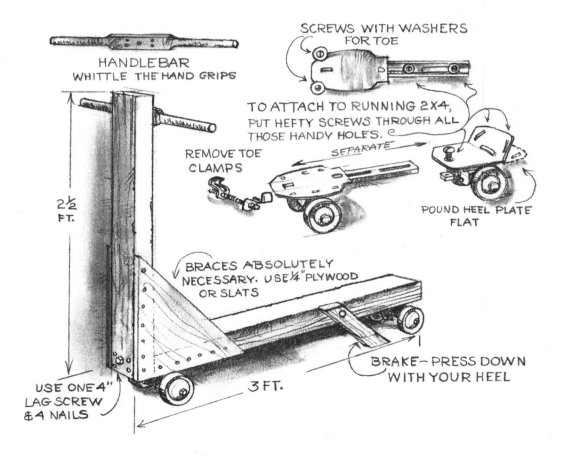

HANDLEBAR
WHITTLE THE HAND GRIPS

SCREWS WITH WASHERS
FOR TOE

TO ATTACH TO RUNNING 2X4,
PUT HEFTY SCREWS THROUGH ALL
THOSE HANDY HOLES.

REMOVE TOE CLAMPS

SEPARATE

POUND HEEL PLATE FLAT

2½ FT.

BRACES ABSOLUTELY NECESSARY. USE ¼" PLYWOOD OR SLATS

BRAKE—PRESS DOWN WITH YOUR HEEL

USE ONE 4" LAG SCREW & 4 NAILS

3 FT.

Scootmobiles were home constructed in an array of custom models you couldn't believe: long, short, squat, wide, monstrous, or streamlined. They were squeaky, rattly, clangy, splintery, smelled of wet paint, and could stop on a dime—or at least a quarter. Some had a cowbell or rubber-bulb horn (to warn pedestrians). But regardless of shape, size, or design, scootmobiles were, without a doubt, more fun than anything on wheels.

Nine-year-old See-Thru Thompson considered himself the best scootmobile builder in Muskogee County. In fact, back in the summer of '34 he seriously thought of going into it as a lifetime business. The first machine to roll off his assembly line, one had to admit, was superb. Pine 2 by 4's, which See-Thru had appropriated from a section of shelving on the back wall of his dad's garage, were used for the bottom board and tongue. It's true that afterward the shelf was too narrow to hold much, and things fell off it every time the side door was slammed. But there was no denying the confiscated lumber contributed immeasurably to the creation of a truly admirable vehicle.

The wheels for See-Thru's basic production model scootmobile came from the discarded roller skates of his older sister, who wore out at least one pair of skates every two or three years. Folks considered her a professional roller skater, as she and her high-school friends would sometimes pay a whole dime per head just to skate around in an indoor roller rink.

For his scootmobile's handlebar, See-Thru took an antique pine board, rotten on one end, which he discovered underneath the back porch and whittled on all morning until it was virtually as round and smooth as a broomstick. A couple of lattice strips borrowed from his mother's climbing rose arbor worked out very well to brace the tongue against the bottom board. After the machine was assembled, he went in search of some cheerful-looking bright-colored paint, preferably red. Red was the "in" color during the bleak years, but as it turned out he was unable to locate any "free" paint at all—much less red. Instead, the scootmobile got a resplendent coat of shellac, unselfishly donated by See-Thru's aunt. There was about a half can of it, well aged, and hardened to the consistency of molasses. The shellac made the machine look extremely shiny, as if it were wet. In fact, it was, and remained that way for almost a week; after that, it was only slightly sticky. The coal oil that he substituted for shellac thinner may have had something to do with this. Anyhow, See-Thru thought the colorful assortment of bugs sticking to it like flypaper created an unusual

crashed into an outhouse, or had a blowout (lost a skate wheel), or got caught in a fence or hopelessly bogged down in mud, or wound up stalled in a deep ditch, he was washed up. The rider immediately behind him became the leader.

From the school road the entourage would careen down the sidewalk in front of the church, barrel through Sudden Canyon, clatter around the Red-Horse Barn, zigzag back through the canyon again, up and down Standpipe Hill, and then roar down the graveled river road to Grandmother Youngblood's house. Finally, a retracing of the route would bring the leader and his faithful followers back to the schoolyard, where skinned elbows and knees were admired and damaged scootmobiles were hastily repaired in preparation for the next thrilling game. Straws would be drawn to determine whether it would be an obstacle race, relay race, cross-country endurance chase, or another—but this time more daring—spectacular performance of follow-the-leader.

Know Your Marbles

Marbles were more than just marbles to kids during the Depression; they were wampum—good as real money. And these brightly colored little orbs, prized above many other possessions, were carried in pocket or purse or special bags, nearly everywhere a kid went. Marble games were many and varied, but as most of them were played on hands and knees on bare ground, marbles were a constant headache to the mothers of young shooters confronted daily with dirty clothes, grubby hands, and pants and overalls worn out at the knees.

Chances are you could run across a kid in the '30s who wasn't up on his three R's—but if he had grimy knuckles on one hand, you could bet your favorite taw he knew his marbles:

DOUGHIES: Another word for marbles. (Oklahoma kids pronounced it dōō jēēz.)

TAW: The special shooter. Usually made of agate. Selected as a shooter because of its hardness and beauty.

AGGIES: Marbles made of highly polished agate stone.

GLASSIES: All marbles made of glass.

SWIRLIES: Marbles made of glass with two or more colors swirled together (reminded a kid of marble cake).

CLEARBELLS: Marbles made of translucent glass of one color. Came in dozens of colors and shades.

MILKIES: Glass marbles of a creamy white color.

CAT'S EYES: Glass marbles of two colors or more. One of the colors formed the shape of a cat's eye. Some marbles made from Mexican agate were also called cat's eyes or "Cyclops," as the pattern in the stone resembled an eye.

PEEWEES: Undersized marbles. Smaller than the regulation size of ⅝ inch.

MOONIES: Oversized marbles, larger than ⅝ inch (named from the expression "big as the moon"). Also called "thumb busters."

CHIPPIES: Cracked or chipped marbles. Made great slingshot ammunition.

effect—sort of polka-dotty. He rolled the beautiful, unique toy into his front-yard showroom, displaying a sign that read: FOR SALE—$1.00. BRAND NEW 1934 MODEL.

Three days later he embellished the scootmobile with a rusty tin-can headlight and dropped the price to 50 cents. By the end of July he threw an "Everything-Must-Go Sale" and lowered the price to a dime. Late one afternoon Kenneth Parker, who already had a fine scootmobile, came by with two Flash Gordon Big Little Books which See-Thru had read three times. Nevertheless, Kenneth rode home on his brand-new 1934 model scootmobile.

The next day Kenneth dismantled See-Thru's first assembly-line scootmobile piece by piece and used the lumber to make rubber guns. Thereafter it was easy to recognize Kenneth's rubber guns. They were the only ones around that were sort of polka-dotty.

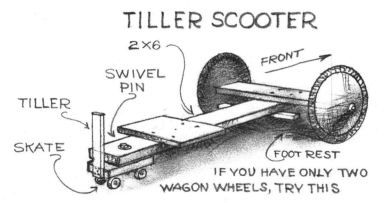

TILLER SCOOTER

The tiller scooter was constructed with a skate-wheel tiller which swiveled. The rider sat facing the front, with one hand behind him on the tiller to guide the scooter. The tiller steered the vehicle in the same manner a tiller attached to a rudder steers a boat. This lazy man's scootmobile, actually a type of pushmobile, was great for coasting down long slopes or hillsides; otherwise it had to be propelled by pushing, requiring the services of an energetic playmate. Sitting on the scooter's wide, comfortable seat, a kid could relax, enjoying the ride, while someone else worked up a sweat pushing the danged thing uphill. On smooth level surfaces, though, one could scoot it along with his feet in the manner of a kiddy car.

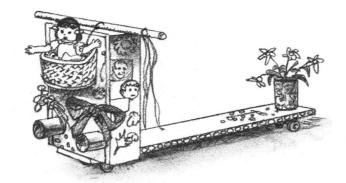

A GIRL'S SCOOTMOBILE

GIRL'S SCOOTMOBILE

To ten-year-old boys it was astonishing the way girls would gussy up their scootmobiles. They'd paint them disgusting, icky colors with leftover indoor wall paint—like pink or light blue—or even whitewash them, then tack on a bunch of magazine cut-out pictures of Little Orphan Annie or some other famous person. And it wasn't uncommon to see a girl's model with as many as four or five tin-can lights positioned in the most unlikely places. For a luggage rack to carry their "girl stuff" around in, they'd tie a cardboard box or a half-bushel basket on front of the handlebars. A girl's interest in her scootmobile was looks, not speed—a fact boys simply did not understand.

CHEAPIES: Marbles made of fired clay (came in tan, brown, and gray). Less expensive than glassies or aggies. Easily chipped.

STEELIES: Steel ball bearings. Usually outlawed as taws. Also made great slingshot ammunition.

IMPORTANT DEFINITIONS

LAGGING: A pregame ritual of rolling or shooting marbles toward a designated line. The player whose marble stops the closest to the line gets to shoot first.

KNUCKLING DOWN: The act of resting a knuckle or knuckles on the ground when shooting.

SHOOTING: The act of holding a taw between the thumb and first finger and propelling it into play by force of the thumb.

FUDGING: Cheating by moving the hand forward toward a target marble or to the inside of the ring line when shooting.

HISTING: The forbidden act of raising the hand from the ground while shooting.

FUNSIES: Marble games played just for fun. No betting allowed.

KEEPSIES: Any marble game where the shooter keeps the marbles he knocks out of the ring. A player could walk away from a game of keepsies with a pocketful of riches—or poorer than a dust-bowl farmer.

RINGTAW: Any marble game played in a circle or ring. Kids in different parts of the country played by different rules.

GRAY MULE: This is the despicable term that a bully or a sore loser would shout as he swooped into the ring to grab a handful of marbles. Whether or not he kept the filched marbles for his own depended on how well he could fight or how fast he could run.

3

Whistles and Other Entertainments

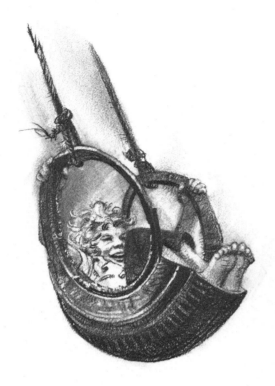

Long before the Depression came, the American farmer was known as a jack-of-all-trades. He was not only an agriculturist but a mechanic, carpenter, doctor, and inventor as well. He was a man who could do just about everything: repair engines, fix broken plows, build a house, cure a sick mule, or make a toy to amuse a child. His reputation for resourcefulness was permanently established during the 1930s. When the hard times came, the farmer was no longer thought of by his city-dwelling relatives as a "poor country cousin." In fact, he was often the most prosperous member of his family. Out-of-work kinfolk whom he had long ago forgotten, or had never even met, would arrive on his doorstep for a good long visit, eager to pool their meager remaining resources, offering their soft hands to help garden-up the soil. The best thing a paupered victim of the times could have was a relative with land. Ironically, the hard times brought many families back together.

For countless farmers, the techniques of survival were a way of life, handed down from generation to generation. For them, the decade that became known as the Great American Depression was just another ten years of "make do, do it yourself, or do without." Farm children labored in the fields and learned early the meaning of hard work and the value of a dollar. Nothing was thrown away. A worn-out tire became a tree swing, the inner tube became rubber bands. Tin cans were converted into planters, roofing shingles, tom walkers, or were hung on strings in the garden to frighten off birds and animals. Everything was used for something else.

A tree was more than just a friend that offered relief from the hot summer sun. It was a storehouse of material and pre-formed parts. The children watched and learned as their father selected a limb curved just right to make a rocker for a chair or cradle, a large forked limb for a cow yoke, or smaller ones for slingshots. They laughed with delight while he whittled away with his pocketknife, transforming a multibranched limb into a doll or an animal, or trimming saplings into stilts. His skilled knife could magically produce tiny cups and saucers from large acorns, or whistles from a green-willow branch.

Often he would take the children's small hands in his large calloused ones and walk with them through woods and fields, sharing with the youngsters his broad *knowledge of the ways of nature. And the children grew up with fascination and respect for the skills and gentle philosophy of this home craftsman who—through bad times and good—tilled the land and helped feed our nation.*

Uncle Dan's Golden Treasure

Uncle Dan always said my cousin Norma was tougher than a nickel beefsteak. And in 1934, with sirloin selling for 29 cents a pound, that meant a pretty durn tough steak—or a mighty small one. I'm not sure she was all that tough, even though she was the reigning scootmobile queen of Standpipe Hill, but I do know for a *girl* she was a lot of fun to play with, and the other guys never called me a sissy for doing so either. I guess they figured Norma would probably clean their plows, if they did.

Norma was six months older than I was, and a lot taller. Her hair was so red it hurt your eyes sometimes to look at it in the bright sunshine, and she had more freckles per square inch than a speckled butter bean.

You've never in your life seen anybody wear out a pair of overalls so fast! But she was real easy on dresses. That's because her folks had to threaten force to get her into one. On these rare occasions (Saturday afternoons and Sunday mornings), she was more fun to watch than Laurel and Hardy. She'd hold her arms down stifflike, a few inches away from her sides, and take little one-foot-in-front-of-the-other steps as if she were walking the top rail of a fence. I could hardly keep from laughing. But I did.

Uncle Dan and Aunt Martha lived on a farm near Fort Smith, Arkansas. They didn't have any kids of their own, so every summer when Uncle Dan had his crops laid by, he would drive over to Fort Gibson in his Model-A Ford pickup and fetch Norma and me back for a long visit. It was always the merriest of times for us, because Uncle Dan could turn anything into a magical and exciting adventure. But best of all, he showed us how to make the finest toys you ever saw: whistles, popguns, peashooters, cigar-box banjos, stilts, tom walkers, and a whole bunch more. He made two persimmon-wood whistles, each having the same exact pitch, for Frosty and me. When we were playing rubber guns, if I got in trouble, I would blow for Frosty to

come to my rescue. I guess we had the only whistles in the world that sounded just alike, and so loud the sound would carry a mile. Uncle Dan made the banjos for Norma and her girl friends. She and Bobby Ann Smith could play "Yankee Doodle" on theirs where you could almost recognize what it was if you listened close enough.

During our summer-of-'34 visit, Norma and I were helping Aunt Martha snap beans in the shade of the back porch one afternoon, when suddenly Uncle Dan, who had gone into town to get the radio batteries charged and play some dominoes at the general store, came skidding the truck around the house. Before the old Ford had come to a complete stop, he was out and running for the toolshed as fast as his short bandy legs would carry him.

"Tarnation!" Aunt Martha said, twisting her 200 pounds around in her creaking rocking chair. "What in the world is that man up to now?"

"Acts like a banshee's after him," Norma said.

"Daniel, you'll have a stroke!" Aunt Martha cautioned. "Where you going in such a fury?"

"To find a treasure, that's where!" He disappeared into the toolshed, and we could hear him thrashing around inside.

"Did he say *treasure?*" I asked.

Norma and I streaked out to the shed and peeked inside. Uncle Dan was rummaging through drawers and along shelves, throwing things into a croker sack: a brace and bit, a chisel, an old butcher knife, and a crazy-looking tin-can contraption with a funnel-shaped spout.

"What's that?" I asked Norma.

"Beats me. Funniest-looking geegaw I ever saw."

"Hey, you kids!" he yelled. "You had my keyhole saw?" We scurried inside and found the saw hanging on a nail. Tossing it inside the sack, he mumbled, "Been a snake, it'd bit me."

"What's all that stuff for, Uncle Dan?"

"We'll need it if we find the golden treasure. Come on, let's get crackin'! You want someone else to find it first?" He ran out of the shed with us following.

"You really know where there's a treasure?" I blurted breathlessly, feeling the excitement in the air. "Buried treasure?" I could see myself knee-deep in a pirate chest full of coins and precious jewels.

"Stop asking ninny questions and scoot down to the barn. Fetch three milk buckets and a coil of balin' wire. Get a bolt of cheesecloth from the smokehouse too. Now, scoot!"

We sped off in different directions while Uncle Dan threw his sack into the truck. When we returned, he told us to put on our lace-up boots and denim jackets—and to bring along gloves and straw hats.

"Gloves?" Norma questioned. "In the middle of July?"

"If you can't hear out of them ears, Norma," he said, "you can just stay here and rinse 'em out with coal oil while me and Hoppy go treasure huntin'. Hurry it up; it's a far piece over to Cypress Creek."

While we were inside the house putting on our boots, he hollered at us to bring along some scissors and a ball of kite string. Norma said she was going to take along her tom walkers too, because she didn't want to step on a snake. And we hung the new whistles Uncle Dan had made for us around our necks. A person could easily get lost treasure hunting.

As we ran back outside, we told Aunt Martha we were off on a treasure hunt. "Not without me," she said. "If you think I'm going to snap beans while you're out having fun, you got another think coming!"

"You gotta wear your overalls and boots," Uncle Dan warned.

"And straw hat and gloves." Norma giggled.

"Don't forget your jacket," I piped.

Aunt Martha said she wouldn't be caught dead dressed like that out in broad daylight.

"Then you can't come!" Uncle Dan yelled and started the engine. "You can just stay here and snap beans till your fingers turn green!"

In the back of the lurching pickup, Norma and I held on for dear life. Uncle Dan hit every hole in the dirt road, while Aunt Martha fumed and tried to fan the dust out of the cab with her straw hat. He swerved the truck off the road and through his unfenced pasture—taking a short cut to Cypress Creek the hard way. The pickup careened over stumps and clods and through two shallow stock ponds, and we held our breaths as it headed at breakneck speed for a dense stand of woods. Just when it seemed we would crash for sure, the truck plowed to a stop inches from the trees.

"Everybody out and grab all that stuff," Uncle Dan said. "We go the rest of the way on foot."

"Thank the Lord," Aunt Martha said. "Never in my life was I so thankful to put my feet down on the good sweet earth!"

"Wait'll I get on my tom walkers," Norma said. She stood up on the tall tin cans, clutched the clothesline cords tight in hand just above her knees, and started high-stepping and jumping around like a kangaroo.

"This ain't no time for circus shenanigans," Uncle Dan told her. "You want to find the treasure or just jumpin'-jack around out here all day like a ninny?"

Hard put to keep up, we followed Uncle Dan through the woods. Trailing behind, Aunt Martha fanned herself and fussed that a person had to be daft to go traipsing around in the jungle during the heat of the day. Norma finally had to abandon her tom walkers because the cans kept sinking deep into the damp earth underneath the trees, cutting out thick dirt pies with every step. She hung her walkers on a bush and ran to catch up with us.

"Okay, this is Peckerwood Point," Uncle Dan said, when we got to the creek. "Kevin and Sean Garrett said they were fishin' right here when they heard it."

"Heard what?" we chorused.

"The golden treasure, you ninnies."

"I knew it!" Aunt Martha said. "He's had a sunstroke! He's crazier than a cow eating locoweed!"

Uncle Dan sniffed the slight breeze. His silvery handlebar mustache seemed to quiver under his nose. "Yahoo!" he yelled, and darted into the woods. Close on his heels, we tramped through tangled briers and honeysuckle until we came to a small clearing. The warm, humid air was heavy with a spicy aroma.

"Ssssh!" Uncle Dan put his finger to his lips. "Listen."

We did and heard a buzzing. "A bee tree!" Aunt Martha screamed with delight. "The old coot has found us a bee tree!"

"And there she is." Uncle Dan pointed to a big dead topless tree about 20 or 30 feet tall. "How's that for some treasure? Tonight at supper you'll think it's better than silver and gold."

"Wild honey!" Norma hollered. "The golden treasure!"

"Hoo-ray," I said, halfheartedly. My visions of doubloons, gold nuggets, and sparkling jewels had suddenly vanished in thin air.

"Gracious, doesn't that honey smell good?" Aunt Martha said.

I breathed deeply. It really did smell good. It was a blend of all the wild fragrances of the nectars the bees had collected from the area. I imagined I could smell wild strawberries, blackberries, cherries, and plums, as well as the apples, pears, and peaches of neighboring orchards. As I inhaled I implanted a perfumed memory in my senses that will be with me forever.

"Dang it!" Uncle Dan said. "I should of brung a ladder."

"Daniel! Such language," scolded Aunt Martha.

"Double dang it!" insisted Uncle Dan. "Their hole is up too high. We'll just have to come back tomorrow. . . . Somebody will beat us to it sure as shootin'."

We looked at the small knothole in the trunk, about 12 feet up, surrounded by a ball of bees the size of a baseball. Uncle Dan explained that they were guards and that most all the other bees were out in the fields working.

"Uncle Dan," Norma said, "I can climb that tree with both eyes shut."

"Me too," I said, even though I knew I couldn't climb a tree any better than a coonhound.

Uncle Dan studied the tree and looked at Norma. "You'll do what I tell you?"

"You betcha. Cross my heart."

1934 Make-do Annual Wages (Average)

U.S. Congressman	$8,670
Airline pilot	8,000
Lawyer	4,218
Doctor (general practitioner)	3,382
College teacher	3,111
Railroad conductor	2,730
Police chief (city of 40,000)	2,636
Engineer	2,520
Dentist	2,391
Fire chief (city of 40,000)	2,000
Electrical worker	1,559
Airline stewardess	1,500
Pharmaceutical salesman	1,500
Bus driver	1,373
Civil service employee	1,284
Schoolteacher	1,227
Secretary	1,040
Stenographer/bookkeeper	936
Nurse (R.N.)	936
Construction worker	907
Priest	831
Dressmaker	780
Coal miner	723
Pharmacist	650
Typist	625
Waitress	520
Clergyman	500
Factory worker	435
Steelworker	424
Store clerk	370
Farm hand	216
Manual laborer	200

"Okey-dokey, let's get at it."

"Daniel!" Aunt Martha said. "She'll get stung to death!"

"No, she won't, either. Besides, a few stings'll never show on all them freckles." Uncle Dan proceeded to "bee proof" Norma. Draping double layers of the cheesecloth over her straw hat and tucking one layer inside her shirt collar, he flowed the other down like a serape and tied it securely around her waist with string. He had her stuff the legs of her overalls inside her boots and relace them. After tying her jacket sleeves at the wrists he went to work on himself, then Aunt Martha and me. In about fifteen minutes we all looked like weird aliens out of Buck Rogers comic strips.

"I'd just die if anybody I knew saw me looking like this," Aunt Martha moaned.

Uncle Dan dumped the sack's contents and explained to Norma what she was to do. "You perch up there on that big limb and pretend there's a window about the size of a bread pan above their hole. Take this brace and bit and drill four holes in the corners of the window; then saw through from hole to hole and cut the window out, so's to get to the comb. First thing, though, loop this balin' wire over the limb so I can send stuff up to you. Move nice and easy. Don't make any sudden moves. . . . Okay?"

Norma nodded and pulled on her gloves, grinning behind her protective bonnet. She was raring to go.

Uncle Dan flipped back the funnel-shaped lid on the funny-looking can, cut a piece from the burlap sack, rolled it up, and lit it. When it was burning he put it inside the can and closed the lid. He pushed the small bellows on the side; smoke poured from the nozzle. "This here was my grandpa's smoker," he said. "He was the most unusual beekeeper in the whole world. . . . He kept *one* bee."

I didn't get the joke, but when the grown-ups finished laughing, Uncle Dan showed Norma how to work the smoker until she had the air so foggy you could hardly breathe.

"Up you go," Uncle Dan said. "I'll send the smoker up when you're set. Puff them bees around the hole first, then stick it in and give 'em five or six good squirts. It don't hurt 'em none. Just makes 'em sleepy so they don't give a dang."

In a jiffy Norma had shinnied up to the big limb. She straddled it, locked her feet underneath, and uncoiled the wire, draping it over the limb. The two ends trailed on the ground. Uncle Dan hooked the smoker on one end and pulled the other, sending it up to her.

Norma promptly became engulfed in a dense white cloud. But we knew she was

SATURDAY NIGHT

still up there because we could hear her sputtering and coughing. When the smoker came down out of the cloud, Uncle Dan sent up the brace and bit.

"Good Lord, Norma! You be careful," Aunt Martha cautioned. "Don't you dare fall! Your mother would kill me if she knew I let you go up there."

By the time the air had cleared so we could see Norma again, she had three of the holes drilled and was working on the fourth.

"Atta girl," Uncle Dan said. "When you get that window cut out, lay it across them limbs."

He sent the saw up; she sawed out the piece of trunk. "Wow!" she gasped. "I ain't seen so much honey in my whole life!"

"*Haven't* seen, dear," corrected Aunt Martha.

Next, Uncle Dan sent up one of the milk buckets with the butcher knife inside. "Cut the honeycombs away from the cavity," he instructed, "but don't squeeze 'em too hard or you'll squish out the honey before you get it in the bucket. Use both hands; I've got the bucket on this end."

She filled the bucket and when Uncle Dan lowered it to the ground, Aunt Martha and I tied a cheesecloth cover over it while Norma started filling another bucket.

"Some combs are dark brown, Uncle Dan," Norma said. "They any good?"

"It's all good. Hurry now . . . when them bees wake up they won't take too kindly to what we're doing to their pantry. You got stung yet?"

"Nope, they're gentle as ladybugs." Bees were crawling all over her.

When we had the three buckets full and covered, Uncle Dan had Norma replace the window in the trunk and wrap the wire tightly around the tree to hold it in place.

Norma came down and licked at her oozing gloves through the veil. "Yum, there's enough honey in there to fill a rain barrel. We'll get the rest tomorrow."

"No sirree," Uncle Dan said. "That's all we'll take. How'd you like somebody to chop into your cellar, Norma, and make off with all the food you're puttin' up? You always leave plenty for the colony to get through winter. That way they'll stay in that tree and be willin' to share with us again next year. The whole trouble with the world nowadays is folks are greedy. They don't want to share or leave nothin' for nature's creatures. If we ain't careful, some day this bounty will also be gone. Okay, time we scoot for home." We scooted.

"Lordy, look at the clock," Aunt Martha fretted. "If we don't hurry with supper, we'll miss *Fibber McGee and Molly*." She asked me to fetch a shoulder from the

Going-to-Town Day

During the '30s Saturday was going-to-town day in much of rural America. Even with no money to spend, this was a primary source of entertainment for young and old. By car, truck, wagon, horseback, or on foot, farm families arrived in town wearing their best clothes, which for many meant home-sewn flour-sack dresses or shirts and patched overalls. Those who had a long way to travel would leave home before daybreak. When the stores opened for business, they would be there. Something of dire need might be on sale.

Some brought along the family pet. Many brought

various items to swap. Some, who couldn't afford to eat at the café, carried picnic lunches. Others came empty-handed, without a dime in their pockets, just to see the sights, admire the automobiles, window-shop, and catch up on the local news. For many, especially the elderly, the day's entertainment consisted of sitting in a car, their necks straining, heads pivoting, to watch the flow of pedestrians go by.

"Wasn't that Tom Block who just went into the feedstore?"

"Naw, I heard he and Fred Paschel—you know, Joan's oldest boy—went to work in that CCC camp over in Joplin, Missouri."

"Well, it sure did look like Tom, the way he walks and all."

"Hey, lookee there! That's Reba Sumars. Lord, I haven't seen her in a coon's age. I'll bet she's finished college by now. Hello, Reba, over here! It's me, Faye Campbell."

Waiting to see their favorite matinee star when the movie theater opened, children romped in the grass on the court square around the shaded benches where old-timers sat, swapping yarns, chewing tobacco, and whittling as they watched the traffic go by.

"Here comes that wild Butch Bunch again. Drivin' like a bat out o' hell. That kid is gonna run over somebody in that car someday for sure, comin' through town like that."

"How come the sheriff ain't ever around when he's needed?"

"'Cause he ain't worth a hill o' beans, that's why! He's so worthless I wouldn't give him hay iffen he was a mule tryin' to graze off a concrete pasture!"

Thus they'd return to their whittling until the next car worthy of discussion rolled by. As the afternoon wore on, the conversation would invariably turn to the hard times. But to many of them there, unless they had lost their land to the Dust Bowl, it was no harder than all the years that preceded the Depression. "I ain't had much or nothin' before; I ain't got nothin' now; and I won't have nothin' after. But with the good Lord willin', we'll get by."

smokehouse and dig a few new potatoes to go in the beans. "And, Norma, if you'll fry the meat, I'll scratch up some biscuits to go under the honey. I sure hope Daniel remembered to get the radio batteries charged. I'd hate to miss *Fibber McGee.*"

". . . And we are mighty thankful," Uncle Dan said softly, his snowy head bowed, "for all the good things You have put on this earth to give us pleasure and to nourish our bodies. And, as always, Your presence is more than welcome at our table. Amen."

"Amen," Aunt Martha said.

"Amen," I said.

"Pass the biscuits and the golden treasure," Norma said.

"Norma!" said Aunt Martha.

"Oh, excuse me. . . . Amen, and pass the biscuits, *please.*"

PLAIN WHISTLE

A branch about ½ inch in diameter from any tree will serve to make a plain whistle, but we preferred to use persimmon or sassafras because the wood had a sweet aroma and taste. The tricky part to making a plain whistle is hollowing out the branch with a ¼-inch drill. Cutting the notch and inserting the split half of a round stick in the air passage is a snap. It was glued securely in place and the glue was allowed to dry thoroughly before the whistle was blown.

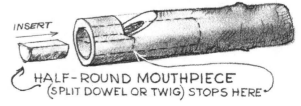

PLAIN WHISTLE

DRILL CENTER OUT OF ANY STICK

INSERT

HALF-ROUND MOUTHPIECE (SPLIT DOWEL OR TWIG) STOPS HERE

GREEN-WILLOW WHISTLE

Any farm kid from Maine to California, growing up in the Depression era, knew that when dogwoods bloomed in the spring, it was time to make green-willow whistles. For only in early spring when the sap is rising will the bark slip easily off a wild willow branch.

To make a whistle, a youngster would select a section of a green branch as big around as his thumb, about 6 inches long and free of burls. With his pocketknife he'd cut a notch 1½ inches from one end. Two inches from the other end he'd cut a ring around the bark. Then, after gently tapping the surface to loosen the bark, he'd hold the branch like a handlebar in both hands, twist that portion that contained the notch, and slip the tube of bark off the branch. The exposed wood of the branch was then whittled to create a narrow air passage and air chamber. When the tube of bark was slid back onto the branch and aligned precisely with the notch over the air chamber, the whistle was ready to blow. And blow it did—so loud it could probably be heard in the next county.

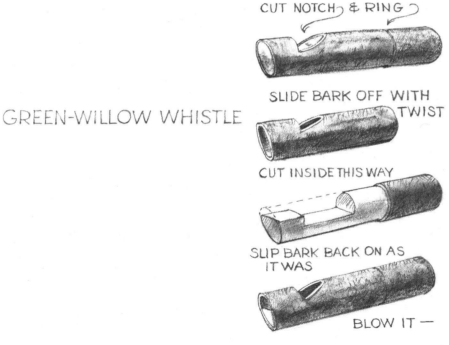

GREEN-WILLOW WHISTLE

Depression-Era Idols

The child's world during the '30s whirled around a group of colorful characters, both fictional and real, who served up splendid, inexpensive, and wondrous dishes of entertainment. On Sunday morning before Sunday school and church, youngsters from coast to coast made a shambles of the newspaper as they scrambled for the funnies to follow the latest adventures of Tarzan, Dick Tracy, Flash Gordon, Little Orphan Annie, Blondie, Buck Rogers, Snuffy Smith, the Katzenjammer Kids, and a score of others.

During the week Dick Tracy came booming over the radio, "Open up in there! I've got a tommy gun in my hand and it's in a barking mood!" The hard-boiled detective was followed by further thrilling episodes of Little Orphan Annie and by teenage football hero Jack Armstrong, "The All-American Boy."

Saturday was movie-matinee day for those who could afford to go: as much as three and a half glorious hours of boisterous entertainment for a 100-percent, true-to-its-value dime. The bill included a full-length movie or two, usually shoot-'em-ups starring favorite cowboy heroes such as Tom Mix or Tim McCoy, two cliff-hanging serials, perhaps featuring Flash Gordon or Tarzan, and an animated cartoon.

In between funny papers, radio shows, and movies the kids squeezed in time to catch up on further exploits of their idols through comic books and Big Little Books (beautifully illustrated, 400-page volumes of half text, half drawings that sold for a dime) or entertained themselves for hours with pop-up and doll cutout books of Buck Rogers, Shirley Temple, or Princesses Elizabeth and Margaret Rose of England (who for reasons unknown were very popular with American kids).

The adventures of these heroes and heroines took place in settings that kids could only imagine—ranging from palaces to the ghost towns of the Old West, from the back streets of gangster-ridden cities to the athletic fields of America, from the steaming jungles of Africa to faraway galaxies.

Spring in the '30s meant warming and greening and barefoot children. When drab gray winter gave way to emerald hues, few emotions could compare with those brought on by discarding shoes and walking barefoot for the first time that year, feeling kinship with the surrounding, changing world. There were caterpillars to contemplate, innumerable species of beetles and ants to appreciate, and dragon-shaped clouds to notice. And out across the meadow, hidden away in the woods, a beckoning creek meandered, swirling and gurgling about the rocks, bubbling a melody as welcome as the springtime. The red-winged blackbird blended its notes in harmony, the mystery and allure of its song irresistible to an adventurous boy or girl. Along the creek bank, the warming of the earth reawakened the sense of smell, and the faint scent of wildflowers (trillium and May apples), wild plum, and honeysuckle blossoms mingled with the rich odor of last year's decaying leaves. Young eyes admired moss flourishing on the bark of trees, forming funny patterns. Ferns and willows grew profusely, and cane stood tall, shutting out the sunlight in places. Bullfrogs serenaded from lily-pad podiums the song of the season. The world was reborn. Spring had come again.

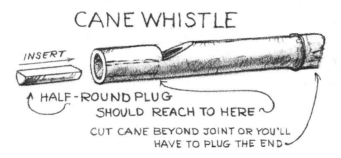

CANE WHISTLE

(diagram labels:)

INSERT

HALF-ROUND PLUG

SHOULD REACH TO HERE

CUT CANE BEYOND JOINT OR YOU'LL HAVE TO PLUG THE END

CANE WHISTLE

Wild cane found growing along creek banks made excellent whistles. And a cane whistle was easy to make, too, because a drill was not needed, nor did the bark have to be slipped off. To make the whistle, a length of cane was cut off just beyond a joint. (This way, one end of the whistle was closed, and there was no need for plugging, as a solid wall membrane grows inside at each joint. Otherwise, the cane is hollow and would have to be plugged airtight on one end.) If a long piccolo-type whistle was desired, a stiff wire was used to clean out the inner pulp and joint membranes. The notch was cut and air-passage stick whittled and inserted the same as for a plain whistle.

In Oklahoma when we took to the pond and creek banks in early spring to gather cane and wild-willow branches, we hunted for bullfrogs too. Armed with homemade spears and arrows, which were tipped with fish-gig points carved from hardwood, we harvested the big croakers that fed off the willow flies. Frog legs were a delicious supplement to the fish diets of people hard-hit during the summer months when rabbits, squirrels, and deer were out of season.

If a kid didn't have a good marksman's eye with spear or arrow, he'd bait his hook with a small scrap of red material and fish for the frogs. An old frog sitting on the bank can't resist what he thinks is a succulent red bug dangling in the air right in front of his nose.

Wild cane and willow branches were used for many things other than whistles. Green-willow branches made decorative grape arbors and lawn furniture, as they would bend easily without snapping and retain their shape when seasoned. Cane was utilized for making cane-bottomed chairs, fishing poles, blowguns, spears, arrows, and peashooters.

The idols themselves were diverse in appearance and personality, but all of them stood staunchly on a common ground for one precious thing: VIRTUE, that sparkling commodity they sold in carloads, proving in each and every installment that clean, wholesome living reaped unlimited rewards. Crime, however petty, was wrong. It definitely did not pay.

Most of these idols were also very successful at selling commercial products. Through radio, films, books, and comics for more than a decade, they had half the children in America convinced that ingesting Wheaties, Ralston, Quaker Oats, and Ovaltine would give them the stamina of Jack Armstrong, the toughness of Tom Mix, the fearlessness of Dick Tracy, and the native wisdom of Little Orphan Annie. At the close of each radio adventure, these idols would fire a salvo of sales pitches on behalf of their sponsors for foodstuffs, trinkets, books, and toys: whistles of every conceivable shape and kind, decoder rings and bracelets, balls, tops, kites, gliders, games, and puzzles. Though advertised as *free*, this was not exactly a cross-your-heart-and-hope-to-die truth. The products from which the box tops or coupons came were expensive for the times, and the nickel or dime "postage and handling" fee would buy a trinket or toy of equal value in any store.

The kids who were hard pressed for cash (or whose parents did not fall for the sales pitches) continued to make do with plainer breakfast fare and homemade toys. But these box-top-deprived children loved the heroes and heroines just the same—and defended their lack of brand-name product consumption by saying things like "Granny told us Ovaltine is full of junk that will grow warts on your tongue" or "My dad says if Wheaties is so good for you, how come FDR doesn't feed 'em to Fala?"

Despite their commercialism, though, the idols created an exciting, beautiful, adventurous world. It was a world that kids loved in an era when, for many, the real world so often appeared to be anything but fun. In fact, more grown-ups than would care to admit it escaped into this make-believe world, too.

PEASHOOTER

The secret of making a peashooter that would shoot hard and far entailed finding a piece of cane exactly the right size in diameter to fit the pea, or vice versa. This was frustrating at times, as both peas and cane came in infinite sizes. However, there was a simple solution to this problem. A dart was made by gluing a small ball of cotton onto one end of a sucker stick, thus converting the peashooter into a blowgun. Who says kids aren't as smart as anybody? If the cotton-ball dart fit snugly into a blowgun about 2 feet long, it would shoot for a mile against the wind. Well, almost, anyway.

NOTE: *A peashooter could really zing a pea—uncooked—in there! Therefore, cautious adults kindly requested that kids confine their target practicing to inanimate objects. And for the shooter's own safety, when shooting he always tried to remember to blow out, not suck in. An inhaled pea was no fun.*

PEASHOOTER
MADE FROM MOST ANYTHING LONG & HOLLOW —
CANE, REED, OR SODA STRAW

SHOOT HEDGE BERRIES, OKRA SEEDS, OR EVEN PEAS

POPGUN

Without a chinaberry tree growing on his property, a child would have about as much use for a popgun as a jackrabbit would for a sidesaddle. So why go to all the effort to make a popgun if you didn't have ammunition available for it? Because you could swap it for an equally good toy to the kid who did have a chinaberry tree, that's why.

Half the fun of making a toy was seeing what barter value it would carry. On a barter-value scale of one to ten, a popgun was normally rated at five. This might fluctuate wildly, though, depending mainly on the weather. If there was adequate rainfall at the right times to produce a bumper crop of chinaberries, the value of a popgun would skyrocket up the scale to eight or nine. If the growing season was unusually dry, a chinaberry popgun's worth would drop like a lead balloon. If a kid did not possess the gumption to gamble on outguessing the chinaberry market, he'd stick to making toys like milk-can tugboats or magic propellers that were so difficult to construct they rated ten on the scale year after year.

Depression Songs Hit Hard and True

That old dust might killed my wheat, boys,
But it can't kill me, Lord, it can't kill me.
That old dust storm, that old dust storm,
It can't kill me, boys, it can't kill me.©

In 1934, recalling a devastating dust storm that swept across a region of the Great Plains, an Oklahoma farm wife said, "In early morning a cold gale began blowing from the northwest, where an enormous black cloud stretched across the horizon as

POPGUN

MADE FROM ELDERBERRY,
A HARD WOOD WITH A SOFT PITH CORE

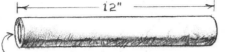

12"

REMOVE PITH WITH A STIFF WIRE

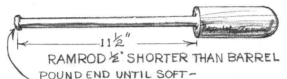

11½"

RAMROD ½" SHORTER THAN BARREL
POUND END UNTIL SOFT —

RAMROD GREAT IF MADE FROM BROOM HANDLE,
BUT WOOD IS VERY HARD. USE PINE IF THE ONLY
TOOL YOU HAVE IS A POCKETKNIFE —

RAM 1 CHINABERRY TO END OF BARREL
IT WILL STOP JUST INSIDE END

PUSH SECOND BERRY IN THIS FAR
BERRIES MUST MAKE A TIGHT FIT!

PUSH RAMROD IN HARD!
AIR WILL COMPRESS, BERRY WILL SHOOT
WITH A LOUD BANG! AND NEXT BERRY
WILL BE READY TO SHOOT

WET PAPER WADS ARE GREAT, TOO, IF
CHINABERRIES ARE OUT OF SEASON

NOTE: *Like the peashooter, the popgun was supposed to be used for target shooting only. And don't forget that chinaberries contain a paralyzing nerve poison, so they were used exclusively for ammunition—never food.*

far as the eye could see. The cloud of dust seemed to fill the sky. By noontime it was darker than night. . . . We lit lanterns to see . . . covered our heads with blankets to breathe. When the howling wind died at dusk we were in another world. The fields were gone . . . only mounds of dirt and sand. Everything in the house was covered with an inch of dust. Even our scant supplies that were to feed us through the winter were ruined."

During the next few years that farm wife's experience was repeated innumerable times. Helplessly, country people in Kansas, Colorado, Nebraska, Texas, South Dakota, and Oklahoma watched in despair as the relentless winds blew away the topsoil of their farms and, with it, their livelihoods and their dreams. Without money or jobs to sustain them, thousands of families fled their homes, many of them heading for California, where they hoped to find work as laborers.

It was during these bleak years of Depression and Dust Bowl that a young Oklahoma-born and -bred folksinger began to write and sing his compassionate songs for hard-hit people. With guitar and harmonica, Woodrow Wilson "Woody" Guthrie entertained the common people all across America, in carnivals, flophouses, roadhouses, migrant workers' camps, hobo jungles, and union hiring halls and, eventually, over the radio. Drawing from the experience of these down-on-their-luck people, Guthrie wrote more than a thousand songs that form perhaps the richest single personal legacy in the history of American folk music. Before he died in 1967, Guthrie saw many of his songs, such as "This Land Is Your Land," win acceptance as American folk classics.

Ways to Produce . . . Music (??)

COMB-AND-PAPER KAZOO: Thin paper was folded over a comb. The player hummed through it loudly.

GRASS-BLADE VIOLIN: One end of a 4-inch blade of grass was held with the thumb and forefinger of the left hand while the other end was brought downward, stretched tightly, and held in place by bringing the hands together in a fist position, forming an air chamber. To make music the player placed open mouth over thumbs and blew hard across the blade of grass, producing an extremely loud, squeaky violin sound.

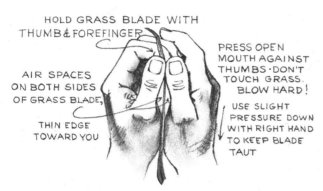

GRASS-BLADE VIOLIN

HOLD GRASS BLADE WITH THUMB & FOREFINGER

AIR SPACES ON BOTH SIDES OF GRASS BLADE

THIN EDGE TOWARD YOU

PRESS OPEN MOUTH AGAINST THUMBS · DON'T TOUCH GRASS. BLOW HARD!

USE SLIGHT PRESSURE DOWN WITH RIGHT HAND TO KEEP BLADE TAUT

DRUMS: Anything could be beaten to generate percussion sounds—an oatmeal box, an oil can, a barrel, old pots and pans . . . or the sunburned back of a fellow musician.

CLAPPERS, KNACKERS, OR BONES: A pair of thin, sanded rib bones from a cow or pig, about 5 or 6 inches long, added spice to the percussion section. They were held loosely between the fingers, one between the thumb and index finger, the other between the index and middle finger. To make a noise they were clacked together at both ends by shaking the hand rhythmically from the wrist. If a musician arrived at a concert with only half the instrument

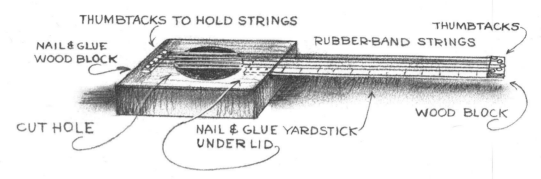

CIGAR-BOX BANJO

THUMBTACKS TO HOLD STRINGS

THUMBTACKS

RUBBER-BAND STRINGS

NAIL & GLUE WOOD BLOCK

WOOD BLOCK

CUT HOLE

NAIL & GLUE YARDSTICK UNDER LID

CIGAR-BOX BANJO

A cigar box with a large hole cut in the lid was used for the sound box of the banjo. Twenty-four inches of a yardstick served as the neck. The five rubber-band strings were tied to, and held in place, by thumbtacks. The tighter a rubber band was stretched, the higher the tone it delivered when plucked.

Now, you've never experienced a real honest-to-goodness hootenanny unless you've heard a rural Oklahoma group of tin-eared kids, youngsters who couldn't carry a tune if it were in a two-gallon milk pail, singing away and playing their homemade toy musical instruments. We fancied we were every bit as talented as Bob Wills, Al Jolson, or Woody Guthrie when we struck up a lively number on our cigar-box banjos, Prince-Albert-can or comb-and-paper kazoos, whistles, washtub bass fiddles, grass-blade violins, oil-can drums, washboards, and whatever else. At the start of each performance, though, two things invariably happened: Dogs and cats ran underneath the house, and all the grown-ups went to visit somebody on the other side of town. However, true music *aficionados* like horses, cows, chickens, and pigs stuck around to enjoy the show.

PRINCE-ALBERT-CAN KAZOO

A Prince Albert tobacco can was just about the most valuable possession a child could have. Its thin rectangular shape made it fit perfectly into his overalls' hip pocket, and its hinged tight-fitting lid kept secret objects secure within its shiny tin interior. It was converted to a kazoo only when it became bent out of pocket shape or was otherwise damaged too severely for the lid to close.

Like a lady's purse, a kid's Prince Albert can held a phenomenal assortment of goodies: things that were absolutely necessary to get one through the day. The contents of a typical (male or female) ten-year-old's can at the start of a summer's day were: two glassy marbles, one agate taw, one steelie, three pretty rocks, four rusty nails, six carpet tacks, half a stick of chewing gum, one ball of tinfoil, a long piece of string, four pop-bottle caps, one Indian-head penny, one buckeye, one scaly-bark nut, six small rubber bands, one fossilized unidentified bug—and two live earthworms (boys only).

At the end of the day the can could either be bulging with additional booty or reduced to the rattling stage, down to just one agate taw, one Indian-head penny, and one dead earthworm.

If a youngster wanted to bury his treasure in the backyard, a Prince Albert can was unexcelled as a pirate's treasure chest . . . because if one waited, say, as long as a whole day before digging it up again, the can and its priceless contents were still just as good as new.

TOBACCO-CAN KAZOO

REMOVE LID, SQUEEZE TOP TOGETHER

FILL WITH PEBBLES

PUNCH HOLES IN BOTTOM

HUM SONGS

CLOTHESLINE XYLOPHONE
PLAY A TUNE!

BOTTLES MUST BE ALIKE
FILL TO DIFFERENT LEVELS WITH WATER
TAP WITH STICK OR SPOON

(because the family dog had buried the other), a thin, flat strip of hardwood would substitute nicely.

WASHTUB BASS FIDDLE: A broomstick was attached to one handle of an overturned washtub with wire or cord. Then a long piece of baling wire (the bass string) was tied to the other handle of the tub and to the top end of the broomstick. The player thumped the string with thumb and forefinger, or toes, or whatever. No matter, as long as the thumps stayed reasonably in time with the beat.

WASHBOARD: A washboard was strummed with thimble-encased finger to jazz up the rhythm of the music.

NOTE: *Washtub and washboard were not available for use as musical instruments on washdays.*

Blowing across the mouth of an empty jug, or slapping spoons together in the palm of one's hand, also produced exquisite tones to the ears of youthful Depression-era music impresarios.

Tarzan Hits the '30s in Full Swing

In 1912 a down-on-his-luck pencil-sharpener salesman wrote a story in longhand on the backs of some old letters and other odd pieces of paper. In October of that year *All-Story Magazine* published that story—"Tarzan of the Apes"—introducing to the world a fictional hero whose popularity has rarely been surpassed.

Two years after the ape-man appeared in *All-Story*, A. C. McClurg & Company, one of the twelve major publishers who had rejected this salesman's submissions, issued a collection of Tarzan stories in book form. Thus, Edgar Rice Burroughs became a multimillionaire author in a few short years. By the time of his death in 1950, Burroughs had published twenty-six Tarzan novels, which have been translated into thirty-one languages and have sold over 36 million copies.

In January 1918, just four years after Tarzan had stormed the book market, the first ape-man movie, *Tarzan of the Apes*, opened in New York. Starring Elmo Lincoln, it played to full theaters all around the country and became one of the first silent-screen movies in history to gross more than a million dollars. Since then, fifteen different actors have worn the loincloth in forty motion pictures, which have taken in over 500 million dollars at the box office.

It was in the Depression years that Tarzan's vine hit full swing. Full-length Tarzan movies and Tarzan serials played to packed houses even when the hard times were at their hardest. In 1929, thanks to the invention of talkies, the ape-man's yell was heard for the first time, bringing moviegoers to their feet. The famous yell was augmented in 1934 by MGM's sound technicians, who combined four different sound tracks—the bleat of a camel, a violin's G-string, the howl of a hyena, the growl of a dog—and recorded them over Johnny Weissmuller's yodel, which was played at a slower speed and an octave higher. Weissmuller, the most popular screen Tarzan, later learned to imitate the eerie guttural yell, and his voice replaced the recording.

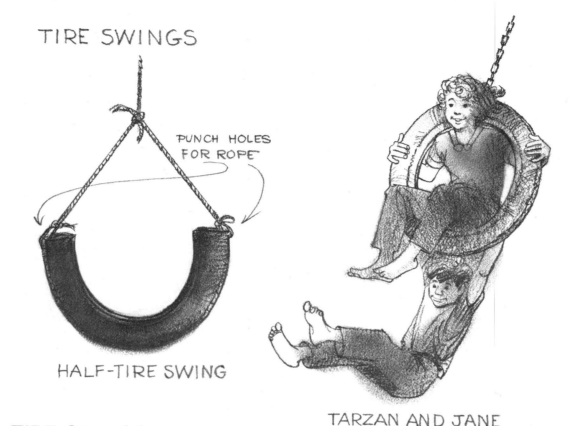

TIRE SWINGS

PUNCH HOLES FOR ROPE

HALF-TIRE SWING

TARZAN AND JANE

TIRE SWINGS

QUESTION: When does an old tire swing become a sturdy jungle vine?

ANSWER: When a young Tarzan swings on it in search of adventure.

The big sweet-gum tree in the cow pasture transforms itself into a steamy dark African jungle as Tarzan swoops from vine to vine through towering treetops and over a dangerous herd of hostile Cape buffaloes (three milk cows). The ape-man's bloodcurdling yodel strikes fear into man and beast alike as it shatters the still, humid air. "Take heart, Tarzan is on his way to the rescue!"

High above the crocodile-infested river (stock pond with pigs rooting around the perimeter), the hero of the jungle releases the vine and dives headlong into the treacherous waters. Armed only with his knife (a short stick), he does battle with the snapping-jawed reptiles to save his pet chimp Cheetah (a turtle) stranded on a floating log in midstream. The water boils as the frenzied crocs are disposed of, one by one, by the ape-man's superior cunning and agile strength. Then with another piercing Tarzan yell, the victorious hero does his famous Olympics-winning backstroke toward the distant shore.

Safely on dry land, Tarzan climbs aboard a friendly elephant (the family mule) and with a ferocious but also friendly lion (the family dog) trotting alongside for protection, they journey homeward. And not a moment too soon either, because Tarzan hears his ape mother, Kala, yelling at him again: "If you don't come to your supper this minute, I'll throw it to the hogs!"

STILTS

By the time they are ten years old, all children, especially those who are short for their age, have developed a perpetual crick in the neck from looking up at tall people. Over the years, every time his six-foot-two dad said, "Look at me when I'm talking to you, young man!" a boy obediently moved his fixed gaze from the belt

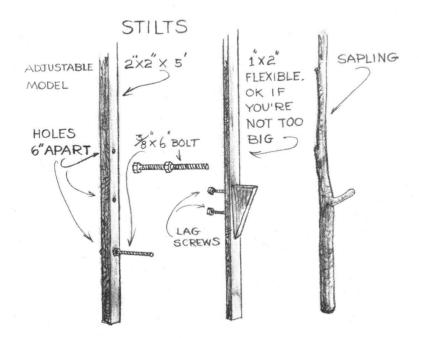

STILTS

ADJUSTABLE MODEL

2"x2" x 5'

HOLES 6" APART

⅜" x 6" BOLT

LAG SCREWS

1"x2" FLEXIBLE. OK IF YOU'RE NOT TOO BIG

SAPLING

The Tarzan yell was heard in living rooms around the country via the radio beginning in 1931, and a year later United Features Syndicate started distributing a Tarzan comic strip internationally. The strip was conceived by Joseph H. Neebe and drawn originally by Hal Foster (of Prince Valiant renown). During the mid-'30s when a family of four could manage to exist on an income of one dollar a day, Edgar Rice Burroughs was reportedly making $5,000 monthly from Tarzan comic strip syndication alone.

With Tarzan turning up everywhere, it was little wonder that children during the bleak years utterly idolized the ape-man. They swung themselves terrifyingly on any available "jungle vine" and gave themselves laryngitis trying to imitate their hero's blood-tingling yell. Tarzan symbolized a call to adventures more exotic than even those young imaginations could conjure.

buckle to stare upward at the underneath portion of a stern chin and flaring nostrils. Standing at attention like this, as if one were looking straight up to see if the sky is falling while simultaneously trying to absorb a long-winded dissertation, put an uncomfortable strain on his trapezius muscles. In other words, the back of his neck hurt like the devil! So kids throughout the ages have tried to alleviate this problem—to put themselves on equal footing with tall adults, so to speak—by climbing aboard a plaything called stilts. This high-minded maneuver could put a child eyeball-to-eyeball with a tall person. And children back in the make-do years found it worked remarkably well to remove some of the pain from a one-sided conversation . . . until the tall person commanded, "Get down off those things and listen to me!"

Adjustable stilts were ideal to work one's way up a step at a time. If long bolts weren't available for footrests, the stilt maker substituted round sticks or tree limbs wired in place with baling wire.

NOTE: *Stilts didn't come with training wheels. Thus younger children—and sometimes clumsy older ones—might require a helping hand from an adult until they learned proper balance. Then it was as easy as riding a bicycle.*

JOHNNY WALKERS

Sturdy johnny walkers were made from tree limbs that had forks suitably broad to support a child's foot.

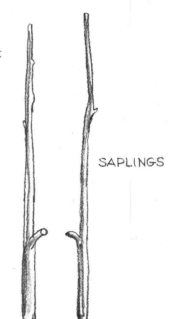

SAPLINGS

JOHNNY WALKERS
(STILTS)

HEAVY
CORD OR
WIRE

TIN
CANS

OPENED
ENDS

TOM WALKERS

TOM WALKERS

A couple of large-size cans (opened on one end) and some heavy cord or wire not only enabled kids to attain a height equivalent to three or four years' normal growth, it gave them a toy that would make the sound of a galloping horse while cutting mud pies at the same time. Fun as they were, though, there was one disadvantage to most tom walkers: If you didn't wear shoes, the raised rims on the cans would leave red indentations on the soles of the feet that wouldn't go away for hours.

NOTE: *Tom walkers, like ice skates, have been known to sprain an ankle or two. Therefore, beginners were instructed to keep the cans pulled tightly against their feet to prevent injuries while tom-walking.*

Remember Annie's Mug?

"Leapin' Lizards!" Little Orphan Annie exclaimed over the radio. "Ovaltine is good!" And it was, too. Especially if one drank it from a mug decorated with a full-color picture of Annie and Sandy, her dog that said "Arf!" The shake-up mug to mix it in was available by sending in inner jar seals from Ovaltine along with a dime for postage and handling. Annie's radio proclamation that this chocolate-flavored powder, when mixed with milk, was highly nutritious had children all over the country believing drinking it was better for them than eating all the vegetables on their plate.

However, if you were a hard-hit kid who could not afford Ovaltine, you didn't have any jar seals or money with which to acquire a Little Orphan Annie mug. Resourceful girls solved this problem by cutting out Annie and Sandy's pictures from the funny papers and pasting them on a jelly jar. Or one could make a reasonable replica of Annie's mug from a gourd.

A flat-bottomed, watermelon-shaped gourd about the size of an iced-tea glass was used. The round end of the gourd was cut off and discarded, the seeds removed, and the gourd was left to dry brick-hard in the sun. Then, with Annie and Sandy's pictures pasted on its side, the mug was ready to be filled with delicious homemade "Ovaltine."

Various Ovaltine substitutes could be concocted, and a young status-conscious hostess could use her imagination to create any of a number of culinary delights to serve to her friends. Typical was this one: to an Annie mug of milk, add 1 teaspoon sugar, 1 teaspoon cocoa, and 1 tablespoon honey and stir well. If the hostess didn't tell her guests any different, they would think she was rich—and was serving them the real thing.

4

Villains and Heroes

In the world of fiction everybody loves a hero . . . and hates a villain to pieces. The heroes have everything going for them: they are outrageously handsome, wear flashy made-to-order clothes, move in the best social circles, enjoy superb transportation facilities, get the pick of the ladies, and bask in public praise while savoring a labor-free, flamboyant life-style.

The villains, of course, are pig-eyed, weak-chinned, and otherwise ugly as sin. Evil seeps from every pore. The aura of meanness that surrounds them is enhanced by unshaven faces, droopy mustaches, and a lackluster off-the-rack wardrobe, usually in basic black. Hissed and booed from all sides and constantly harassed by hero-type persons, they try day and night—unsuccessfully—to grub out a meager living in crime.

In all walks of life, a villain gets the dirty end of the stick. If he happens to be a cowboy villain, he unfortunately ends up with a gun (or guns) that won't shoot straight—and a horse, always of a dark color, that doesn't perform any smart tricks and can't run any faster than a mule with a spavined knee. If the cowboy villain is forced to catch the first stage out of town, his luck will have it that all good seats by the windows will be occupied and he will have to sit facing the rear, unable to enjoy the scenery or see where he is going. Because females abhor him, his love life is in the doldrums. His only contact with the fair sex is through abduction or coercion, and even then he doesn't enjoy their companionship much, as they are screaming all the time at the top of their lungs.

But, even so, children in the '30s who loved to play make-believe games of "Cowboys and Indians," "Rangers and Desperadoes," or "Cops and Robbers" gave villains their rightful due. Shrewdly, kids discovered early on that without a villain, a hero would have nothing to do except sit around and play mumblety-peg. Somebody had to be the bad guy. Therefore, when a bunch of creative youngsters got together for a day of play, the volunteer Simon Legrees, who were "necessary evils," received profound praises from the heroes of the game for their unselfish contributions. Of course, no one wanted to play the role of a villain, and it took a kid with a fertile imagination to do so. He had to pretend to act contemptible and ruthless, knowing all the time that down deep he was just as much the hero as the boy next door.

Six Graves in Sudden Canyon

Dressed all in black, the stranger appeared from out of nowhere like the sinister shadow of Death. He rode slowly down the nearly deserted street, looking neither left nor right. Everything he wore was black: shirt, pants, cowboy hat, and boots. Even the fringes on his shirt sleeves were black. And in his black holsters, made of *real* leather, he packed a pair of black rubber guns with barrels so long they hung below his knees. He dismounted at Mr. Boatwright's store and looked our way. The hot wind swirled dust around his black boots, and in the distance the door of the Red-Horse Barn seemed to scream a warning on its rusty hinges.

I shuddered and told myself it must be the ice-cream cones we had sweet-talked out of my dad, or the squealing hinges, that caused my sudden rash of goose bumps. Frosty squinted across the street at the stranger and licked his cone, and we both sat up straighter on the bench outside the drugstore.

The Black Stranger parked his recently painted black bicycle (which I would have given my eyeteeth for) and walked into the general store. I saw right off that this was not just another run-of-the-mill ten-year-old kid. He didn't even glance at—much less stop to admire—the fishbowl of jawbreakers displayed in Mr. Boatwright's window. And he walked right by the penny gum-ball machine without checking the delivery chute. I sensed that this stranger dressed all in black meant only one thing—*trouble!*

Our worst suspicions were confirmed that afternoon when the town grapevine (See-Thru) brought us the bad news. He said that the Black Stranger was Killer's cousin from Kansas City and that he would be in town for two whole weeks. "And," See-Thru added, his eyes bigger than roller hoops, "Killer told Bluegill he's the fastest gun this side of the Rio Grande!"

"Well, there goes our barn," I said decisively. Fighting off the Renegades was bad enough; I wasn't about to go up against a professional gunslinger to boot. I told them so, too.

Frosty just grinned his famous "wait-just-a-minute, don't-get-excited, I'll-handle-everything-from-here" grin and took a plug of Day's Work chewing tobacco (coal tar) from his bib pocket. While he rolled it around in his mouth, he told us that a man's reputation usually didn't amount to a bag o' beans when it came right down to it, and that nobody was going to take over the Red-Horse Barn, especially a stranger. Actually, what he said was, "If the Black Stranger draws down on me, I'll blow him clean out of his fancy black boots!"

Frosty always could bolster my courage somewhat in the face of grave danger.

FROSTY & HOPPY'S LAST CHANCE SALOON (NO GIRLS ALLOWED) always did a land-office business on Saturday afternoons. After the scootmobile races, the crowd would converge on the barn to have a few drinks and play some Old Maid poker. The red-eye whiskey (iced tea without ice) flowed like water, and a lot of silver nuggets (tinfoil balls) and cash money (pop-bottle caps) changed hands. The girls flew kites or rolled their hoops around the barnyard and usually didn't come inside, because it wasn't ladylike for a girl to be seen patronizing a saloon.

Now, I wouldn't for the world say that someone wasn't ladylike, but Norma and Bobby Ann either ignored our sign or didn't give a hoot about protocol, because we had to watch them like a hawk every minute. They were always climbing up the sweet-gum tree and sneaking down inside through the loft. The next thing you'd know, there they'd be, bellied up to the bar, drinking right along with the boys—and not paying for a drop. Frosty and I tried in vain to hire a bouncer, but not even Bluegill, the bravest kid in town, would take the job. He said he wouldn't tangle with those two tomboys for all the tinfoil and bottle caps in Muskogee County.

On the first Saturday afternoon following the Black Stranger's arrival in town, I was tending bar (an old plank set across two barrels) when, without warning, he entered the saloon accompanied by Killer and Whetstone. I was the first to see him come in, because Frosty, Eskimo, Bluegill, and Pete were deep in a hot game of poker, and Kenneth and See-Thru were target shooting with their three-shooter pistols at a straw-filled Duke's Mixture tobacco sack swinging on a string from a rafter. Bobby Ann and Norma were up in the loft, driving everyone crazy with their old cigar-box banjos, waiting for their chance to sneak down and join the crowd.

When Killer escorted his two cronies up to the bar, I couldn't help noticing that I no longer had a strong craving for his Hopalong Cassidy hat because it looked terrible where he had tried to remove the creosote stain with naphtha. I wanted to tell him so but figured it might be wise to wait for a better time. He didn't exactly seem to be in the mood for idle conversation. I took one look at the Black Stranger and swallowed hard. He was the meanest-looking kid I ever saw: steely blue eyes, yellow hair, and flappy ears that would have stuck out as far as his hat if tabs of adhesive tape weren't holding them flush to his head where they belonged. (I had had this trouble a few years back, but thanks to my mother and eighteen rolls of tape, I turned out to have beautiful ears.)

When he banged his fist down on the bar to call for a drink, his hand looked as big as a bicycle saddle. With nerves of steel, I poured him a shot glass (snuff can) of red-eye without spilling a drop and said, just as nice as you please, and at the top of my lungs, "Howdy, stranger! You new in town?"

This got everybody's undivided attention, and it became quiet as a tomb. Except for Norma and Bobby Ann still banging away on their banjos, you probably could have heard the tobacco-sack target swishing back and forth through the air. When the Black Stranger tossed a Nehi cream-soda cap on the bar to pay for his drink, it rattled around and sounded as loud as a pie pan. I started to tell him a drink cost *five* bottle caps; on second thought, I told him instead that it was the age-old custom of the Last Chance Saloon to give all strangers their first drink on the house. Without even saying thanks, he tossed down the red-eye, banged his glass hard on the bar, and turned around to glare at Frosty. Killer and Whetstone turned too, both grinning like possums.

"I hear tell you're the yellow skunk that messed up my cousin's hat," Black Stranger hissed at Frosty. Frosty ignored him and raised Pete two Coca-Cola caps and one grape-soda cap.

Black Stranger took three threatening steps toward the poker table, then stopped. His giant-sized hands hovered over his black, long-barreled guns. And I saw they were loaded with *long-range stringers!* None of us local kids could handle a pistol with a barrel so long it took a stringer. There had to be so much tension on the clothespin jaws to hold a stretched stringer on the gun that it was impossible for us to squeeze the clothespin open with just the strength of one hand. It was as difficult to load as it was to shoot.

"I hear you're fast," Black Stranger taunted Frosty. "Killer, here, tells me you're so fast you can outdraw any girl in town!" At this degrading insult, Killer and Whetstone burst into laughter and poked each other in the ribs. All eyes turned on Frosty.

He got up slowly from the poker table, reached behind him for his guns hanging from a nail on the wall (he always took off his hardware while playing cards), and strapped them around his waist. Bluegill and Eskimo winked at me, and I winked back. We knew precisely what the outcome would be, because there wasn't a gun-

slinger alive who could outdraw Frosty Youngblood. Stepping away from the table and moving catlike toward Black Stranger, Frosty looked him square in the eye and said softly, "When you say that, Black Stranger, smile."

We couldn't believe what Black Stranger did then. He smiled. He really did.

It was a leering, jack-o'-lantern smile that knifed from ear to ear over his face, and before Frosty could get close enough for his short guns to be effective—the Black Stranger struck!

Not one of us there saw his lightning move. One second his huge hands were empty; the next, like magic, they held long black guns that fired simultaneously. *Thump! Thump!* Two long-range stringers smashed into Frosty's chest. Unbelieving, I saw him go down, to sprawl grotesquely in the sawdust, littered with poker-chip bottle caps and candy-cigarette stubs. Both his guns were still in their holsters. Frosty hadn't even cleared leather.

From above came the mournful strains of Norma and Bobby Ann singing "The Streets of Laredo," and to make things even gloomier a gust of wind caught the barn door just right. The eerie sound sent shivers down my backbone more than it ever had before, because my best friend and co-owner of the Red-Horse Barn Last Chance Saloon was—without a doubt, right on the spot—dead-and-out!

The next day, as Sunday school and church let out, I made it a point to avoid the Renegades and the Black Stranger like the plague. But Killer ran up and, while giving my folks the sweetest hello-smile in the world, jammed a letter into my hip pocket.

That afternoon Frosty and I must have read it over a hundred times. It was printed in blood-red Crayola on the back of a crumpled Baby Ruth wrapper. The awesome thing said:

DEAR HOPPY AND FROSTY,

THE RED HORSE BARN IS NOW THE SOUL PROPERTY OF RED RIVER RENEGAIDS. WE HAVE PUT A KEEPOUT SIGN ON IT SO YOU READ IT GOOD! IF YOU DON'T MY CUZIN WILL GIVE YOU THE SAME THING HE GAVE FROSTY. HA-HA. WE HAVE 16 GUNS, 5 RIFLES, 3 SHOTGUNS, AND 105 LONG-RANGE STRINGERS. COME GET US IF YOU AIN'T YELLER KYOATS.

YOURS TRULY,
KILLER

Now, to call a man a coyote is one thing, but a *yellow* coyote is something else! The more we thought about it, the more riled we got. We vowed that before the sun set on the Red-Horse Barn Monday evening, Killer and the Renegades—and the Black Stranger too—would be pushing up daisies in Boot Hill.

Eskimo and Pete said they were just itching to help us get the barn back from the Renegades, but it would be a few days before they could get around to it, as they had already made extensive plans to devote a lot of time to slingshot shooting. They wanted to be in top form for the big shoot coming up on Labor Day. We reminded them that Labor Day wasn't until September. "True," Eskimo said, "but you know how time has a habit of slipping up on you."

Over at Bluegill's house, he showed us a big can of newly gathered catalpa worms and said it would be a crying shame to waste such marvelous bait. He was going fishing down at Skull-Head Cove. "But if the fish happen not to be biting, I'll drop by the barn to give you a hand."

Kenneth wasn't at home, but his mother told us the dear boy had volunteered to help her put up sauerkraut all next week. Then See-Thru informed us that the arthritis in his trick knee was back with him again. He thought it would be beneficial to his health to remain off his feet for maybe a week or so.

Thus deserted by our best friends in the direst of times, Frosty and I reconciled ourselves to the sad fact that the barn would remain in control of the Renegades until the Black Stranger left town. Frosty still thought he could outdraw him if he could just get close enough to use his short guns. Our only alternative—to storm the barn using rifles and shotguns that shot long-range stringers—would be suicide. Two against five wasn't exactly the best odds in town, especially with us being the two.

After sundown, Frosty and his folks came over to my house for a Sunday evening front-porch visit. While our parents chatted, Frosty and I sat on the steps and fanned the mosquito repeller (smoldering rags in a tin can) to keep it smoking a lot. Hershel Murray came running up to take my sixteen-year-old sister, Beverly, out on a date. I figured he had been running so hard because he was late picking her up. But Hershel jokingly told us there was so much smoke coming from the can he thought our porch was on fire, whereupon my dad informed me we only wanted to chase a few mosquitoes away from the porch, not all the people out of town.

Seeing Hershel gave me an idea. I told Frosty about it, and he got so excited he wanted to talk to Hershel right then, but I said we'd better wait till later as he might be more responsive when he didn't have his mind on my sister. Hershel was seventeen, and a legend in his own time. When he was a kid he'd had a reputation as the most notorious rubber-gun gunslinger that ever lived in these parts. For many years he had successfully defended the Red-Horse Barn against hordes of undesirable owl-hooters. The story had it that, one Saturday afternoon in 1927, Hershel had single-handedly wiped out the Apache-Jack Marauders and run Apache-Jack Wingfield clean out of the county. (The Wingfields moved to Oklahoma City when Mr. Wingfield got a job there in the oil fields.) Hershel retired back when he was twelve and hung up his guns forever.

Monday morning we found Hershel working over at Mr. Buford's place. He was moving the "convenience" (outdoor toilet) up closer to the house because Mr. Buford, now in his eighties, confessed he no longer enjoyed quite such a long walk every morning before breakfast.

Frosty and I pitched right in and helped Hershel set the two-holer over the new pit he had dug. While we gave the structure a fresh coat of whitewash, we burdened Hershel with our problem and asked his advice. Hershel didn't give us an answer right away. He sat down and thought long and hard about it until Frosty and I finished painting the privy. There was little wonder he'd been such a famous gunfighter. He was clearly a man who thought things out very carefully—no hasty decisions for him.

We sat down on the ground with Hershel, and he told us the situation called for cunning, strategic planning, and the development and use of sophisticated weaponry. Actually, what he said was, "Build yourselves a big cannon and ambush 'em at the pass!"

Hershel took a sharp stick, and we watched spellbound as he drew in the dirt a set of plans for the most devastating weapon ever imagined in rubber-gun warfare. Thanking Hershel from the bottom of our hearts for his valuable time, we rushed off to Granny Porter's house. There were several fine-looking 2 by 4's leaning up against her smokehouse that I had had my eye on for months.

Our spirits dropped to find that Granny was not in one of her overly generous moods. But our charms finally won her over, and three hours later, after picking her garden clean of green beans for canning (about a hundred bushels), we walked away the proud owners of four of the nicest four-foot-long 2 by 4's you ever saw.

For our plan to succeed, absolute secrecy was imperative, so we didn't say a word to the other guys. It wasn't that we didn't trust our sidekicks with restricted information, but as Frosty put it as we sneaked the boards into his dad's toolshed, "If See-Thru was an Indian, he'd be called 'Running-Mouth.'"

That afternoon the Fort Gibson Firearms Foundry went full speed ahead. For three hours the two-man crew sawed, hammered, nailed, chiseled, wired, argued, and cussed (dang it!)—only to discover that somewhere along the assembly line we had not followed the blueprints exactly and would have to start again from scratch. Frosty, sucking his hammered thumb, said, "That's the dangdest-looking gun I ever laid eyes on!"

But we persisted and later, when my mother called us over to have some ice-cold grape penny drinks, we had—concealed under some old croker sacks—the most destructive dead-and-out-maker rubber gun ever imagined by mankind. We named it "Old Hershel."

Old Hershel was a six-shot cannon with three barrels, each four feet long. They were nailed 3 inches apart onto a crosspiece, which was mounted on top of a nail keg by a rusty stove bolt so the barrels would swivel 180 degrees. The receiver of each barrel was notched to hold two rounds of ammunition (each round was four rubber bands knotted together), and these extra-long long-range stringers were so powerful it took both of us to stretch them back to load them into the notches over the leather-strap triggers.

That evening as we admired Old Hershel, Frosty suggested it would behoove us to test the cannon's accuracy on a living target. With an instinct born of experience, my dog Nicky, who was chewing on one of my double zingers, returned the rubber band to me and went directly underneath the back porch. And I suddenly remembered the coverless Big Little Book that I had recently swapped Eskimo thirteen unchipped marbles for and told Frosty I thought it was time I caught up on some reading. Frosty explained that he was more than willing to volunteer to be the target himself, but as he made a much larger target than me, to do so would not prove the absolute accuracy of the cannon. In other words, he said, "Do you want to get the barn back from Killer or not?"

While I continued to remind him that my fragile-boned body had a very low tolerance to pain, he padded my backsides with croker sacks stuffed under my galluses and into the seat of my overalls and gave his cross-my-heart assurance, "You'll never know when it hits ya."

Surprising myself that I summoned up enough courage to speak further, I told him that in case I didn't come back, I wanted him to have my scootmobile and whistle slingshot for his very own and that my superb collection of Big Little Books was to be donated in my name to the school library. We shook hands, as best friends do on such poignant occasions, and I walked slowly out of the toolshed, stopping about 20 feet away. With eyes closed tightly, I gritted my teeth.

"Okay, that's fine," Frosty yelled from inside the shed. "Ready . . ."

I had forgotten to tell him he could have Nicky too—

"Aim . . ."

I don't believe he ever did say "fire," because all I heard was an angry whirring sound like a rainmaker, just before it felt like Mr. Buford's mule had kicked me in the back of the neck. The ringing in my ears was so loud I didn't hear exactly what Frosty said then, but I think he said, "It shoots a might high and a smidgen to the left."

Tuesday morning, from my lofty position on the roof of Frosty's house, I had a commanding view of the Red-Horse Barn and the road to town. I heard the ice truck somewhere in the vicinity of Uncle Eura's and knew it would come up the road any minute. The tin roof was hot enough to fry an egg on, but I flattened myself out

behind the chimney anyway and told Frosty on our tin-can telephone that I thought it was time he took over the lookout post, as I had sustained third-degree burns on 90 percent of my body. From the cool comfort of the toolshed, Frosty said there must be a kink in the wire on his end because he couldn't hear me too well.

When Mr. Brown stopped his ice truck at my house, I saw it had already attracted half the kids in town, as well as two of the Renegades, Sticker and Kong. Kong was chomping on a chunk of ice big as his fist, making me so thirsty I was tempted to shuck the plan right then and there. But I continued to endure the excruciating pain while watching the Pied-Piper truck suck up kids like a magnet as it came closer. Killer, Whetstone, and the Black Stranger came running out of the barn too. In a few minutes the truck, with everybody tagging along behind it, would be on its way up the hill, out of sight of the barn. It was time to make our move.

Sweating like sinners on Sunday, we dragged Old Hershel across the road, behind the barn, and into the shelter of Cherokee Pass in Sudden Canyon. Sudden Canyon was an erosion ditch that started as a small rut in the pasture below the barn but deepened and widened out where it cut across Mr. Sudden's farm. It was a canyon to us, because in some places it was four or five feet deep, and this made the walls higher than our heads.

We situated Old Hershel in the middle of the canyon floor about 25 feet from Cherokee Pass (a narrow, sharp-curved portion of the ditch) and hastily went over Frosty's three-part brilliant and flawless plan once again.

1. Frosty would provoke, taunt, cajole, or otherwise entice the Renegades to chase him into the canyon, whereupon he would then run like the wind through Cherokee Pass and take an unobserved position on the rim to cover me with his Greener (double-barreled shotgun).

2. When the unsuspecting outlaws came through the pass, one at a time, the cannoneer (me) selected over all others because of his outstanding courage and marksmanship would systematically and without qualms send each and every one of the Red River Renegades directly to Boot Hill, not excluding the despicable Black Stranger.

3. The cannoneer would not, under any condition, panic or abandon his post—even though he might miss a shot or two—because he would be safely out of range of the enemies' guns and would be adequately protected at all times by Frosty from above.

I told Frosty I wasn't overly thrilled with Part 3 of the plan. He said we'd bush-whack the Renegades right after noontime dinner, as he always fought better on a full stomach.

The afternoon was hot as a blacksmith's forge. Along the sun-baked floor of the canyon, heat waves shimmered, danced upward, and distorted images into hazy mirages. Above, a solitary hawk made endless circles in the cloudless sky. The far-off sound of a howling wolf split the air. A small gray lizard scurried into the shade.

Frosty's warning wolf cry was soon followed by shouts, threats, and war whoops, as thundering feet echoed off the canyon walls. I shakily braced myself behind Old Hershel. With the speed of an arrow, Frosty came running through the pass. Breathing heavily, he scrambled up onto the rim of the canyon above me, loaded his Greener, and cautioned, "If you miss 'em we're done for! They're madder'n hornets!"

With nerves of iron, which is the common trait of all brave men, I swung Old Hershel toward Cherokee Pass and grasped the leather-strap trigger of the middle barrel. Killer came storming through first, running hard. His mouth opened in astonishment and he braked to a stop as Old Hershel roared. The long-range stringer slapped him square on the belt buckle. But as usual the cheat yelled, "Ya, you only winged me—"

Ka-thump! I gave him another one. It smacked into his chest, and he went down like a fallen tree. "Yip, yip, yahoo!" Frosty war-whooped. "Attaway, Hoppy!"

Whetstone and Sticker galloped into view at the same time. Sticker tripped over Killer's body, and before he could regain his feet, Old Hershel gave him a one-way ticket to the happy hunting grounds. Whetstone went into a crouch and circled toward me, firing his repeating rifle as he came, but his stringers fell far short of their mark.

Deliberately, I swung away from him and put a quick dead-and-out shot into Kong, who had gotten himself temporarily stuck in the narrow opening of the pass. Whetstone threw down his rifle and raised his arms in surrender. I looked up at Frosty. He pointed his thumbs downward. We both knew Whetstone carried a Yankee hideout pistol in the right rear pocket of his overalls. Without even saying "sorry," I dropped him in his tracks.

Four down, one to go, and one more shot left on Old Hershel. Sardonically, I chortled to myself, "*I saved the last one for you, Black Stranger!*" I aimed at the pass and waited.

And I waited some more.

In fact, I waited so long I had cramps in my hind end. Sweat streamed down my face, stinging my eyes and blurring my vision. Something was bad wrong. I knew the Black Stranger probably couldn't run very fast in his cowboy boots, but he should have arrived long before now. "Where is he?" I asked Frosty. No answer came. I turned around, looked up, and could have died. Frosty was gone!

I whirled back around as a movement in the pass caught my eye. Aha! The Black Stranger's hat came into full view as he peeked cautiously around the corner of the canyon wall. Taking a deep breath, I held it, took dead aim on the black crown, and squeezed off the shot. *Thwack!*

The hat spun in the air; I screamed victoriously. "Yippee! I got him, Frosty. He's dead-and-out!" Overjoyed, I got to my feet and gave Old Hershel a big hug. Then I froze in terror. The Black Stranger, with a long stick in his hand, stepped into view, retrieved his hat, and stuck it over the end of the stick. Then he backtracked into the pass, and I saw his hat peek around the corner at me again. But this time I saw the stick. I couldn't believe that the spitting image of Hopalong Cassidy (me), the smartest gunslinger who ever cleaned out a nest of outlaws, had fallen for the old "put-your-hat-on-a-stick-and-make-the-other-guy-shoot-at-it" trick. And to add insult to injury—even though they weren't supposed to because they were dead-and-out—the bodies of Killer, Whetstone, Sticker, and Kong chuckled and shook with glee.

Swaggering, the arch-enemy approached slowly; the black deadly guns in his hands pointed their long death fingers at me. I was trapped like a rabbit in a box. My short pistols were useless against his long ones, and if I tried to climb out of the canyon, he'd shoot me in the back.

He came closer, the evil grin grew wider, and his steely blue eyes bored into mine. Hoping against hope that Frosty hadn't abandoned me and had just run home to use the privy, I reached for my persimmon whistle and blew loud as I could.

"Whatcha doing, baby," the Black Stranger rasped, "whistling for your mama?" I saw his big hands tighten, ready to squeeze the gun butts. Courageously, I braced myself against the inevitable.

And then it happened.

The most earsplitting, spine-chilling war whoops ever heard by any living creature in Muskogee County turned the Black Stranger to stone. It even caused one of his ears to come untaped. Rolling like a rain barrel, Frosty, with pistols in hand, came spinning down the canyon wall. He rolled right over the body of Killer, squashing his hat flat, then came up running fast, still whooping like a pack of wild dogs. He

The Decade of Real-life Villains

On a hot summer morning in 1933, a well-dressed couple in a shiny new Ford coupé drove along Robinson Avenue in downtown Oklahoma City. As they neared an intersection, the pretty young woman driving braked to a stop and asked a traffic cop for directions. The policeman approached and politely answered her questions. Smiling sweetly, the woman thanked him warmly—before she shot the startled man in the face with both barrels of a sawed-off shotgun. The woman let out a squeal of elation, her youthful companion laughed heartily, and the car sped away, leaving the officer lying dead in the street.

This was the cold-blooded act of real-life villains. These were Bonnie and Clyde.

The Great American Depression brought good times to at least one profession—crime. While factories closed, legitimate businesses folded, and Dust

galloped in circles, hopped, danced, and zigzagged. You've never in all your travels ever seen such goings-on! I was as stunned and perplexed as the Black Stranger. (Frosty told me later it was his famous "make-'em-think-Indian-gone-loco-on-firewater" trick.) After running up, down, and around the canyon walls a few times he did three somersaults, two cartwheels, flip-flopped around on the ground like a fish out of water, zigzagged again, in low between me and the Black Stranger—and put two double zingers into the villain's dastardly black heart.

Simultaneously, reflex action triggered the Black Stranger's guns. And with my luck running true to form, they were still pointing directly at me. The powerful long-range stringers parted Frosty's hair on the wrong side and slapped into my chest so hard they knocked all the dust out of the bib of my overalls

But before I went down to lie staring up at the sky with sightless eyes, I saw the Black Stranger crumple in a heap—his face a picture of shock and disbelief—the jack-o'-lantern smile erased from his face forever.

Frosty continued his frenetic shenanigans for a full five minutes.

The Renegades were so captivated with Old Hershel they helped Frosty and me move it up to the barn. Jason (alias the Black Stranger) said he was going to build one just like it when he got back to Kansas City. While we were taking turns shooting the cannon at Killer's Hopalong Cassidy hat (which Frosty's antics had rendered unsalvageable), Bluegill arrived to say the fish weren't biting worth a hoot. Eskimo and Pete straggled in, informing us they had perfected their slingshot shooting earlier than expected and noting that Kenneth was on his way over too, as his mother had relieved him of his sauerkraut duties. See-Thru ran up and said his arthritis was so much better he felt spry as a kid again.

Frosty and I cautioned Killer that Old Hershel would be on guard duty twenty-four hours a day, in case he and the Renegades had any more ideas for taking over our barn. Killer said he thought it was a shame that such a magnificent weapon couldn't be displayed for all to see, and that it might be a nice gesture on our part to donate Old Hershel to the Honor Heights Park Veterans' Hospital over in Muskogee. It would look absolutely splendid alongside the other cannons there on the lawn.

After supper I finally located Frosty by investigating the strange hammering noises coming from Sudden Canyon. He was busy making crosses out of sticks and shingles. I agreed with him wholeheartedly that the least we could do was to give the departed a decent burial, and I congratulated him on the professional lettering job he had done on the markers. The names of the deceased, printed in creosote on the shingles, were just as clear as they could be. Frosty explained that "Black Stranger" contained too many letters to go on a shingle, so he abbreviated one cross with the initials B.S.

As Frosty pounded six grave markers into the ground, I couldn't believe my eyes! But there it was plain as day on one of them in big black letters—HOPPY. Horrified, I told Frosty, if it was all the same to him, I'd rather not be buried within a hundred-mile radius of a bunch of owlhooters like the Red River Renegades. He was most understanding and sympathetic but reminded me of the centuries-old Code of the West: "You gotta plant 'em where they fall."

BASIC STOCK (rifles, shotguns, etc.)

Rifles and other long-barreled guns were often made from a single piece of lumber. The problem was, good solid 1-inch-thick boards long enough to make rifles, tommy guns, or shotguns were at a premium. Such boards were usually hoarded by grown-ups for shelving or mending fences and outbuildings. Shorter boards, though, less than 2 feet long, suitable for gunstocks, could most likely be retrieved in time if one searched woodsheds and kindling boxes. We always took great pains in sawing out a stock, for it needed to be just right to fit the individual user's size and arm length. A carefully made stock would last for years, and with the use of different barrels it could easily be converted into the type of rubber gun one needed for the game to be played: rifle or shotgun for cowboy shoot-outs, tommy gun for cops and robbers.

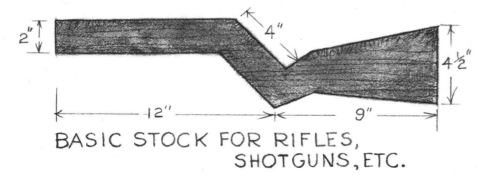

BASIC STOCK FOR RIFLES, SHOTGUNS, ETC.

Bowl farms lay deserted, unprincipled, down-on-their-luck individuals in alarming numbers went in search of easy money outside the law. Across the nation, marauders in fast cars, armed to the teeth with pistols, rifles, shotguns, and tommy guns, began robbing small-town banks, post offices, and savings and loan associations. In large cities organized crime escalated rapidly, raking in millions of dollars from gambling, prostitution, bootlegging, auto theft, assassinations, extortion, and kidnapping. By 1935 the Justice Department estimated so many people had turned to crime that crooks outnumbered plumbers, carpenters, and electricians by four to one, grocers by six to one, and physicians by twenty to one.

Most children growing up in the '30s knew where fictional villains left off and the real ones began. We were constantly exposed, through newspapers, radio, and newsreels, to the killing sprees of gangsters who plagued the Depression years. No fantasy here. When these bad people shot real bullets from real guns, their victims did not jump up and brush themselves off, ready to play the game again. They were dead—not just make-believe "dead-and-out."

There were none among us who hero-worshiped a gangster. We didn't even rally around "Pretty Boy" Floyd, the boy-faced killer who holed up in the nearby Cookson Hills close to Akins, Oklahoma, and reputedly gave half his bank-robbery loot to the grubbing Dust Bowl farmers. We felt justice had prevailed when his life of crime came to an end; he was killed by FBI agents on October 22, 1934. And six months earlier, in May 1934, when the notorious Bonnie Parker and Clyde Barrow were killed by a posse that pumped 187 bullets into their car, my friend Frosty Youngblood, a ten-year-old arithmetic buff, said, "I'd give anything to have been there and counted the bullet holes in that car! I'll bet a thousand marbles they counted 'em wrong."

At the Top of the 1930s' Thug Parade:

• BRUNO RICHARD HAUPTMANN: On March 1, 1932, Hauptmann kidnapped the infant son of aviation hero

Charles Lindbergh. The child was found dead six weeks after a ransom of $50,000 had been paid. Hauptmann was caught by New York police two years later. He was tried, convicted, and electrocuted on April 3, 1936. His execution was registered with deep satisfaction by the nation.

• JOHN HERBERT DILLINGER: Dillinger was a U.S. Navy deserter who started as a small-time thief in 1923, later emerged in the '30s as a Robin Hood folk hero to his own kind. He reportedly was very generous in nature and would stop by Chicago movie theaters to give each kid waiting in the matinee line a quarter. When he took hostages for a ride, he invariably gave them carfare home. Constantly in and out of prison, he escaped once from the Crown Point, Indiana, jail, bluffing his way out with a gun he had carved out of wood. Between June 10, 1933, and July 22, 1934, he allegedly killed ten men and, with accomplices, robbed twelve banks for a total take of $308,000. The FBI claimed to have killed Dillinger outside Chicago's Biograph Theater on July 22, 1934. But some people have suggested that another man, James Lawrence, a small-time hoodlum, was shot down in his place, and that the Indiana gangster disappeared to live out his life in obscurity.

• MACHINE GUN KELLY: It was said that George Kelly was so good with a tommy gun he could write his name with bullets on a barn wall. This could be seriously doubted, though, since he couldn't even write his name with a pen or pencil. An illiterate, good-natured drunk, Kelly started out as a bootlegger and would have been content doing just this for the rest of his life, had it not been for his ambitious wife, Kathryn Shannon. Kate put a shiny new tommy gun in Kelly's hands and pressured him into pulling big-time capers like bank robbery and kidnapping. Kelly tried knocking over a couple of small banks but didn't like it because he was afraid of getting shot. So while Kate passed out souvenir bullets from his tommy gun and bragged that her husband was shooting down lawmen and cleaning out cashier cages by the dozens, Kelly went back to running booze and playing poker

NOTE: *It was important that all barrels on rifles, shotguns, tommy guns, and cannons be scoop-shaped on the end (the same as the pistols shown earlier) for safety while loading and firing. (See "Rubber-Gun Safety" on page 7.) All these guns shot long-range stringers for ammunition, and those with clothespin triggers were loaded and fired in the same manner as the basic pistol. (See page 8.)*

SINGLE-SHOT RIFLE

1"X2"X24"

SCOOPED END

NAIL OR SCREW BARREL TO STOCK

SMALL NAIL

BASIC STOCK

RUBBER BAND FOR JAW TENSION

SIMPLE SINGLE-SHOT

TO FIRE, PUSH KNOT OFF WITH THUMB

TIE KNOT IN STRINGER

SINGLE-SHOT RIFLE

To some unscrupulous rubber-gun gunslingers, the single-shot rifle was an illicit backup weapon. Before a planned shoot-out started, it was stashed away in some concealed spot—behind a bale of hay or down in the storm cellar—to be there loaded and ready for its owner to grab after he had managed to get himself chased directly to it.

But this deceptive sidewinder's prank could turn sour, for the instigator of the trick might run down into the cellar to find his favorite rifle had vanished, replaced by a chilling note on the cellar door: TO WHOM IT MAY CONCERN—IF YOU WANT YOUR OLD RIFLE BACK LEAVE 26 MARBLES, OR 2 GOOD TOPS, OR 3 YARDSTICKS, OR SOMETHING JUST AS EXPENSIVE IN THE HOLLOW STUMP IN SUDDEN CANYON. YOURS TRULY, THE RED BANDIT.

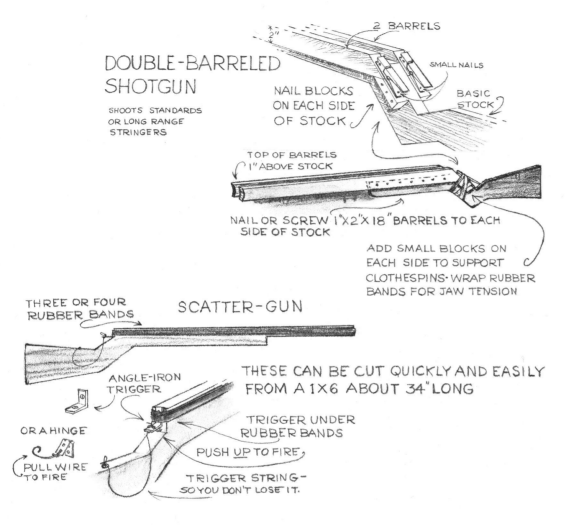

DOUBLE-BARRELED SHOTGUN

SHOOTS STANDARDS OR LONG RANGE STRINGERS

2 BARRELS

SMALL NAILS

NAIL BLOCKS ON EACH SIDE OF STOCK

BASIC STOCK

TOP OF BARRELS 1" ABOVE STOCK

NAIL OR SCREW 1"X2"X18" BARRELS TO EACH SIDE OF STOCK

ADD SMALL BLOCKS ON EACH SIDE TO SUPPORT CLOTHESPINS· WRAP RUBBER BANDS FOR JAW TENSION

THREE OR FOUR RUBBER BANDS

SCATTER-GUN

THESE CAN BE CUT QUICKLY AND EASILY FROM A 1X6 ABOUT 34" LONG

ANGLE-IRON TRIGGER

TRIGGER UNDER RUBBER BANDS

PUSH UP TO FIRE

OR A HINGE

PULL WIRE TO FIRE

TRIGGER STRING— SO YOU DON'T LOSE IT.

DOUBLE-BARRELED SHOTGUN (Greener)

Every day of the week, including Sundays, a youthful Depression-era toy maker kept his eye peeled for little things, like how near the lard can was to being empty, how many pipefuls of tobacco were left in Granddad's Prince Albert can, how many cigarettes to go in Uncle Frank's Bull Durham sack, the exact number of cigars left in a given box, and how soon would a broom or mop see its final leg. His timing had to

with the boys. But in 1933 Kate pinned poor Kelly down and talked him into kidnapping millionaire oilman Charles Urschel of Oklahoma City for a ransom of $200,000. When the ransom was paid (in marked bills), the Kellys went on a cross-country spending spree with the FBI right on their tails. They were finally caught and arrested in Memphis, Tennessee, on September 26, 1933, without a shot being fired. Thereafter, George was laughingly referred to by the press as "Pop Gun Kelly." They both got life in prison, where Kelly died in 1954. Kate, who never saw her dreams of becoming a famous gun moll materialize, was paroled four years after her husband's death.

• PRETTY BOY FLOYD: Born and raised in Akins, Oklahoma, the son of a poor-dirt Cookson Hills farmer, Charles Arthur Floyd turned to crime at the age of eighteen. When the family farm was lost to the Dust Bowl and bank foreclosure, the hardworking Floyd could not find a job to feed his pregnant sixteen-year-old wife, Wilma Hargrove, so he pulled a payroll robbery. He was caught and served three years for the crime. When released he headed for Kansas City, where he joined up with big-money gangsters like Red Lovett, Tom Bradley, and Jack Atkins, to serve his bank robbery apprenticeship. It was there he was given the nickname he detested, when a Kansas City madam said to him in her brothel, "I want you for myself, pretty boy." The nickname stuck throughout his career.

In the Depression years to follow, the charming, good-looking gangster robbed three dozen midwestern banks—so many in Oklahoma during 1932 that the state's bank insurance rates doubled and the governor placed a $6,000 reward on his head, dead or alive. Floyd was said to have confiscated and destroyed farm mortgages while looting the Oklahoma banks and to have shared his ill-gotten gains with his neighbors, other Cookson Hill victims of the Dust Bowl. While doing his Robin Hood act, Floyd was also machine-gunning lawmen and innocent bystanders. He kept score of his killings by filing notches on his gold watch fob. When he was killed by FBI agents on an Ohio farm in October 1934, Melvin Purvis, agent in charge, removed Floyd's watch from his pocket and counted the notches on the fob. The number agreed with FBI records. "Ten," Purvis said to his men. "Who would have thought the pretty punk could count?"

• BONNIE AND CLYDE: Clyde Barrow was twenty-one and Bonnie Parker nineteen when they met in a Dallas café in 1930. For the next four years this handsome farmhand and golden-haired waitress made headlines robbing and killing their way through the South and Midwest. The star-crossed lovers stayed on the run, sleeping and eating on the road as they robbed grocery stores, gas stations, and other small Depression-hit businesses. Their biggest haul was $1,500; their average take was only $40 or $50. John Dillinger, while serving time in the Michigan City, Indiana, penitentiary, called them "a couple of penny-ante killers. They're giving gangsters a bad name!" The trigger-happy pair killed for the sheer joy of killing and are perhaps the most illogical and murderous couple ever recorded in the annals of American crime. During their short career they shot and killed twelve people and seriously wounded twenty-seven more.

The nation breathed a sigh of relief when the bullet-riddled lovers went to their graves. The kill-crazy Bonnie fancied herself a poet and liked to glamorize her exploits in verse. Shortly after her death, several newspapers ran one of her poems, titled "The Story of Suicide Sal," in which she painted Clyde as being "honest, upright, and clean"—an innocent victim of the times. The last stanza of the poem, ironically, came closer to the truth than Bonnie ever dreamed:

> Some day they will go down together,
> And they will bury them side by side.
> To a few it means grief,
> To the law it's relief,
> But it's death to Bonnie and Clyde.

be perfect if he hoped to acquire the empty can, bag, box, or discarded broom or mop. If he was off lallygagging around when one of these priceless items was thrown out the door, he was out of luck—because another more attentive toy maker would be there to catch it before it even hit the trash can.

Sometimes smart little kids would resort to adult psychology (which occasionally backfired) to speed up the procurement of a valuable toy-making item such as a mopstick: "Mom, that old mop is so scraggly, it's working you to death."

"You're right, I'm pooped. Here, you finish. Mop it, rinse it good, and give it two coats of wax. When you're through in here, do the dining-room floor too."

One-by-twos were fine for shotgun barrels, but for the look of the real thing, broom- or mopsticks couldn't be beat. And if they were painted black, waxed, and polished to resemble blued steel, the shotgun could pass for a genuine Greener, the famous shotgun of the Old West, made in England by the prestigious gunsmith W. W. Greener.

REPEATER RIFLE

Notches for a repeater rifle were sawed out carefully and about 1 inch deep to allow space for both the trigger strap and the rubber-band ammunition to fit securely in place when the firearm was loaded. A thin leather strap cut from an old belt made the best trigger. But strong cloth such as denim or canvas would do fine.

Whether the barrel was mounted to the stock with nails or screws was not important. It was important, though, to predrill holes to prevent the wood from splitting. People who say, "I never cried over spilt milk" evidently never split a beautiful rifle stock they had worked hard on all day.

How the Repeater Rifle was Loaded and Fired

Step 1. The trigger strap was held so it rested along the top of the notches cut in the barrel.

Step 2. The first rubber band was looped over the end of the barrel, then stretched back and into the first notch (the one closest to the end of the barrel), making sure the trigger strap was underneath the band. The second rubber band was put into the next notch, and so on, until the last notch—the one closest to the butt of the gun—was loaded. This was the rubber band which would fire first.

Step 3. To fire the repeater rifle, the trigger strap was pulled upward, releasing the rubber bands from their notches, one at a time. The faster and harder the trigger strap was pulled determined how quickly the repeater rifle would repeat. All guns that had notches and trigger straps (including cannons) were loaded and fired in this manner.

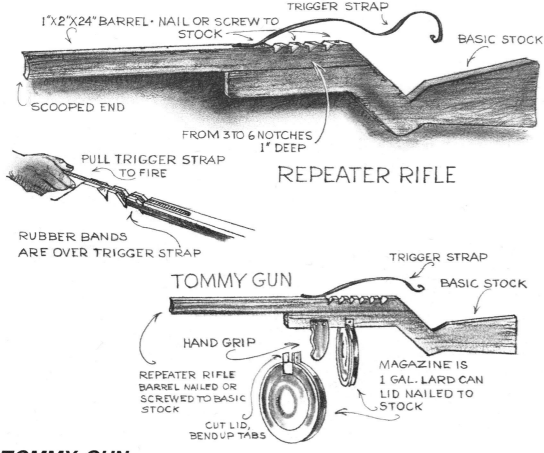

1"×2"×24" BARREL · NAIL OR SCREW TO STOCK

TRIGGER STRAP

BASIC STOCK

SCOOPED END

FROM 3 TO 6 NOTCHES 1" DEEP

REPEATER RIFLE

PULL TRIGGER STRAP TO FIRE

RUBBER BANDS ARE OVER TRIGGER STRAP

TOMMY GUN

TRIGGER STRAP

BASIC STOCK

HAND GRIP

REPEATER RIFLE BARREL NAILED OR SCREWED TO BASIC STOCK

MAGAZINE IS 1 GAL. LARD CAN LID NAILED TO STOCK

CUT LID, BEND UP TABS

TOMMY GUN

A wood hand grip and a lard-can lid would transform a repeater rifle into a tommy gun in the time it took to read a Dick Tracy comic strip. Painted black, it looked authentic and was ready to spray rubber bands faster than a blinking eye.

The Johnny-on-the-Spot Named Dick

Talk about being in the right place at the right time! The timing was perfect for Dick Tracy, the hawk-nosed, sharp-chinned detective hero who hit the comic strips in the early '30s when swarms of gangsters were running wild. Chester Gould, the clever artist who created the cartoon character, was quoted as saying, "I believe people are fed up with gangsters taking over the country. Even when they are caught, which is seldom, they come out of the courts scot-free. So I thought: What if you had a detective who doesn't mess around taking the hoodlums to court, but shoots them instead?"

Putting his ideas to paper, Gould launched a comic strip that was loaded for bear. In the very first week Tracy—and a million readers—witnessed the slaying of his sweetheart's father, Jeremiah Trueheart. This marked the first time that anyone in the history of the funnies had been gunned to death in cold blood. But many, many more were to follow, for Dick Tracy was so embittered by the foul murder of Tess Trueheart's dad that he swore to avenge all such killings and signed on as a policeman for life.

While Tracy mowed 'em down with his tommy gun on the funny pages, Quaker Oats cereal brought him to the radio too—and with him a cunning, and immensely successful, sales gimmick called the Dick Tracy Secret Service Patrol. A kid could join the patrol for only one box top, but if he desired to escalate higher in rank, say to a sergeant, the badge would cost him five box tops. It was seven box tops for a lieutenant's badge, ten for a captain's, and so on. In other words, a kid's rise in the Dick Tracy Secret Service Patrol depended mainly on the quantity of Quaker Oats he could stuff down at breakfast.

Are You Hurt Bad, Tom?

To strengthen his screen image as the toughest hombre in town, Tom Mix's publicity agents had a field day in the '30s promoting him as a cowboy hero who had an authentic background to start with. In the course of his many adventure-filled occupations, he reportedly sustained numerous injuries, any one of which would have incapacitated an ordinary guy for a period lasting from six months to life. These included twelve gunshot wounds, thirty fractured bones, twenty-two knife wounds, and a 4-inch-square hole many inches deep blown in his back by dynamite. A line drawing of Tom Mix with an X or O marking the spot of these injuries was furnished free to all Ralston Straight Shooters.

The day Killer (Carl Peterson, our favorite local villain, who always played the part to the hilt) received his official Ralston Straight Shooter illustration portraying the location of Tom Mix's wounds, we gawked at it all day. This cowboy was truly, honest-to-goodness tough as a boot! Frosty Youngblood, however, believed the gunshot count on the picture was less than accurate . . . because in a single movie, one we had sat through twice, he had counted Tom Mix being shot *seven* times.

The real-life tommy gun was named after John T. Thompson, a retired army officer, who patented it in 1920. Weighing about 10 pounds, it fired standard .45-caliber ammunition at the rate of 450 rounds per minute. It would empty the circular drum magazine holding 50 rounds in less than eight seconds. Despite its inaccuracy, limited range, and tendency to jam easily, it gained notoriety as the weapon of gangsters and lawmen alike during the late '20s and '30s, when crooks were monopolizing the headlines. Toy manufacturers put several toy replicas of the famous tommy gun on the market. One, a windup model, made a feeble *rat-tat-tat* sound as sparks flew from the muzzle. Its exorbitant cost of $3.00 put it out of reach of most children. They reached for their homemade tommy gun instead, and while rubber bands spewed from its barrel they shouted out a *rat-tat-tat* that beat the sound of the $3.00 gun any day.

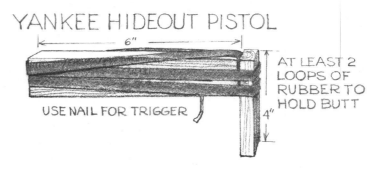

YANKEE HIDEOUT PISTOL
6"
USE NAIL FOR TRIGGER
AT LEAST 2 LOOPS OF RUBBER TO HOLD BUTT
4"

YANKEE HIDEOUT PISTOL

According to southern children, kids in the northern part of the United States not only had a strange way of talking, they had a peculiar way of making rubber guns too: the hideout pistol, for example. A couple of small boards held together with rubber bands appeared to be anything but a rubber gun. Yet it was a cleverly conceived product resulting from sly Yankee ingenuity. It was fast and simple to make, worked like a charm, and was small enough for a shifty-type person to hide in a pocket, sock, or sleeve. It had one drawback, though: If carried concealed in a hip pocket, it had a tendency to discharge when sat on. When a kid jumped up out of his chair all of a sudden, as if stung by a bee, he was branded as one who should be watched closely during rubber-gun battles.

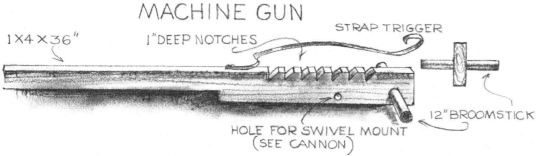

MACHINE GUN

1 X 4 X 36"   1"DEEP NOTCHES   STRAP TRIGGER

12"BROOMSTICK

HOLE FOR SWIVEL MOUNT
(SEE CANNON)

MACHINE GUN

The machine gun, sawed from 1-inch stock lumber, was essentially an enlarged version of the repeating rifle. The barrel, being much longer than that of the rifle, required long-range stringers for ammunition. Machine guns were frequently mounted on the hoods of scootmobiles. And when a kid came *clack-clack-clack*ing lickety-split into the midst of a battle with the chin straps of his Jack Oakie cap flapping in the breeze and his machine gun swiveling and firing to beat sixty, one would think a World War I tank had arrived on the scene. The swivel mount for the machine gun was the same as that used for the cannon. (See the illustration of the rubber-gun cannon on page 79.)

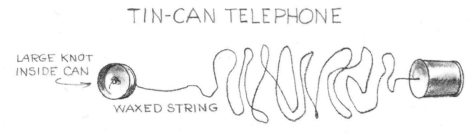

TIN-CAN TELEPHONE

LARGE KNOT
INSIDE CAN

WAXED STRING

TIN-CAN TELEPHONE

Young children have never had a problem with long-distance communication, as most of them are endowed with amplified voice boxes that can easily send a message across the Grand Canyon. However, when devious plans were in the works and secrecy was imperative, the volume of a kid's voice was reduced to a whisper over the tin-can telephone.

The reason Killer was the solitary, bona fide Tom Mix Ralston Straight Shooter among us was that he happened to be the only kid we knew who could afford to eat a lot of Ralston. He once confessed, however, that he didn't like it all that much. Good tasting or bad, Ralston cereal rendered box tops that were better than real money.

Occasionally, when Killer felt so magnanimous he forgot to project his villainous image, he'd invite all of us who didn't own a radio over to his house to listen to Tom Mix or some other show. We liked Dick Tracy a lot too. Killer's folks had a battery-operated radio similar to my Uncle Dan's over in Fort Smith, and Mrs. Peterson was real nice, not at all the way you'd expect a villain's mother to be. She always made us feel right at home with cookies, popcorn balls, or other treats. And for some reason Killer seemed a different person when she was in the room; he was just as sweet as he could be.

KEEP STRING TAUT

MAKE IT AS LONG AS YOU LIKE

If Alexander Graham Bell could have seen two kids transmitting and receiving lengthy coded messages over a contraption consisting of two tin cans tied to the ends of a long piece of string, he probably would have said, "Amazing! Why didn't I think of that?"

Howsomever, this toy was instrumental in deciding the outcome of many make-believe games. Mock wars were averted or won, daring escapes were successfully perpetrated, rubber-gun artillery fire was accurately targeted, and wily gangsters were brought to justice. At times just when it was needed the most, though, it was unavailable for use as a communication device—because some gossipy, giggling girls would stay on the danged thing all day.

RUBBER-GUN CANNON (and mount)

Cannons were constructed in a variety of shapes and sizes according to the materials available. The illustration shows a typical model with a 2-by-4 barrel. Any large board would serve as well. The swivel mount (which was used for machine guns too) might appear complicated to build, but it wasn't. It was merely two boards nailed or screwed together to form an L-shape, with a hole drilled in each, to take the bolts (metal or wood) for mounting the cannon to a base. Some soap or a drop of oil on the bolt and washer permitted the cannon to swivel easily, up and down and around.

The rubber-gun cannon was indeed a neat toy. It was not used much in hot cowboy shoot-outs, as it was bulky and too heavy to move around. But in a situation where one was drastically outnumbered, the superior range of the cannon would at least hold the opposition at bay until reinforcements arrived.

NOTE: *Because rubber-gun cannons would shoot rubber-band ammunition harder and farther than other rubber guns, they were never fired at anyone at close range. A long-range stringer fired from a cannon would leave an uncomfortable welt on bare skin. (See "Rubber-Gun Safety" on page 7.)*

We played a great game with cannons called Annie Over Artillery. Two cannons were positioned about 40 feet apart, one in the front yard, one in the back, so they would shoot over the house. (If the house happened to be two-story, a low outbuilding was used instead.) A washtub containing 2 or 3 inches of sweet lime was placed a few feet away from each cannon. (Most rural children had access to lime, as it was used to spread over potatoes to preserve them during storage.) The washtub of lime served as the target, and the artillery team that shot the first long-range stringer over

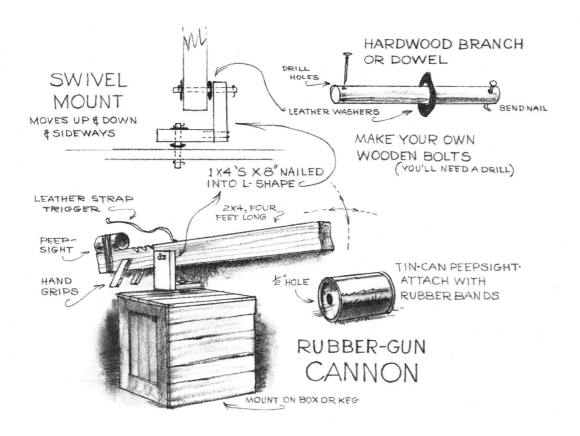

SWIVEL
MOUNT
MOVES UP & DOWN
& SIDEWAYS

DRILL
HOLES

HARDWOOD BRANCH
OR DOWEL

LEATHER WASHERS

BEND NAIL

MAKE YOUR OWN
WOODEN BOLTS
(YOU'LL NEED A DRILL)

1 X 4'S X 8" NAILED
INTO L-SHAPE

LEATHER STRAP
TRIGGER

2 X 4, FOUR
FEET LONG

PEEP-
SIGHT

HAND
GRIPS

½" HOLE

TIN-CAN PEEPSIGHT·
ATTACH WITH
RUBBER BANDS

RUBBER-GUN
CANNON

MOUNT ON BOX OR KEG

the house to land in the washtub won the game. When a direct hit was made, the lime would puff into the air to simulate a bursting artillery shell. Each team was allowed an "observer" who would get into a position to see the enemy target. He or she would instruct the cannoneer over a tin-can telephone as to where the shells were hitting in relation to the target.

Tap! Tap! Tap! "Observer to cannoneer: That last shot went all the way over on Mrs. Smith's back porch. I think it landed in her African violets. Bring it up a little and a teeny bit to your left. . . . No, you dummy, left! *Left!* That's the hand you don't write with. . . . You're still hitting Mrs. Smith's—hold it! *Hold your fire!* Somebody just came out on the porch. I—I think she's coming over here. . . . This is the observer signing off—I gotta go home now!" *Click!*

5

Rainy Days

Why is it that rainy summer days put grown-ups, especially mothers, in an edgy mood? Snug indoors, surrounded by her loving children and perhaps several of their little playmates, why does a mother become restless, uneasy? Why does she peer out the rain-streaked window every five minutes, exclaiming, "Lordy! Will it never stop?"

Depression-era children always seemed to enjoy a nice rainy day. It gave them the opportunity to do a lot of things they ordinarily did not have time to do when frolicking outdoors in fair weather. Things like playing hide-and-seek in every room in the house; things like singing songs in the living room, accompanied by the piano (even though no one quite knew how to play it). Rainy days were also fine for whipping up a batch of toy-making glue on the kitchen range by bringing a thick mixture of flour and water to a boil, or trying out the new taffy recipe published in Grit newspaper—which somehow always managed to turn out about the same as the glue. Most of all, though, a rainy day was spent in a house-wide treasure hunt for spools, buttons, beads, needles, string, pasteboard, matchboxes, and other toy-making materials, followed by some serious building.

When a summer thunderstorm came bristling through a hot June day, aglitter with streaks of lightning and a stiff wind, it added yet another dimension of excitement to the children's world. Interrupting play, it sent them scurrying homeward (or perhaps to a storm cellar), their footprints already filling with raindrops as they ran. Oh, to be blessed with a tin-roofed house! How welcome the pouring rain sounded on unmuffled rusty tin. . . . Not so at first, for the drumming would be so loud that voices were muted. But as the storm slowly tapered off, a gentle lulling rhythm followed. A person could build dreams while listening to nature patter contentedly overhead.

Then, as suddenly as it began, the rain stopped. Drops sparkled on the leaves of thirst-slaked trees and clung in running rows down tall grass stems. Crickets, frogs, and birds sang. A butterfly unable to fly spread its moisture-covered wings to dry in the sunshine. Refreshed, after days of dust and heat, the cooling ground offered up steamy waves of thanks. The earth had enjoyed its bath.

When a summer rain ceased, children with homemade toy boats always came out faster than the sun. Bare feet couldn't resist shin-deep puddles and ditches that ran gurgling swift like white-water rapids. And when boys or girls were playing with boats and waterwheels, they just naturally had to resort to cavorting

*(wading, splashing, and squishing mud between bare toes)—whether or not they
were wearing Sunday clothes. Ofttimes a boating excursion ended on a sour note.*

*"Just look at your clothes! Didn't I tell you to stay out of those puddles?
Come in the house . . . this instant!"*

*"Aw, gee, Ma, I'm sorry. I had to go down into this little ditch, just for a
second, to get my paddle boat, and then there was this big deep hole—"*

"Your shoes! Where are your shoes?"

Nicky and the Devil's Tongue

In most southern and midwestern states, especially Oklahoma, growing up in rural
areas meant spending a lot of time in storm cellars. This was something most kids
hated even more than being purged with Black Draught tea. During the spring,
summer, and fall, whenever a thundercloud approached, night or day, we were herd-
ed into an underground shelter comparable to a torture chamber straight out of

Edgar Allan Poe: a dark, damp tomb, infested with spiders, mildewy odors—and, worst of all, bossy adults who would stare down our throats constantly. We didn't dare scratch, much less misbehave.

Frosty, who loved to count everything—the peas on his plate, the bullets in Tom Mix's gun belt—kept count of the many hours we spent in storm cellars every year. One year, back in '32, I believe it was, his calculations revealed we spent two hours more in cellars than we did in church. And the church had held extra tent revival meetings that summer, too.

A storm cloud never seemed to materialize when one was doing something not particularly enjoyable, like sitting in church or painting the front porch. But just as soon as you got in the middle of the greatest kite fight of your life, or a rubber-gun battle to end all battles, you could bet your last lucky buckeye that that was when Uncle Frank would start blowing away on his old cow horn to signal everyone in earshot that a storm was brewing. When we heard the horn's warning, we would scramble to his backyard cellar. And down we'd go! The entombment might last less than an hour or seemingly forever, depending on the severity of the storm.

Sometimes the thunderclouds would spawn a "devil's tongue" (which was what the old folks called a tornado), and when this occurred we knew we were in for a long, miserable stay. Most children learned from past experience to keep a supply of spool tractors stashed safely away in the cellar on a shelf behind the canned goods, to keep them from going crazy as bedbugs. Our favorite storm-cellar game was Climb-the-Hill. We'd pile some old *Reader's Digest, Collier's,* and *Saturday Evening Post* magazines down on the floor into a stair-stepped mountain shape and see whose spool tractor could climb the highest.

It wasn't unusual for the countryside around Fort Gibson to experience several bad thunderstorms a year, including two or three tornadoes. A twister had never struck the town itself, though—not in my ten-year lifetime, at least. But in the summer of '34, a tornado that would long be remembered by folks in our town came too close for comfort.

The day was hot and muggy, with a pinkish haze in the sky that seemed to magnify the intensity of the sun. It was one of those sweltering summer days that Granny Porter called a "stump burner," a day when heat waves danced across tin roofs, and barefoot children sought grassy paths to avoid walking on scorching hard earth and gravel. Around five o'clock in the afternoon, though, a few gray clouds scudding along the horizon promised cooling relief, as folks began to gather at my Uncle Frank and Aunt Opal's house for an outdoor fish fry. Uncle Frank, a retired barber, enjoyed fishing, and a couple of times a year, when his catch was exceedingly good, we got treated. Aunt Opal's invitations were extended to just about everyone around with a simple "Come if you can."

The women would arrive loaded down with covered dishes, and the checkered oilcloths spread on the ground beneath the trees would soon be heaped with bowls of slaw, potato salad, corn relish, baked beans, pickles, and all types of desserts. There were good things to drink, too, like iced tea, lemonade, and penny drink in sweating pitchers. And in an iron wash kettle of boiling lard, Aunt Opal would fry enough catfish and Indian cornbread to feed practically all the people who were out of work in the big cities.

That afternoon Frosty and I arrived early to build the hickory-and-oak fire under the pot for Aunt Opal, as well as to pilfer a few samples of her pies and cakes. Afterward, we went down to the Red-Horse Barn to practice shooting at tin cans with our slingshots until the main course was served. Naturally, Nicky tagged along with bright-eyed enthusiasm, making a pest of himself. He never missed an opportunity to pounce on a target can and carry it off into the hedgerows.

Old Nicky was the one and only dog I had ever owned, and I liked him almost as much as I did Frosty. He wasn't quite *all* Airedale, but he was all dog. He loved smelly bones, hamburgers, secondhand chewing gum, ice cream, and sleeping on my bed. He hated lye-soap baths, high notes on a whistle, and cats—especially George. George was the big calico that belonged to Bobby Ann Smith, and he was ten pounds of patchwork meanness that couldn't be trusted. One minute he could be a gentle, fluffy bundle of purring multicolored fur; the next, a spitting claw-and-fang circular saw. If you happened to be caught in a storm cellar with him, you had to watch him constantly. He could either rub up against your leg or take it off at the knee, depending on his mood of the moment. Nicky carried numerous scars on his nose as proof of George's sneaky, unpredictable disposition.

Anyhow, we'd been down at the barn plinking cans for about an hour when we heard more folks arriving at the house, and the aroma of frying fish started drifting our way. The smell of food took Nicky's mind off the cans, and he scooted for the house. Just at that moment the sound of Uncle Frank's cow horn rent the air.

"Aw, for cryin' out loud," Frosty moaned, and missed the can he was aiming at by a mile.

The horn bellowed again.

"Maybe he's wrong this time," Frosty suggested hopefully, as we made a beeline for the house.

"Not a chance," I said, looking at the sky. Over in the southwest it was black as coal tar. "He's never been wrong about a storm in his whole life."

And he hadn't. Not as long as I'd known him anyway.

All at once a yellowish-orange overcast bathed everything in an eerie light. "Gonna be a ripsnorter," Uncle Frank told us between blasts, his face and bald head red as a beet. "You young'uns get that fire put out and help Granny Porter down the cellar. We ain't got much time."

I threw water on the fire while Frosty helped Granny. She was spry enough but had trouble with the uneven dirt steps. Then I went and got her "spittin'" can for her (she dipped snuff constantly), and Frosty dashed down the street to her house to fetch Princess, her canary. My sister, Beverly, came driving up from the drugstore in town to drop my father off; then she accelerated down the rutted river road to fetch Miss Bowen, our teacher, and Grandmother Youngblood, who didn't have a storm cellar. Grandmother Youngblood, with unerring accuracy, had predicted only yesterday that there would be a bad storm today.

Bobby Ann and Norma cornered George, scooped him up from the spot in the garden where he was trying to dig out the fish heads Uncle Frank had buried for fertilizer, and carried the bushy-tailed cat into the cellar. Nicky followed close behind, keeping his eyes on the struggling, square-eyed animal.

When most of the others were safely down in the cellar, Frosty and I stood just outside with the men watching the dense cloud as it crackled with lightning. It spread like a massive blue-black awning, south to north, as it came toward us across the flat farmland. A narrow band of bright sky separated the cloud from the horizon. Occasionally, a feathery finger of the swirling dark mass would dip earthward, then contract.

"He's tasting the icing," Uncle Frank said. "If he likes it, he'll eat the cake."

"And it's a devil's-food cake sure as shootin'," Mr. Buford said.

The breeze suddenly stopped; not a leaf or a blade of grass moved. Like magic, all the birds had vanished from sight.

We heard the devil's tongue before we saw it.

A far-off sound like a highballing freight train broke the silence. As we watched, an inky ice-cream-cone-shaped tongue licking at the earth from the cloud base moved slowly northward, spinning like a top.

"It'll miss us if it doesn't hit the river and follow it," Uncle Frank said, "but they usually take to water like a duck."

The distant, deadly funnel appeared to stand still and began to take on a fatter look. The speeding freight-train sound grew louder, and a cold blast of wind-driven rain tugged at us. I found one of my father's hands and hung on. Frosty took hold of the other.

"You think it's on the river, Frank?" Dad asked.

"Yep, and coming this way. Let's pray it stays on it now. If it jumps the bluff on this side, we're goners!"

The afternoon had become nearly dark as night when Beverly drove into the yard with her passengers and we all ran for the cellar. Frosty and I found seats under the shelves of canned goods where Aunt Opal kept Mason jars of parched corn and peanuts for nibbling. We reconciled ourselves to another miserable evening in the cellar that Uncle Frank had built himself and bragged was the best in the county. (If it was, I sure would have hated to see the worst one.) It was a pit about 10 feet square, excavated down into hardpan. There was 6 feet of headroom between the clay floor and the black-locust beams that supported the roof: sheets of galvanized tin topped with a 3-foot-thick mound of dirt and Bermuda sod. The heavy hinged door fit unevenly in its frame. A clay tile pipe running through the roof provided ventilation. The crude wood benches along the earthen walls would seat about twelve people in a pinch. And that day there was a definite *pinch*—standing room only.

First off, Mrs. Tucker, our Sunday-school teacher, led us in a prayer, after giving Frosty a jaundiced eye. (Last Sunday he had disrupted her entire class with his funny-noise maker.) After the prayer, Granny Porter told us again about the devil's tongue in the 1880s that blew their log cabin "clean off" the Kiamichi Mountain. She and Grandpa Porter had saved themselves by hanging down in the cistern on the bucket rope. Granny always could tell real scary stories.

As the storm built in intensity, I felt goose bumps running up and down my spine. The wind coming down the vent pipe made ghostly calliope whistles, and the kerosene lantern nearly flickered out in the draft. Nightmarish conjectures of being blown down the river and out to sea, or buried alive forever, came to my mind as we kids sat shivering, watching Nicky and George glaring at one another while the wind screeched and the thunder crashed outside. Every few minutes Uncle Frank would force the door open a crack and peek out to give us a play-by-play report, such as "The house is still standing" or "Can't see a danged thing!" Then—"Lordy!"

The raging wind tore the door out of his hands and with hurricane force ripped it off its hinges. We huddled against the back wall while the strong suction from outside pulled at us. Loose magazine pages and small objects went flying out the opening.

My eardrums felt as if they would burst from pressure. I hung onto Frosty while he clung to the bench. The noise and flying debris must have terrified George, for he suddenly clawed his way out of Bobby Ann's grasp and shot outside, with Nicky right on his tail. Horrified, I yelled at Nicky to come back, but he and George kept on going out into the storm. Bobby Ann attempted to dash out after them, but Uncle Frank restrained her with the warning: "You could get yourself killed out there, child. Calm down now, your kitty's got nine lives, remember?"

I, instead of panicking, consoled myself with the thought that my dog was just as smart as Little Orphan Annie's Sandy, and surely he would find shelter in the garage, or under the car, or somewhere. An uneasy feeling haunted me, though, that this time Nicky's penchant for chasing cats had gotten him into serious trouble.

Later as the wind subsided, it started raining harder than I had ever seen it rain before, and continued for about ten minutes. "Mercy me! It's a goslin' drownder!" Granny said, as a muddy waterfall rushed down the steps to fill the cellar ankle-deep. After the downpour came hail—then some more rain—and then again more thunder and lightning. Nearly two long hours passed before the last faint rumbles of thunder died away in the distance and Uncle Frank finally gave us the all clear.

We emerged from the shelter into a cool, starry, moonlit night. "Thank the Lord!" someone said. "The worst of it missed us."

"It must've followed the river till it petered out," Uncle Frank said. "We're danged lucky it did."

Frosty and I were relieved to see the Red-Horse Barn was still standing, although it appeared to be leaning a little more than usual against the old sweet-gum tree and looked as if more shingles were missing from the roof. I whistled for Nicky, but he and George were nowhere in sight.

Bluegill and Eskimo arrived with their parents to relate the good news that no injuries had been reported so far. And while some folks ran home a minute to check on their property and livestock, Aunt Opal began to fry the rest of the fish on the kitchen range. But I couldn't enjoy the late supper, for when I whistled for Nicky, he still didn't come. George had showed up earlier, however, and was underfoot mewing and begging for handouts.

At bedtime I called and whistled for Nicky again, but to no avail. My mother told me not to worry, he'd been out in storms before. But I knew something terrible had happened. For over seven years he hadn't missed a night sleeping in my room (on my bed when Mother didn't catch him).

During the long night, time and again I thought I heard him scratching at the back door, and I jumped out of bed to look. But he wasn't there. The singing of crickets and frogs was the only sound in the darkness. It was sad and lonesome music.

Early the next morning, Frosty and I set out to form a search-and-rescue party— after we faithfully promised that we'd return in time to clean up before Sunday school and church. Even after I put up a reward (my scootmobile, minus accessories) for the lucky person who found Nicky, we only recruited two members: Bluegill and Eskimo. See-Thru wanted to go in the worst way, but his mother, who had already dressed him for Sunday school, said, "If I turn him loose for as much as five minutes, he'll look like he's been run over by a thrashing machine!"

Together the four of us searched, whistled, and shouted. We must have fetched up every dog in the county except Nicky. While Bluegill and Eskimo went to Standpipe Hill to look, Frosty and I covered Sudden Canyon and Skull-Head Cove down on the river, where Nicky liked to splash around chasing minnows, frogs—and our paddle boats, when we had races.

Next we went over to see if Mr. Buford would let us borrow his famous black-and-tan coonhound, Rosemary. We reasoned if anyone could sniff out Nicky, she could. Mr. Buford informed us we were more than welcome to her services, but she was so old and lazy nowadays that she wouldn't hardly track a soupbone. Downcast and discouraged, we decided to give up the search until after church and Sunday dinner.

During the service, after Uncle Eura had warned us all—at least seven times—that we were doomed to fire and brimstone if we didn't change our ways immediately, he announced to the congregation that Nicky was missing, and if anyone should see him to report to me. But no one did.

We continued the search all Sunday afternoon. Even Killer and the Renegades joined in. Killer liked Nicky a lot, I guess because he was the only dog in town that didn't try to bite him all the time. By sundown I had given up all hope of ever seeing my dog again. I slept fitfully through the night.

The next morning as I started out to meet Frosty, I heard my mother call, "Come quick, son. Nicky's under the porch!" I hurried back to find Mother on her hands and knees, peering through the narrow crawl opening. "I heard him whining but he won't come out."

With my head bumping the joists, I squeezed under the porch. When my eyes finally adjusted to the darkness I saw Nicky lying back in a corner. I crawled over to him, and he gave my hand a feeble lick. Patiently, I half-dragged, half-coaxed him outside. In the light we could see he was badly hurt; his coat was heavily matted with dried blood and dirt, and he couldn't get to his feet. An ugly wood splinter skewered his left eye, protruding through the upper side of his jaw.

Frosty, who had come over on his bike, said he'd ride down to the drugstore to fetch my father. While we waited, I went inside so Mother wouldn't see me, in case I started to cry.

There wasn't a veterinarian in our town, but Dad, being a pharmacist, knew a lot about doctoring. He got home quickly and examined Nicky. The prognosis was grave. Dad told us he would do what he could. He sent Frosty back to the store to get some chloroform from the clerk, Mr. Spera, and had me cover the kitchen table with newspapers.

When Frosty returned with the chloroform, Dad gently placed Nicky on the table and had him asleep in a few seconds. I couldn't stand to watch, so I turned my head aside while he removed the splinter and poured alcohol into the wound. When we carried our patient out into the fresh air to sleep it off, Dad told me, "He might recover if he isn't hurt internally. I'm sorry, son; that's all we can do."

For three whole days Nicky didn't move from the back-porch bed which I had made for him out of an old quilt. He drank a lot of water, but he wouldn't eat a bit, not even raw meat. Then on the fourth day, Eskimo, who had come over to play, offered him a bite of his Eskimo Pie. Nicky ate it! And begged for more. I ran down to the drugstore and blew an entire month's allowance (20 cents) on Eskimo Pies. Proudly I told Dad he could have been a famous surgeon!

Fortunately, the awesome devil's tongue that nearly killed Nicky did only minor damage in our town. It shattered windows, partially deshingled or stripped roofing tin from a few houses (ours included), and scooted Granny Porter's old chicken house from way out behind the hog lot to within 30 yards of her back porch. She swore until her dying day that not an egg had been broken and that a "settin' hen" was still on the nest. Granny's no longer having to walk so far to gather eggs gave further strength to her sagacious proverb: "You can find something good in everything the Lord does."

The church house suffered the most damage of all. It lost its bell tower. Nothing was left of it except some kindling—and, of course, the bell, which Uncle Eura discovered partially buried where it had landed on the front lawn.

Old Nicky lost the sight in his damaged eye. It didn't seem to bother him much—he just appeared to be winking at you all the time. But I'll tell you one thing: He never was caught out in a storm again. Whenever Uncle Frank blew his warning beneath a threatening Oklahoma sky and the blare of the old cow horn echoed across the river bluff, Nicky was the first one in the cellar. And even though he didn't like it too much, he stayed put—and was always the last to leave.

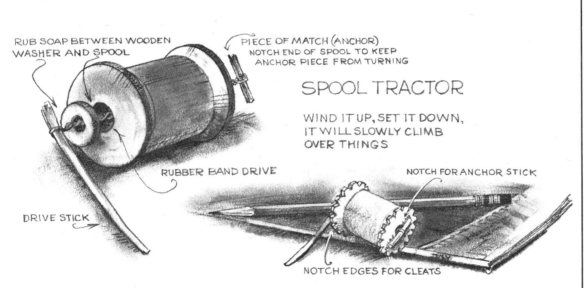

RUB SOAP BETWEEN WOODEN WASHER AND SPOOL

PIECE OF MATCH (ANCHOR) NOTCH END OF SPOOL TO KEEP ANCHOR PIECE FROM TURNING

SPOOL TRACTOR

WIND IT UP, SET IT DOWN, IT WILL SLOWLY CLIMB OVER THINGS

RUBBER BAND DRIVE

NOTCH FOR ANCHOR STICK

DRIVE STICK

NOTCH EDGES FOR CLEATS

SPOOL TRACTOR

This was a superb toy that could be put together in a minute. The size and number of rubber bands used, and the type of washer, determined the speed and/or power of the tractor. A washer of wood, cardboard, or leather would work, but for a powerful,

Spool-Tractor Horse Racing

If inclement weather had you stuck indoors or down in the storm cellar, spool-tractor horse racing was a popular sport. The tractors were identified by numbers, and these same numbers were written on individual slips of paper and put into a hat. Example: If there were six tractors numbered from 1 to 6 in the race, six slips of paper numbered from 1 to 6 would go into the hat.

The racetrack was laid out on the floor or on a tabletop. About 2 to 3 feet apart, a starting gate and a finish line were established. This might sound like a short track, but tractors were not long-distance runners. The space between start and finish still gave the spectators ample time to shout encouragement to the favorite. Tractors, even the speedy ones, crept along like turtles.

Each spectator drew a number from the hat; the tractors were wound up and placed in the starting gate. When all was ready, the starter blew up a candy sack and burst it, or popped a paper popper (see page 94). "They're off and running! . . ."

Suppose you drew number 5: If tractor number 5 won the race you held the winning number. Then, to establish the pari-mutuel odds, you drew from another hat in which slips numbered from 1 to 100 had been placed.

"What number did you get? Wow! Forty-seven! How come you're so danged lucky? I've never in my whole life had a winning horse that paid forty-seven to one!"

"Well, you know what they say: 'That's horse racing.'"

slow-moving climber a short length of crayon or a piece of soap inserted between the winding stick and the spool made the best washer. The winding stick (the long one) could be a sucker stick, a kitchen match, or a tree branch. The tractor was set in motion by giving the winding stick several turns.

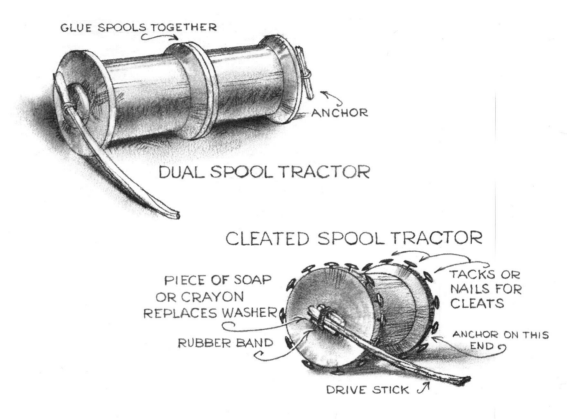

GLUE SPOOLS TOGETHER

ANCHOR

DUAL SPOOL TRACTOR

CLEATED SPOOL TRACTOR

PIECE OF SOAP OR CRAYON REPLACES WASHER

TACKS OR NAILS FOR CLEATS

RUBBER BAND

ANCHOR ON THIS END

DRIVE STICK

DUAL SPOOL TRACTOR

Two spools of the same diameter glued together end to end made a tractor that would accommodate longer rubber bands. This greatly extended the toy's running time between rewindings. The dual model wasn't the best climber, but it was a speedster that would really move out—comparatively speaking. All spool tractors were slow movers.

CLEATED SPOOL TRACTOR

For added climbing power, notches were cut into the rims of the spool. And if one wanted a super climber, the tractor could be equipped with steel cleats: carpet tacks or small finishing nails. Dual tractors normally weren't cleated; they were racers or long-distance haulers, not climbers.

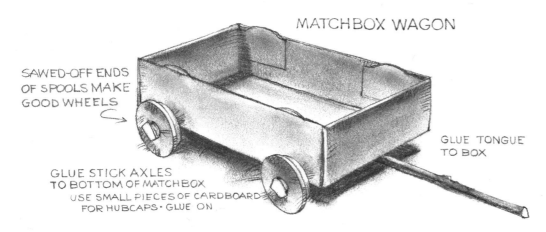

MATCHBOX WAGON

SAWED-OFF ENDS
OF SPOOLS MAKE
GOOD WHEELS

GLUE TONGUE
TO BOX

GLUE STICK AXLES
TO BOTTOM OF MATCHBOX
USE SMALL PIECES OF CARDBOARD
FOR HUBCAPS · GLUE ON

MATCHBOX WAGON

Matchboxes were the best for making small wagons. And from them, children manufactured flatbeds, buckboards, buggies, even Conestogas. They consulted pictures of the real ones in magazines or catalogs and tried to make their models look authentic. Buttons were sometimes glued on for wheels, or spool ends with painted-on spokes were used for a really genuine wagon-wheel look. Kitchen matchstick axles with cardboard hubs caused the matchbox to wobble like an old wagon when it rolled. Miniature penny-matchbox wagons could be hitched up to spool tractors (mechanical mules).

TREE-BRANCH ANIMALS

There was no better way to while away a rainy summer afternoon than to sit out on the screened-in back porch and whittle tree branches into toy animals. We kept a box

TREE BRANCH ANIMALS

PAPER EARS   DRILL HOLE FOR NECK

CARVE EYES & NOSE

USE BRANCHES FOR LEGS, BUT WHERE EXTRAS ARE NEEDED, DRILL HOLE & PLUG IN STICK

of twigs and branches on the porch just for this purpose. A pocketknife with a sharp-pointed blade was the only tool needed. The sharp point was necessary for boring the small holes in the animal's body in which to insert the twigs that resembled legs, ears, tails, etc. Just about any kid could make a recognizable farm animal. But it took considerable skill and imagination to turn out an exotic species such as a giraffe or camel that could be immediately identified as such.

PAPER POPPER AND PAPER PUPPET

Hundreds of fascinating toys can be constructed by merely folding a sheet of paper. Many books have been published on origami, the ancient Japanese art of paper folding, but rural hard-times children, whose knowledge of the subject was limited, made do with simple airplanes, and the like, objects that did not encompass complicated folding procedures. Paper poppers, which could be folded in a jiffy even by five-year-olds, were gala noisemakers and when distributed as party favors contributed a raucous atmosphere to Halloween or New Year's Eve. They also added inexpensive

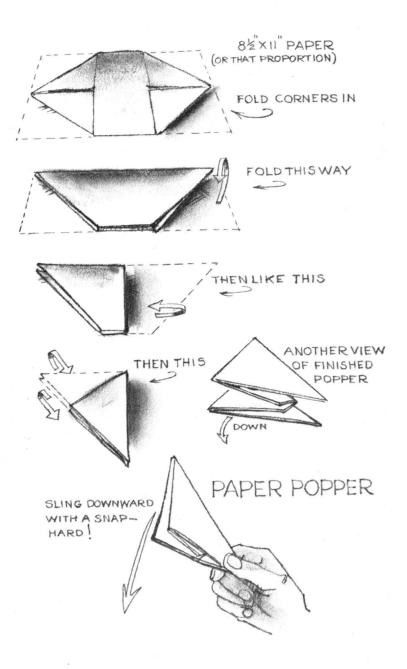

8½" X 11" PAPER
(OR THAT PROPORTION)

FOLD CORNERS IN

FOLD THIS WAY

THEN LIKE THIS

THEN THIS

ANOTHER VIEW OF FINISHED POPPER

DOWN

SLING DOWNWARD WITH A SNAP— HARD!

PAPER POPPER

A Toy Maker's Tools

When it came to making toys, Frosty Youngblood and I were more fortunate than some of our friends; we had access to a lot more tools than they did. Frosty's father was a carpenter and a good all-around fix-it man. He never objected to our using his tools any time. But there was one stipulation: Afterward they went back in their proper place in the toolshed, or else!

"The first time I reach for a chisel or a screwdriver and it isn't there, I'll hang both of you on the nail where it belongs!"

Those weren't exactly Mr. Youngblood's words verbatim. He threw in a couple of expletives for even greater effect. Mr. Youngblood always had a knack for making himself understood. Never once did I ever hear Frosty say back to him, "Whatcha mean by that?"

95

Most of our homemade toys were so easy to construct that only a few basic hand tools were needed. A hammer, saw, screwdriver, scissors, and a pocketknife would usually suffice. For some toys, however, such as plain whistles, you needed a brace and a large bit. Small bits—drills—came in handy too, for predrilling nail and screw holes to prevent delicate wood parts from splitting. And tin snips were a must for cutting cans and other sheet metal.

Mr. Youngblood did not seem to appreciate our using his soldering iron, because we never took the time to clean and tin the tip properly; consequently, we devised a small homemade one out of a piece of copper rod and an ice-pick handle. It took a little longer than a store-bought model to get hot on the coals, but it worked just fine for what little soldering tin-can boats required.

Store-bought glue was so costly it was used only where the homemade type would not suffice. A thick mixture of flour and water brought to a boil turned out a glue that dried quickly—almost transparent— and worked well on paper, cardboard, and most fabrics. For paper-doll cutouts, doll clothes, and kite-making the flour glue was indispensable; it would hold up quite satisfactorily if it didn't get wet—or if bugs didn't eat it.

START WITH A SQUARE OF PAPER, FOLD CORNERS IN

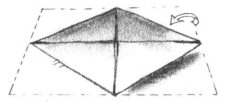

FLIP OVER, FOLD CORNERS IN AGAIN

PAPER PUPPET
(COOTIE PICKER)

DRAW EYES

FOLD UP, STRAIGHTEN OUT, THEN FOLD UP IN OTHER DIRECTION

TURN IT OVER & IT LOOKS LIKE THIS

STICK FINGERS INTO COMPART-MENTS & SQUEEZE TOGETHER

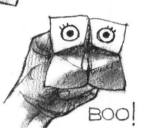

BOO!

bangs to the Fourth of July if one could not afford firecrackers. The puppet, which was a little more tricky to fold than the popper, delighted little kids and kept them entertained for hours. They were appreciated as birthday presents too.

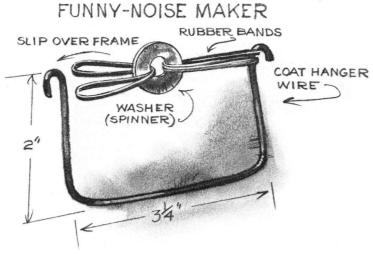

FUNNY-NOISE MAKER

The rubber gun was, without a doubt, the favorite toy of most ten-year-old boys living in our small Oklahoma community during the '30s. But ask any boy (or girl) what homemade toy was absolutely, positively more fun than a barrel of monkeys, and he (or she) would unhesitatingly reply, "The funny-noise maker." We constructed our funny-noise makers by bending an 8-inch piece of coat-hanger wire into an elongated U-shape. Rubber bands were looped through a penny-sized metal washer to suspend it between the frame, allowing adequate tension on the rubber bands to prevent them from slipping down the frame. If this toy had been store-bought, the manufacturer's instructions for its use would probably have read as follows:

Instructions for Playing with the Funny-Noise Maker

This toy may be used to scare your sister! Wind the spinner about twelve turns and, being careful not to let it go, put it inside an envelope marked: THIS ENVELOPE CONTAINS RATTLES FROM THE WORLD'S LARGEST RATTLESNAKE. With your thumb and

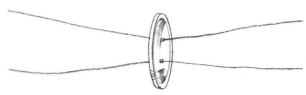

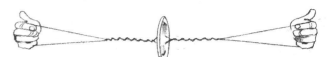

forefinger still holding the spinner from outside the envelope, show it to your sister and say, "Hey, look what our teacher gave me at school today!" See her eyes grow big with wonderment as she reads what's on the envelope. See her reach for the envelope to see what's inside. Wait until it's in her hand before you release the spinner. See her drop the envelope and scream as the spinner makes the appropriate funny noise.

IMPORTANT: Make sure your escape route is clear.

CAUTION: Do not pull this trick on your sister if she faints easily.

To make another outrageous noise with your funny-noise maker, wind the spinner up tightly and, being careful not to let it go, sit on it. Now, remove your hand and allow the pressure of your body to hold the spinner securely in place against the bottom of the chair. (A firm upholstered chair works best.) Then, leaning forward, raise up very, very slowly to release the spinner, so it will spin noisily between you and the chair seat.

WARNING: *Grown-ups who think children should be seen and not heard will find little humor in some of the funny noises the funny-noise maker makes.*

MILK-CAN WATERWHEEL

CUT VANES WITH POCKETKNIFE, BEND OUT — TAKE CARE - DON'T CUT YOUR FINGERS ON THE SHARP EDGES

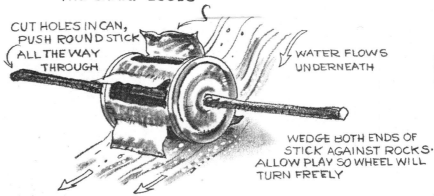

CUT HOLES IN CAN, PUSH ROUND STICK ALL THE WAY THROUGH

WATER FLOWS UNDERNEATH

WEDGE BOTH ENDS OF STICK AGAINST ROCKS. ALLOW PLAY SO WHEEL WILL TURN FREELY

BOTTLE SUBMARINE

AIR

AIR

PILL BOTTLE UPSIDE DOWN

WATER

FIRST

FILL LARGE BOTTLE NOT QUITE TO TOP

FILL PILL BOTTLE, DUMP INTO OTHER BOTTLE, UPSIDE DOWN.

YOU'LL LOSE ENOUGH OF CONTENTS TO LEAVE AN AIR POCKET

USE FINGER OR THUMB TO MAKE A TIGHT FIT.

PRESS DOWN, SUB WILL GO TO BOTTOM

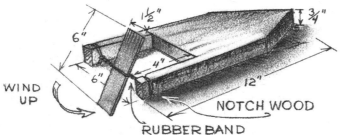

PADDLE BOAT

WIND UP

NOTCH WOOD

RUBBER BAND

PADDLE BOAT

Just about any piece of scrap lumber from 6 to 12 inches long—even a wood shingle—launched a seaworthy paddle boat. The ideal wood for the hull was a piece less than 1 inch thick, for the lighter the boat, the faster it would go. And the paddle was cut from the thinnest stock one could find, so that the rubber-band motor wouldn't have to carry any excess weight. A small strip from a fruit crate made an excellent paddle if painted or waxed to prevent waterlogging and warping. For durability the hull was also painted. After winding the rubber-band-powered paddle several times, the boat was placed in water and the paddle released. "Watch 'em go! Bet mine goes farthest."

SARDINE-CAN PADDLE BOAT

During the Depression a sardine can was considered the Cadillac of cans by young toy-boat builders. Perhaps this is the reason some rural children claimed sardines were a "special treat," and on a Saturday going-to-town day you might see a kid with a newly purchased can of sardines peeking out of his shirt pocket, rather than a licorice stick or a Black Cow sucker. When empty, the sardine can was exactly the right size and shape for the hull of a flatboat, and it would last for many voyages. A can of sardines cost a whole nickel, but it was worth every penny—even if you happened to be one of the few who hated the little fish worse than castor oil and slipped the smelly things under the table to the cat when no one was looking. (Parents sometimes wondered why Tabby had such a beautiful, shiny coat.) Anyhow, the nickel spent for sardines resulted in a purring, appreciative pet and a happy toy-boat builder.

Going-to-Muskogee Day

"Going-to-Muskogee day" came on a Saturday five or six times a year for us: a magical day of wish-shopping at Kress's, visiting the library, eating at the café, and going to the *movies!*

Frosty would scoot over to my house early, before the rooster crowed twice, to help me wash the car— my father's most luxurious possession. We'd soap, rinse, and polish until it sparkled show room new. It was a beautiful maroon '29 Model-A Ford sedan with yellow wheels. My father had paid $65 for it used back in '31. And there were no prominent dents in it at all, except for a bad crumple in the running board. My mother refused to drive a dirty car into Muskogee. "If folks see your car's filthy," she'd say, "they'll think the same of your house."

By eight thirty we'd be on the road: Norma and Aunt Opal up front with Mother; Frosty, Bobby Ann, and me in the back. All of us were dressed fit to kill for the big day on the town: Frosty and I in our one-and-only set of Sunday clothes (store-bought shirt, pants with suspenders, and spit-shined shoes), the females in multicolored freshly starched dresses and smelling overwhelmingly like rose gardens in summer.

As we bumped along the graveled highway, windows closed tightly against the choking dust, I would, for the hundredth time, mentally recount my coins, which were burning a hole in my pocket, and contemplate how to spend them wisely. I knew Frosty was doing the same. *Twenty-three cents!* A dime, two nickels, and three pennies. A fortune! The dime would go for the movie ticket. One of the nickels for a half pound of candy, the other perhaps for a new top, or a can of sardines for later boat-building. That would leave three cents! *Whooee!* Three whole pennies to blow on something frivolous or save toward the next trip in.

Sometimes if Frosty and I had an extra penny or two, we'd chip in and treat Bobby Ann to a Black Cow sucker or something equally nice, because she could seldom scrape together more than the dime it

SARDINE-CAN PADDLE BOAT

CANDLES, CRAYONS, OR ROUND STICKS FOR SMOKESTACKS
2 MATCHBOXES FOR CABINS
SOLDER COAT HANGER WIRE
WIND UP
RUBBER BAND
HOLES
TIN KEEL 3" LONG· SOLDER TO BOTTOM
WOOD PADDLE ⅛" X 1" X 2"

SARDINE-CAN SAILBOAT

4 INCH SUCKER STICK MAST
PAPER SAIL
SARDINE CAN
2 PENNY MATCH BOXES GLUED TOGETHER & TO BOAT

A classy-looking paddle boat that would perform beautifully was constructed by inserting a coat-hanger wire through two holes in the can and bending it to shape. The wire was soldered at the holes in a position to assure that about half the wood paddle (same as in a real paddle boat) would ride beneath the water's surface. If you wanted the boat to be a racer, a small tin keel had to be soldered to the bottom or the boat would not steer a straight course, but kept paddling around in a circle. It was up to the builder how elegant to make the cabin and smokestacks. But lightweight materials were best. Crayolas, round sticks, or birthday candles, melted in place, made colorful smokestacks. And the candles were sometimes lit for dishpan night cruises on the front porch, while the adults swapped yarns and discussed the hard times.

NOTE: *Builders of tin-can toys learned early on that sharp edges could cut fingers. Therefore, sharp edges on boats and other toys (such as waterwheels) made from tin cans were filed smooth, and the toys were handled very carefully during construction and play.*

SARDINE-CAN SAILBOAT

Two penny matchboxes (one atop the other) glued together, and then to the can, formed the cabin. The addition of a sucker-stick mast and paper sail completed a sailboat that would sail like a champion. Cloth sails, two or three masts, or a keel were optional modifications.

SARDINE-CAN FISHING BOAT

Ten-year-old Bluegill Turner, an ardent fisherman, was also a master boatbuilder. Every kid in our town envied his skill with tin snips and soldering iron. Mr. Turner loved to tinker, and obviously his hobby had rubbed off on his son. Bluegill made the best tin-can boats around. In fact, most people guessed he was the genius who invented the sardine-can fishing boat, although we never heard him boast about it. He knew his boats were top of the line and therefore asked, and got, exorbitant prices for them. One of his fishing boats would cost anywhere from 20 marbles (unchipped) to one Big Little Book (cover intact). For a sardine-can motorboat, a customer would have to lay out twice this amount, or two tops (spinnable), or a nice slingshot. One of the magnificent milk-can tugboats Bluegill and his dad built was practically beyond price.

During the off-season, though, good old generous Bluegill would make you a fishing boat almost for free (10 marbles) if you furnished the corks, the sardine can, the mast, and the sail. While the customer watched (it took about four minutes), Bluegill would stick the mast and sail in one cork, insert a piece of wire through the other, tie it in place, twist it into an eye, then glue both corks inside the can, clamp-

cost for the movie. Her father was out of work and her folks were *really* hard-hit. Bobby Ann tried to supplement the meager family income by selling *Grit* newspaper. But this didn't bring in much money.

It was only twelve miles to the big city, yet it took about an hour to get there. My mother never drove over 25 mph, and we stopped along the highway to visit and inquire if any of our neighbors needed something from the city—perhaps some knitting or crocheting materials or snuff. Many were elderly and could not be persuaded to leave their front-porch rocking chairs. Not even to go to Muskogee.

Our first stop in town was the public library. While Mother and Aunt Opal visited friends in the Broadway Apartments across the street, we kids would check out our favorite books. Possibly we'd find a Tarzan or Hopalong Cassidy, one we hadn't read before. If not, we'd fall back on Zane Grey westerns, *Robinson Crusoe*, or *Gulliver's Travels*. Norma and Bobby Ann pored over the Nancy Drew stories.

Leaving the library, we'd drive downtown and find a parking spot on the main drag. This wasn't always easy, as every Tom, Dick, and Harry came to town on Saturday. With eyes big as saucers, we marveled at the sight of so many people and cars and trucks. Why, sitting in front of just one store alone were more vehicles than we had in the entire community of Fort Gibson! Once parked, we'd scramble out of the car and make a beeline for Kress's, followed by Mother and Aunt Opal's stern warnings: "Don't run through the store! And don't touch anything you don't intend to buy! We'll meet you at the café at eleven o'clock sharp!"

Oh, the breathless, indescribable wonders of the five-and-dime store! So much enchantment that it blurred before your eyes. Candy! Glass showcases as big as chicken coops displayed mountains of it: chocolates, caramels, licorice ropes, kisses, cinnamon red hots, gumdrops, bellyburner jawbreakers, candy corn, candy orange slices, and on and on and on . . . the delicious smell of it made us giddy. There were so *many* different kinds! Which to buy? The clerk on the opposite side of the counter kept pace, white paper bag in one hand, a large scoop in the other, as sweaty little forefingers pointed against the glass. "A penny's worth of this . . . and a penny's worth of those—no, wait! Gimme two cents' worth of that. . . ."

Then there were the toys. Acres and acres of toys! Row after row of long counters piled high with the things that dreams are made of: boats with masts two feet tall, kites large as cellar doors, airplanes that would really fly, windup cars and tractors, balls the size of pumpkins, tin tops that would hum a tune, true-to-life baby dolls that cried and said "Ma-ma," six-shooter cap pistols silver shiny with simulated pearl handles, tooled-leather holster sets studded with star-shaped *conchas*, and a trillion other delights that always brought the promised thought: *Someday, when I'm rich* . . .

Later, having dinner (the noon meal was "dinner" in Oklahoma) at Ray's Café was exciting, but rough on the digestion. Eating in the midst of a lot of strangers, and in plain sight of pedestrians watching you through the big plate-glass window, was unnerving. We had to mind our table manners every minute. Mother and Aunt Opal usually had the plate lunch special, but for the rest of us it was a hot dog or a hamburger. Ample room was saved for candy to be eaten during the movie. We never wasted our money buying the theater's popcorn as the city kids did; we raised our own corn and popped it all the time at home, so it wasn't a treat for us. Aunt Opal always paid the check for everyone's lunch—Bobby Ann's too—saying it was the least she could do since Mother furnished the car and gas to drive all the way over.

At eleven thirty, Frosty, Norma, Bobby Ann, and I would join a hundred other kids in the long line that snaked noisily along the sidewalk under the marquee of the Broadway Theater: SAT. MATINEE SPECIAL! 12 NOON. Inside we'd part company. Frosty and I wouldn't be caught dead sitting with girls. Anyway, we liked to sit way down in the front row where we could get in on the action. Norma and Bobby Ann

ing with rubber bands to hold them in place until dry. After tying on a bream rig (hook, line, and sinker), he'd then hold out his hand for 10 marbles—all in one smooth, proficient operation. Sometimes when a first-time customer walked away from Bluegill's boatbuilding shop with a brand-new fishing boat, a thought flickered through his mind: *You've been took, dummy. Hook, line, and sinker!*

Still, there was no denying a fishing boat made fishing a doubly pleasurable pastime, helping to combat the boredom that came between bites. The two large corks prevented the boat from sinking, and so, tied to a fishing line, it became a fishing float that would move the bait slowly through the water. Every fisherman knows that redear sunfish, bluegill, and bass just can't resist moving bait. When a fish struck, the buoyancy of the boat would usually set the hook and prevent the fish from throwing it until the fisherman reeled it in. Unfortunately, there was still one problem that could curtail a day of fishing. More than once a brand-new, tediously built, sardine-can fishing boat ended up in Davy Jones's locker, towed away by a large fish, never to be seen again. Big ones have a way of breaking a fisherman's lines—boat or no boat.

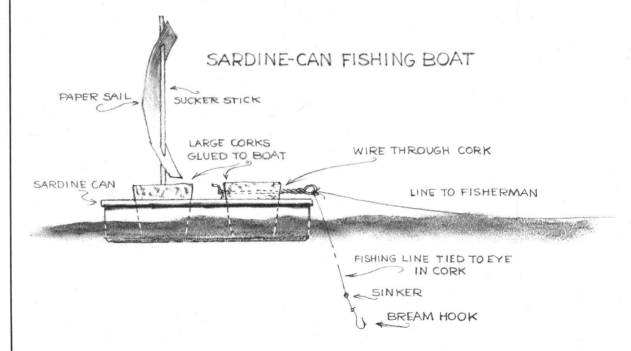

SARDINE-CAN FISHING BOAT

PAPER SAIL

SUCKER STICK

LARGE CORKS GLUED TO BOAT

WIRE THROUGH CORK

SARDINE CAN

LINE TO FISHERMAN

FISHING LINE TIED TO EYE IN CORK

SINKER

BREAM HOOK

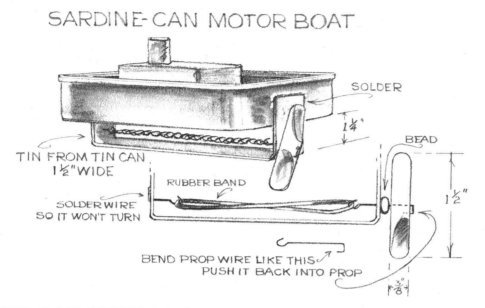

SARDINE-CAN MOTOR BOAT

SOLDER

TIN FROM TIN CAN
1½" WIDE

SOLDER WIRE
SO IT WON'T TURN

RUBBER BAND

BEAD

1¼"

1½"

BEND PROP WIRE LIKE THIS
PUSH IT BACK INTO PROP

⅜"

SARDINE-CAN MOTORBOAT

Sardine-can motorboats were built for speed. Bluegill could put one together in an hour's time—that was after the prop was carved, of course. The prop had to be made from a piece of hardwood about 1½ inches long, ½ inch wide, and ⅜ inch thick. This thickness was needed because the prop required more pitch than a windmill propeller. The boat was propelled by a rubber-band motor, much like the ones that powered store-bought model airplanes. After winding the prop until the rubber bands were virtually in knots, you could speed the motorboat on its way.

MILK-CAN TUGBOAT

The milk-can tugboat, powered by carbide gas, was considered the Queen Mary of homemade toy boats. It took considerable time and effort to construct, as the boiler assembly had to be airtight, and cutting out the hull to the right shape with tin snips was arduous. After cutting, all rough edges were filed smooth. The secret to bending the copper tubing tail pipe without its kinking was to insert a piece of coat-hanger

preferred the center-section seats where they could watch the aisle traffic and giggle at the older boys showing off.

At last the houselights dimmed, and we were drawn into three and a half hours of thrilling make-believe, where brave and daring heroes and heroines came thundering across our horizons, unyielding in their efforts to bring to justice the evil, greedy, dastardly villains.

When our idols disappeared in a cloud of dust and glory and we came back to the real world, we couldn't believe the time had passed so quickly. Sticky hands were sore from clapping. And the yelling had left us hoarse, our throats dry.

On the last leg of our going-to-Muskogee day, we'd stop at the big grocery store out on Okmulgee Avenue, where one might save as much as 5 cents on a 50-pound bag of flour. The huge red-and-white banners in the windows advertised specials: T-BONE STEAK 30 CENTS LB, IDAHO POTATOES 2 CENTS LB, COFFEE 25 CENTS LB, FRESH GULF SHRIMP 32 CENTS LB. "Lord have mercy," Aunt Opal would say. "If food keeps going up, folks won't be able to eat!"

Driving through the outskirts of town, we'd roll down all the windows and open the windshield to catch the cool air. It didn't matter if you got dusty or the wind mussed up your hair on the trip home. We'd sing or act a little crazy and wave at city folks—people we didn't even know—sitting on porches or on lawns. These were the affluent who lived in elegant white houses, or opulent domiciles of brick with green shingled roofs . . . roofs that did not reverberate with the sound of rain as our rusty tin-topped homes did. During those moments there was no envy in our hearts, even though some driveways contained a shiny new bicycle or a store-bought scooter. For we were rich too. We had been to town! And I had blown a bundle—a whole 23 cents—and had loved every minute of it.

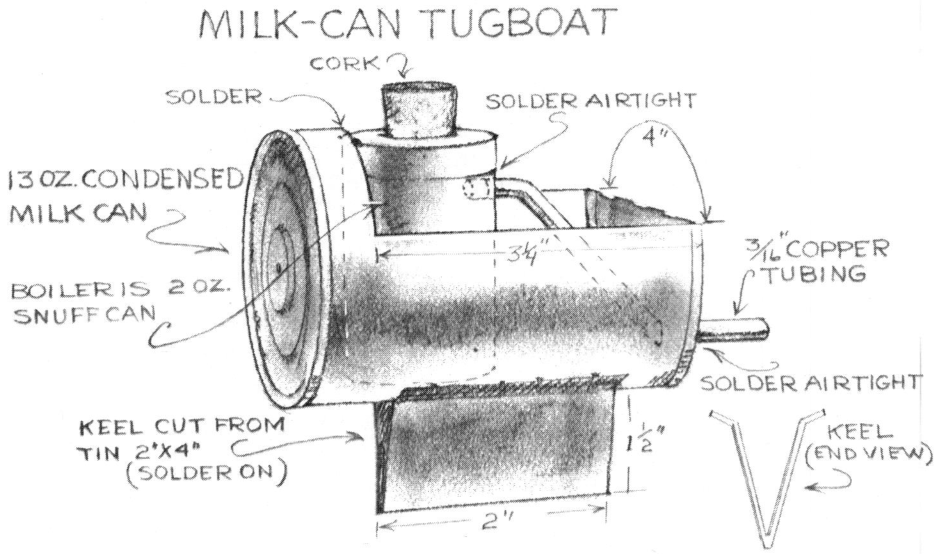

MILK-CAN TUGBOAT

CORK

SOLDER

SOLDER AIRTIGHT

4"

13 OZ. CONDENSED MILK CAN

3¾"

3/16" COPPER TUBING

BOILER IS 2 OZ. SNUFF CAN

SOLDER AIRTIGHT

KEEL CUT FROM TIN 2"X4" (SOLDER ON)

1½"

KEEL (END VIEW)

2"

wire through the tubing before bending. After the tubing was bent to the desired shape, the wire was pulled free.

If the lid of the snuff-can boiler did not fit airtight, it was made so by soldering. The tail-pipe connection into the boiler was soldered airtight too, and the boiler cork had to fit snug as could be. All this was important because if there were any leaks in the boiler assembly, the boat was robbed of the propulsion power of the carbide gas. For the tug to operate efficiently, all the gas had to be expelled out the tail pipe with as much pressure as possible.

The keel, which balanced the boat in the water, had to be positioned accurately onto the hull. To find the exact balancing point by hit or miss, the keel was first stuck to the hull with a couple of dabs of well-chewed gum, then moved this way or that until the boat floated in a perfect upright position. After the keel was soldered to the hull permanently, the milk-can tugboat was ready for its test run: in at least 4 inches of water—perhaps in a dishpan, an old cattle-watering trough, or a rain puddle. Sometimes puddles of sufficient depth could be found in the yard where chickens had scratched. A bunch of chickens, fluffing and dust bathing, could dig a hole deep enough to drown a duck . . . well, almost, anyway.

Into the boiler went about 1 teaspoon of calcium carbide crystals and 3 tablespoons of water. The boiler was corked quickly, as the gas started forming immediately. "Stand back. There she goes!"

One whiff of carbide gas would tell you why we weren't allowed to play with tugboats indoors. "Whew-eeee! Who broke the rotten egg?" It stank to high heaven, true, but it worked okay as fuel for carbide cannons (see page 24) and tugboats. Watching your boat sputter, spew, gurgle, and bubble as it chugged through the water very, very slowly—just as real tugboats do—was indeed a joy.

We decorated our tugboats by sticking flags in the boiler cork or by painting funny faces on the bow. And after a period of boating, we'd flush out the boiler and tail pipe with water to prevent a buildup of residue and keep the machinery in good running order. After all, a kid would be a ninny not to take proper care of his milk-can tugboat, the most difficult of all Great American Depression toys to construct.

NOTE: *It was always a good idea for children to have adult supervision while playing with carbide-gas-operated toys. As carbide gas is highly inflammable, our parents cautioned us to be careful never to play with these toys around open fire or flame, to heed all the warnings on the carbide container, and to follow them faithfully.*

6

Windmills and Kites

The mysterious wind is forever with us, sometimes wild and restless, whistling a song as old as the earth; sometimes sultry, gentle, so languid it almost seems to be waiting. You cannot touch it, but it can touch you. A child need only set foot outdoors on a windy day to feel its breath. Children have always enjoyed the wind as a playmate, taking pleasure in the flight of a feather, a maple or a cottonwood seed, a dandelion puffball—anything that can be carried along by a breeze. These simple toys of nature, along with handmade ones that are powered by the wind, have provided children with thousands of years of entertainment.

The Bufordville Ace

Silently, the great Red Bomber flew through the cloudless blue Oklahoma sky. The morning sun brightly reflected the aircraft's chilling insignia, a grinning skull and crossbones painted starkly in black. As the massive craft gained speed, the dark, menacing shadow it cast on the ground glided stealthily across the peaceful countryside. The warm, strong breeze from the southwest lifted the bomber even higher. Its two sharp-edged propellers whirred ever faster, humming a song that only the high-flying birds could hear: an evil song of premeditated destruction.

Like a huge crawling monster, the bomber's creeping shadow skirted the foot of Standpipe Hill, wormed its way through Mr. Buford's cow pasture, and over to Sudden Canyon. There it edged snakelike along the canyon's rim to make an unswerving approach toward the Red-Horse Barn.

Suddenly a signal from the ground activated a sophisticated mechanical device within the bomber. It shuddered momentarily before releasing from its belly an awesome bomb: a bomb more deadly than any kid could ever imagine. . . .

The devastating missile came through the skeletal roof of the barn and exploded violently against a rafter, spraying Frosty and me all over with a white cloud of Light Crust flour.

Although stunned at the sneak attack, we recovered sufficiently to run outside and shoot a couple of shingle darts at the raiding box kite, but it was out of range, speeding for Standpipe Hill. Diabolical laughter from the unseen pilot and bombardier drifted on the wind from that direction.

"Whew! That was close!" Frosty said, slapping flour from his overalls, "Danged near blew us to smithereens!"

"Too *danged* close!" I said, in a voice cracked with shell-shocked strain, digging flour out of my ear.

We went back inside the barn to survey the damage. That was when we found The Note. It was written on the ruptured housing of the flour bomb (a small paper bag from Kress's). We knew right off it was from Killer because it was printed in red Crayola that looked a lot like blood. And red Crayola and the skull-and-crossbones insignia were the Renegades' trademark. The threatening thing read:

DEAR FROSTY & HOPPY:

WARNING! AFTER DINNER WE ARE GOING TO BOMB YOUR SECRET BUFORDVIL HEADKWARTERS TO PEACES. WE HAVE 6 MORE BOMBS. OUR WAR KITES ARE THE BEST IN THE WORLD. WE DUBLE-DOG-DARE YOU TO STOP US!

YOURS TRULY,

BARON VON KILLER
(THE RED ACE)

Overwrought and madder than wet hens, Frosty and I went over The Note several times before sticking it up on the wall behind the bar. It would be there forever for future generations to plainly see, written proof that Killer and the Red River Renegades had broken the peace treaty. The air war was on *again*.

Inwardly, we chastised ourselves severely for not being more alert. We should have known the sneaky Renegades were just sitting back waiting for another nice, windy day—waiting for the chance to get even for the humiliating defeat they had suffered at our hands during the big air battle a week ago Tuesday. On that memorable day, which will go down in Okie air-war history as "Terrible Tuesday," the troops of Frosty's Fearless Flying Circus had taken a direful toll of Baron von Killer's war kites when they had tried to bomb our squadron headquarters in Bufordville (Mr. Buford's cow pasture). I had come within an inch that day of receiving the Blue Max (the distinguished air medal made from blue foil Christmas wrapping paper) and becoming the first Bufordville Ace of 1934 (one who shoots down three enemy fighters in a single day).

On Terrible Tuesday I flew (as was my custom) my sleek, trusty three-prop Spad named "Hoppy's Hawk" which was constructed by my own two hands from brand-new Pittsburgh-paint yardsticks and butcher twine and covered with pages from a *Grit* newspaper Bobby Ann had given me; its spectacular tail was made from colorful quilt scraps knotted together (courtesy of Granny Porter). Between each knot a deadly twist of sharp tin glistened.

Demonstrating simply unbelievable dogfighting skills, I had caused Kong's Fokker to collide with Whetstone's. Frosty's black Spad "Midnight" had been grounded temporarily for repairs; so, on my own, I lit out hot and heavy after Killer's Fokker "Red Lightning." And I almost had it, too, when See-Thru—in his own inimitable fashion—came flying his "Katzenjammer Spad" in from out of nowhere and got his tail tangled in my string. We won the battle, but I lost my kite. The horrible crash to earth snapped both of Hawk's spars (yardsticks) in two. The Katzenjammer Kids funny papers on See-Thru's Spad were torn to shreds.

Now, after the Red Bomber's sneaky retaliatory flour-bomb attack, Frosty and I sprang to action. We made a dash for Mr. Youngblood's toolshed. En route, Frosty checked the time of day the old Indian way by squinting solemnly at the sun with one eye closed, and said, "We got about two hours to fix your kite. We're in bad trouble!" This was true, because locating two dependable war-kite spars in just two hours was like finding a four-leaf clover in four minutes—highly unlikely.

We searched Mr. Youngblood's toolshed and garage thoroughly, and my garage too, but did not find an adequate stick for a kite spar. "You'll have to use a tree limb," Frosty suggested, knowing full well that a tree limb wasn't worth hog slop for a war-kite spar. You couldn't find one straight enough, and even if you did it'd make the kite too heavy for dogfighting. "How about a piece of cane?"

"Not on your life!" I said, determined to get the Hawk, the best danged war kite ever made, back in the sky again good as new. "Hurry! Let's go to town."

We did.

And without obtaining permission, too. For the first time in our lives we went down to Boatwright's store before asking our mothers. This brash decision was necessary, for if we took the time to ask, we'd be too late to save Bufordville headquarters; the Renegades' skull-and-crossbones bomber would wipe it off the face of the earth. As we scootmobiled into town I tried to make myself semi-invisible by keeping Frosty and his machine between me and the drugstore where my father worked, just in case he was looking out the store window.

Mr. Boatwright gave us the appalling news we'd expected. He had given away the last free yardsticks—those advertising Dutch Boy or Pittsburgh paint—only yesterday. "But I still have some Cardui calendars and a few church fans if you want one of them."

We each took a Muskogee Funeral Home church fan, as the wood handles made great propellers, but were too embarrassed to accept a Cardui calendar. I told Mr. Boatwright I needed some yardsticks in the worst way ever. And he tried to make me feel better—but didn't—by informing me that poor souls in Hades needed ice water in the worst way, too.

The yardsticks for sale—those without any advertising on them—cost two cents apiece. I was a trifle short of cash because last Saturday had been a "going-to-Muskogee day." Mr. Boatwright said, No, I could not borrow a yardstick for the rest of the day even if I promised to return it good as new; and, No, my credit was not good unless the purchase was for my father or mother; and, Yes, he would give me one for free if I'd sweep out the store for him every morning for a week. Elated, with yardstick and fan in hand, I dragged Frosty away from the BB gun he was admiring, and we sprinted for his father's toolshed.

An hour later, Hoppy's Hawk was once again ready to do battle with the evil forces in the sky. The Hawk's vertical spar was now the brand-new, soon-to-be-paid-for yardstick. The cross spar was a nice window-shade slat I had "borrowed" from Granny Porter's living-room window. This particular window was on the shady side of the house, and Granny wouldn't miss the slat until she lowered the shades after dark. By then, I planned to have it back in its rightful place.

While I twisted some new strips of tin (which served as cutters) into Hawk's magnificent tail, Frosty gave his fighting Spad Midnight a fresh coat of black Shinola; in some spots the paper wasn't as black as Frosty liked it to be. He then adjusted the rubber-band tension on the clothespin of the pilot's parachute release, oiled the three tin propellers, and tried to sharpen Midnight's tail cutters with a file. "If I had some razor blades, I'd use 'em too," he said. "It ain't fair for Killer to use 'em."

I shuddered, thinking what the consequences would be if he did do such a thing and got caught. Frosty would be grounded for life! Our folks sternly forbade using razor blades on our war kites. Too dangerous, they said. If a kite should fall on someone it could injure him seriously. Nevertheless, we suspected that Killer did not always obey this parental command and had at least one double-edged razor blade wired into the tail of his Red Lightning. His war kite was murder on our strings and bridles. One good solid swipe from Red Lightning's tail and you were a goner! Sure, our old tin props and cutters would cut through a kite string, but not clean as a whistle; only a razor blade could do that. Thus it boiled down to one of two things: either Baron von Killer was the best danged fighter pilot that ever flew a Fokker, or he had a razor blade hid in his tail.

It was a hot, lazy summer afternoon in Fort Gibson, Oklahoma, an afternoon that called for all chores to be forgotten. An afternoon for seeking the welcome shade of front porches, grape arbors, or the giant whispering umbrellas of trees. An afternoon for sipping iced tea and for watching the wind make dancing green waves across fields of grass, for contemplating the mystery of a dust devil as it did a whirling dervish down the river road, dissipating as magically as it started somewhere in the cow pasture . . . where the cattle lay underneath persimmon trees, their tails swishing lazily, jaws chewing cuds in unison. . . .

A frenzied dust devil swept across the airstrip, causing the colorful Spads of Frosty's Fearless Flying Circus parked there to flutter nervously. Before it disappeared, the small whirlwind collapsed one of the headquarters buildings (a cardboard-box lean-to) that housed spare parts for the Spads (string, paper, rubber bands). Hanging from a low branch of a persimmon tree behind Mr. Buford's hen house, the wind sock (Bull Durham sack) indicated the wind was coming from the southwest. And the anemometer (tin-can windmill) showed it was blowing at 10 knots, gusting to 12.

From inside the squadron's briefing room, which consisted of a larger cardboard-box lean-to, a sharp-eyed observer scanned the endless skies with binoculars (corncobs). He relaxed his vigil temporarily, turned to the captain, and said, "You keep lookout; I got a piece of this danged cob in my eye!"

Captain Frosty took his turn at watch while Lieutenant Bluegill tried to dislodge the speck by pulling his upper eyelid down and over the lower one. And I said, "Maybe we should have told See-Thru. It doesn't seem right to leave him—"

"Forget it," Frosty said, peering over the binoculars. "He almost made us lose the battle on Terrible Tuesday."

"Yeah," Lieutenant Eskimo said, slapping at ants crawling up his pants leg. "He flies his Spad like he was choppin' cotton. Who needs *him*?"

"We might," piped Lieutenant Kenneth. "With Laughing Pete gone to Muskogee, we're one fighter short. And I got a bad feeling about this. Bobby Ann's cat ran across the road in front of me this morning."

"Her cat ain't black."

"I know it, dummy. But one of the other kittens in the litter was."

"Hey, that's right, it was. One of 'em was as black as coal tar!"

"I think I'm getting a bad headache."

"Hey, I gotta idea," Bluegill said. "Let's go fishin' down on Skull-Head Cove. I've got a couple of new fishing boats—"

"Here they come!" Frosty yelled. "To your fighters, men! Let's get 'em in the air!"

What we saw as we ran for the airstrip chilled us with a foreboding of doom. In the eastern sky, high above Mr. Buford's house, the big Red Bomber stood out against the blue like a scarlet drop of blood. And flying escort were several other dots of color, wicked tails streaming. We couldn't believe our eyes; horrified, we counted the enemy Fokkers. One, two, three . . . six. *Six!* Where there should have been only three fighters, there were six! War kites in the air were thicker than hair on a dog's back.

"We're done for!" Bluegill cried, running to get his "Blue Bandit" airborne. "Who're the other three?"

"Can't tell," shouted Eskimo, feeding his "Cyclone Slasher" string. "One of 'em looks like Luther Spera."

"Luther!" I yelped, as Frosty handed me Hawk's reel. (He always launched my kite for me in the heat of battle as I couldn't run very fast.) "No fair! He's three years older than us!"

"And Waldo too!" screamed Kenneth, fighting to keep his "Battle Bat" away from the persimmon trees. "They've brought Waldo and his cousin Jake!"

As the dreaded enemy war kites approached, the five of us spread out in formation to protect our headquarters, each flying at different altitudes. Through my kite-string reel I could feel Hawk wasn't flying well, a little sluggish. I reeled in sharply. He climbed, but not fast. Too much tail, or the window-shade stick had added more weight. Jerking back fast and hard, I put Hawk into a roll-over dive. It was sloppy, and he came out of it much too slowly—a bare inch from the ground.

"What's wrong with Hawk?" Frosty yelled, putting Midnight through his dazzling wigwag sky dance.

"Beats me; I think he's got arthritis!"

"Don't matter, we'll blow 'em out of the sky!" With this he lowered Midnight's altitude and ran across the pasture, emitting war whoops that sounded so formidable they would have put a yellow stripe a mile wide down the *real* Red Baron's back. For a moment I thought Frosty was going to attack the Red Bomber (piloted by Kong), which was strictly against the rules. Bombers were too expensive to shoot down. But he didn't. He flew straight for Killer's Red Lightning—where they engaged in a ferocious dogfight.

Waldo, by this time, had skirted the pasture close enough for me to see he was grinning like a sheep-killing dog. He waved at me cordially as he nursed his war kite toward mine. It was obvious Waldo was just along for fun and had come because Killer had bribed him with something uncommonly expensive, probably a candy bar. Well, I'd show old Waldo a thing or two. . . .

I let Hawk sidle up alongside Waldo's ancient kite. It was puttering along on just one propeller, flying as if it were pasted in place in the sky—the way a store-bought kite from Kress's flies. Then, before you could say "Watch this trick, Waldo," I gave Hawk some slack. He dropped like a rock, came up again in front of Waldo's kite, and looped over and around his string. Hawk's coiled tail snapped Waldo's string as if it were a rotten thread. The untethered kite fluttered down, tail first, to crash in the hedgerow.

"Hey, that was great flyin', Hoppy!" Waldo hollered, reeling in his empty string. He sat down in the shade to watch the battle and started eating a candy bar. It looked like a Baby Ruth. Any other time I would have asked him for a bite.

But at the moment I had my attention back on the air war that was raging furiously. I brought Hawk over to hover close to the persimmon grove and surveyed the situation. Killer's Red Lightning was still squared off with Frosty's Midnight. Bluegill was doing a great job of keeping his Blue Bandit in front of the Red Bomber, preventing Kong from getting in position to bomb our headquarters. Otherwise, though, there were so many war kites all over the sky I couldn't make head nor tails—

A whirring green streak came out of the sun, missing Hawk by mere inches. Leaves rained down from the persimmon tree where a deadly green tail, flashing steel meant for Hawk, had slashed a branch. Razor blades!

Quickly, I brought Hawk down lower, and even closer to the trees. Then I saw it for the very first time: the "Green Eagle"! The legendary war kite I had heard stories about all my life but had never seen. It hovered now treetop high, a glimmering green dragon's eye, its three sharp 6-inch propellers humming like angry bees, the razor-blade-encrusted tail swishing catlike. The most destructive war kite in the world was stalking Hoppy's Hawk!

I followed the Green Eagle's string down to the reel in Luther's hand. I blinked and found it hard to swallow. Luther, Sticker's thirteen-year-old brother, was not only the greatest top spiker in school, he was the builder, owner, and pilot of the war kite that old-timers like Waldo and Jake said *had never in its whole life been defeated in combat*! Luther, a Bufordville Ace many times over, supposedly had put his war kite in moth balls two years back when he had become a professional top spiker. But now here Luther stood thirty yards away from me, legs spread, his flinty blue eyes watching the Green Eagle and Hawk. Over the screaming and hollering of the other pilots I heard him yell at me. "Say your prayers, Hoppy. The Green Eagle is gonna strike again!"

In desperation I looked around for Frosty. Surely Midnight would come to my rescue. But a quick glance told me that Killer was giving Frosty more than he could handle. So taking a firm but still sweaty grip on my reel and remembering what my Grandfather Porter once said, "You'll never know how good you can fight until you're backed into a corner," I brought Hawk out and away from the trees. And into the greatest dogfight of his life!

The Green Eagle's first sneaky stratagem took a few of Hawk's feathers and made him fighting mad. Pieces of *Grit* newspaper flew when the Green Eagle's tail flicked Hawk's left side just above the propeller. With this Hawk shook himself like an angry wet dog and took for the high blue. The Green Eagle followed right on his tail.

From a great height I let Hawk fall, fluttering—my famous "dead-leaf" trick—but the Green Eagle didn't buy it. He went into the dead-leaf, too, and pulled out of it squarely on top of Hawk, the green tail slashing like a saber. Hawk streaked to one side and flew low to the ground, down the hedgerow over Waldo, making him duck.

It looked hopeless. Hawk had thrown every trick in the war-kite book at the Green Eagle, to no avail. Luther's legendary war kite was too fast, too clever, too well armed. As a last resort—as a farewell salute, so to speak—to the gallant Hawk, I had him gain altitude once again, determined to put him through the most beautiful and difficult war kite stunt of all: the split-S dive. The Green Eagle shadowed Hawk all the way. Then; it happened. Don't ask me how—it just did.

The very instant that Hawk went into the dive, the wind died like closing a valve; then it gusted. The sudden strong gust flipped Hawk around to fly directly into the Green Eagle, face to face. Even from such a great height, the crash was audible to those on the ground, and tiny flakes of green and *Grit* snow shimmered downward. I jerked back hard on my reel to release the pilot chute in case Hawk's bridle string had been severed. Astonished, I watched as Hawk actually flew out of the entanglement—at an odd tilted angle, but flying just the same. The crippled Green Eagle rolled over on its back to spiral downward faster and faster, the bridle string broken. As it slammed into the ground, a green pilot's chute floated lazily on the wind toward Standpipe Hill. Luther's chute had opened. According to the rules, he could put the Green Eagle back into the battle if repairs could be made in time.

I couldn't believe it. First, I had shot down Waldo's kite and now the infamous Green Eagle. Two down! Just one more to go. I would be the first Bufordville Ace—

An earsplitting screech suddenly rent the air, sounding as if a giant hand was scraping its fingernails across a gigantic blackboard. Through the pasture came Lieutenant See-Thru, running hard, chin straps of his Jack Oakie aviator cap flapping like hound's ears. Certain that we were losing the battle, he screamed, "I'm comin', men, don't despair!" as he fed out string to his Katzenjammer Spad.

What happened next can best be described as absolute chaos. And the notable event went down in air-war history as "Wipe-out Wednesday."

First off, See-Thru galloped at a dead run smack into Frosty, knocking them both flat. (See-Thru's goggles were so scratched they impaired his vision.) This caused Frosty to lose his reel, freeing Midnight, which dropped like a rock onto Killer's Red Lightning. Both kites were thrown into the spider web of strings controlling three other kites. Then, when See-Thru's Katzenjammer Spad had most of its tail bitten off by Eskimo's Cyclone Slasher, it went into a series of crazy, wide loop-the-loops. The Cyclone Slasher spit the severed tail into Whetstone's Fokker, throwing it into a dive that splintered Kenneth's Battle Bat, which immediately entangled more strings and tails. The chain reaction reached me and Hawk through Kong, who stumbled backwards over a cow chip. Sprawling on his back, he involuntarily jerked the bomb-release string attached to the Red Bomber. The flour bomb scored a direct hit on See-

Thru, who naturally thought Kong had done the dastardly deed on purpose. In flour-blind fury he chucked a clod at Kong, which missed and struck me on the nose with considerable force. The stinging clod jarred the reel out of my hand, sending Hawk plummeting to earth.

When the dust had finally settled, Bufordville was the scene of utter destruction. The crumpled remains of Fokkers and Spads dotted the pasture from the foot of Standpipe Hill over to Mr. Buford's house. The solitary kite remaining in the air was See-Thru's Katzenjammer Spad. It continued to fly in crazy, uncontrollable loop-the-loops. Lieutenant See-Thru pushed up his floured goggles, took a good look around, then pointed up to where something red and shapeless hung in the very top of the tallest persimmon tree. A tattered black skull and crossbones waved in the wind. The Red Bomber would fly no more.

Later, sitting on the back porch contemplating the sad condition of Hoppy's Hawk, I figured that, all in all, it hadn't been exactly what I'd call a terrific day. My victory over the Green Eagle had been a hollow one. Nobody but Waldo had witnessed it, and he didn't count. When Granny Porter had caught me trying to sneak her window-shade stick back in its place, her house was placed off limits to me for two days (which meant none of her home-baked, melt-in-your-mouth tea cakes for forty-eight long hours). The new two-cent yardstick, that I would have to work my fingers to the bone paying for, had a major fracture that would take a miracle to fix. No wonder I wasn't overly thrilled as I might have been during the impressive medal-presentation ceremony. Sure, Lieutenant See-Thru shot down three enemy planes and that made him the first Bufordville Ace of 1934, very true. But somehow it just didn't seem proper to bestow the prestigious Blue Max on a fighter pilot who had knocked down all of his buddies' planes too.

Just as I decided to try splicing the yardstick, my father came home for supper. I couldn't hear all the conversation he was having with Mother in the kitchen, but I did hear her say, "No, I did not."

The way she emphasized the words "did not" left me feeling somewhat apprehensive. When heavy footsteps headed my way I bent to my work, whistling what I hoped sounded like a merry tune. Dad opened the screen door, gave me a look that implied he would like to feed me to the hogs, and inquired in a tone that was definitely not sympathetic to my cause, "Did you get your mother's permission before you went down to Boatwright's store today?"

Harnessing the Wind

Along with waterwheels, windmills were among the earliest machines that replaced man as a source of power. Their use was widespread in Europe until the early twentieth century. The earliest known references to windmills are in the story of a Persian millwright in A.D. 644. Chances are the windmill's discovery happened like this:

One day in A.D. 644 a young Persian gristmill owner, who had customers waiting in line to get their grain ground, found himself in deep water when the creek went dry. Standing dejectedly, looking at the now dry-as-a-bone waterwheel of his mill, he noticed it was moving ever so slowly. The wind that whistled through the valley daily, so strong it practically blew him out of the millhouse, was turning the wheel—but just barely. Quick as a wink, he grabbed up some old boards and a couple of pieces of baling wire and converted the waterwheel into a big propeller. "Okay, who's next?" the triumphant millwright said, as the mill's wheel whirled merrily in the wind.

From that day over a thousand years ago until World War I, the wind was the main power supply worldwide for grinding grain and pumping water. The windmill's demise began rapidly, after the Great War, with the full-scale development of the internal-combustion engine and the spread of turbine electric power. But for decades wind-power energy has been

PAPER WINDMILL

Windmills made of folded paper or celluloid gained general popularity in America in the early 1900s. The toys, sometimes called pinwheels, sold faster than peanuts and popcorn at fairs and carnivals. A whirring windmill in a kid's hand added even more excitement and thrills to the midway rides. In the '30s rural children delighted in holding homemade toy windmills out the open windows of automobiles and feeling the wind's force as they chugged along a country road. Since there was very little traffic, youngsters were often seen riding outside on the running board. As Father sped along at 10 miles an hour, Mother sat with arms extended through the window, clutching Junior by the galluses. Junior, meantime, was clutching his paper windmill, twirling away to beat sixty.

PAPER WINDMILL

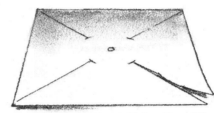

START WITH A SQUARE PIECE OF PAPER· DRAW LINES FROM CORNERS· CUT ON LINES ⅔ WAY TO CENTER

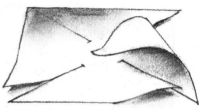

BEND IN TO CENTER

ATTACH TO STICK WITH STRAIGHT PIN THROUGH CENTER—IT'LL SPIN AT A WALK

WINDMILL

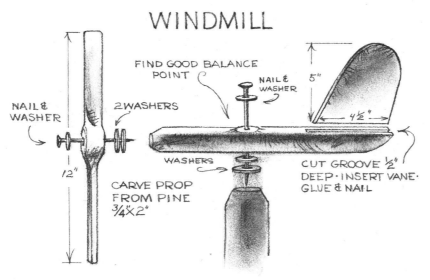

NAIL & WASHER

FIND GOOD BALANCE POINT

2 WASHERS

NAIL & WASHER

5"

12"

4½"

WASHERS

CARVE PROP FROM PINE ¾"×2"

CUT GROOVE ½" DEEP·INSERT VANE· GLUE & NAIL

WINDMILL

When a young Depression-era toy maker discovered for the first time how easy it was to whittle a wood propeller, he would soon have such an impressive array of windmills stuck around in the yard that a person put his or her life on the line on every trip out to feed the chickens.

Homemade toy windmills came in more sizes and varieties than puppies, but the construction and operating principle of all of them was pretty much the same: The prop spun easily in the slightest breeze, and the complete unit was balanced so that the vane kept the toy pointed into the wind. As a well-designed windmill made an excellent weather vane, it was not unusual to see one on a farm atop the steepest roof of house or barn, spinning away, pointing into the wind the same as its big, mechanical, store-bought brother that was busily pumping water from the well.

TIN-CAN WINDMILL

During the lean years, nearly everyone who had access to a piece of ground large enough to shoot marbles on planted a vegetable garden. Even in cities, gardens were as numerous as pigeons on a park statue. Sure, vegetables were cheap as dirt at the

the subject of extensive experimental studies. In 1979 the world's largest windmill went into operation atop a mountain in Boone, North Carolina. From winds blowing at 24 mph or stronger, the ten-story machine with its steel blades 200 feet in diameter was designed to generate 2,000 kilowatts of electricity (enough to supply 300 homes).

Toy windmills appear on woodcuts and engravings dating back to medieval times. The sails of these early toys were two crosspieces of wood nailed loosely to the end of a stick. Engravings dated 1774 show children playing with toy windmills that have a miniature mill affixed to the end of a stick on which the sails are attached. In America, toy windmills of wood and iron became popular in the late 1800s. Some were quite elaborate and as mechanically intricate as a clock mechanism. The sails activated a moving figure: a woodchopper, a cyclist, a runner, a man rowing a boat, etc.—all powered by the wind.

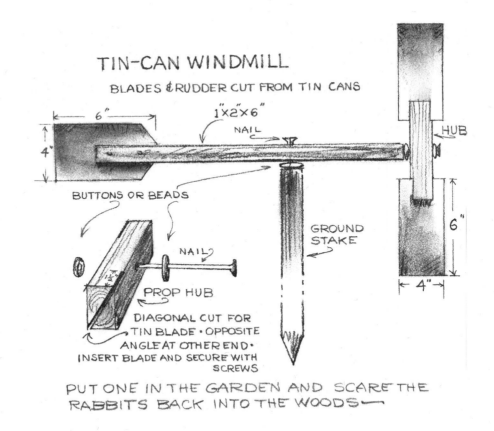

TIN-CAN WINDMILL

BLADES & RUDDER CUT FROM TIN CANS

6"

4"

1"x2"x6"

NAIL

HUB

BUTTONS OR BEADS

6"

GROUND STAKE

NAIL

4"

PROP HUB

DIAGONAL CUT FOR TIN BLADE · OPPOSITE ANGLE AT OTHER END · INSERT BLADE AND SECURE WITH SCREWS

PUT ONE IN THE GARDEN AND SCARE THE RABBITS BACK INTO THE WOODS

grocer's, but that was of little use to those who didn't have any money coming in. So many families turned to gardening. One seldom needed to purchase seeds; they were gathered yearly from mature crops, dried, and sealed in Mason jars to keep through the winter. There was a comfortable reassurance in providing your own food that seemed to breed confidence in the natural order of things. Most rural Americans found it difficult to believe that anyone could have actually starved during the Great American Depression. The forests supplied wild game, the lakes and rivers were abundant with fish, and a dime would buy enough garden seeds (if they had to be bought) to supply a household with vegetables for a year. In reply to the rumors that people were starving to death, an old-timer would say, "Well, if that's true, they're too lazy to breathe!"

The tin-can windmill was useful in the garden. Its shiny 6-inch tin sails made it surprisingly effective in repelling certain garden pests. Rabbits, chipmunks, squirrels, and birds were frightened away by the large revolving propeller, which did not move as fast as a wooden one but emitted a low *flap, flap, flap* sound. Three or four tin-can windmills placed around in a small garden would keep it pest free for quite a while. Sooner or later, though, the bravest of the varmints would overcome its fear of these strange-sounding, rotating monsters to sneak in for a snack.

NOTE: *Kids gave a whirling tin-can windmill a wide berth. Like an electric fan, the tin blades could cut fingers, toes, or whatever.*

MAGIC PROPELLER

One got the impression that the magic propeller (also called "Gee-haw-whimmy-diddle") was a wind toy. But it was not. The prop, a flat piece of wood, would not spin in the wind. It was not carved in the shape of a propeller. You could hold it into a gale, and it wouldn't turn a lick. But hand it to the kid who made the toy, the one who knew "the magic," and he could induce it to whirl faster than any wind prop ever devised. And to beat all, he seemed to be able to change the spinning direction from clockwise to counterclockwise by just shouting the magic words: *"Gee! . . . Haw!"*

For the toy maker who enjoyed whittling, the magic propeller was a piece of cake. A seasoned hardwood branch about 8 inches long (the prop stick) was whittled flat on two sides until the top of it (where the notches were to be cut) was about ¼ inch wide. The first of the nine notches was then cut 1½ inches from the propeller end of the prop stick. The next step consisted of getting comfortable under a cool shade tree with a fistful of homemade tea cakes and a tall glass of lemonade. The tea cakes supplied the toy maker with stamina; the lemonade prevented dehydration as he sweated over the remaining task. It was essential that notches be cut more or less uniformly about 3/16 inch apart and ⅛ inch deep. The better the quality of workmanship in this step of construction, the stronger the magic of the finished toy.

The rubbing stick was whittled from another hardwood branch, about 4 inches long. Half of it was whittled down to an edge almost sharp as a knife (this edge when rubbed back and forth over the notches activated the magic).

MAGIC PROPELLER

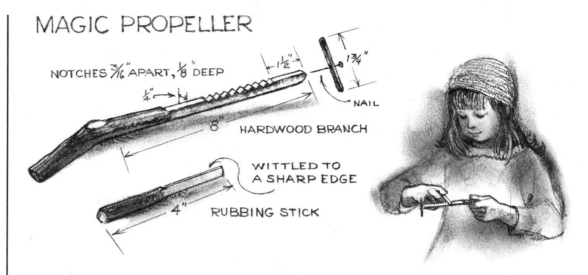

NOTCHES 3/16" APART, 1/8" DEEP

1 1/2"

1 3/4"

NAIL

1/4"

8" HARDWOOD BRANCH

WITTLED TO A SHARP EDGE

4" RUBBING STICK

To complete the toy a small hole was drilled in the exact center of the flat wood propeller, which was then nailed to the end of the prop stick. A space of about 3/8 inch was left between the head of the nail and the prop stick. It was most important that the propeller spin free y on the nail and be perfectly balanced.

The Secret of the Magic Propeller

When the sharp edge of the rubbing stick is rubbed rapidly back and forth across the notches of the prop stick (which is held in a horizontal position), the prop will begin to turn slowly. The faster the notches are rubbed, and the faster "whimmy-diddle, whimmy-diddle" is chanted, the faster the prop will spin. To make the prop turn to the right (the operator's right) the rubbing stick is held at an angle to contact the left side of the notches To turn left, reversing the prop's direction, the right side of the notches is rubbed. So observers won't notice the shifting of positions, let the forefinger ride on top of the rubbing stick.

This sorcerer's toy is made even more mysterious if the commands given to plow horses or mules are called out when the prop reverses direction: "Gee" for a right turn, "Haw" for a left. The toy will appear to reverse direction at your command. How the magic propeller became known as the "Gee-haw-whimmy-diddle" is a mystery. Gee and Haw are self-explanatory . . . but what is a whimmy-diddle?

KITE-STRING REEL

A young kite flyer who preferred something more elaborate than an old stick or a corncob to wind his kite string on built himself a kite-string reel. All that was needed were five thread spools, a ¼-inch bolt with nuts and washers, a broomstick, two ¼ by 6-inch-square boards, and a few wood screws. Operating on the same principle as a fishing reel, it provided quick and effortless control of any kite. It was particularly desirable for putting a war kite through its paces, where a fast release or pull on the string meant the difference between victory or defeat.

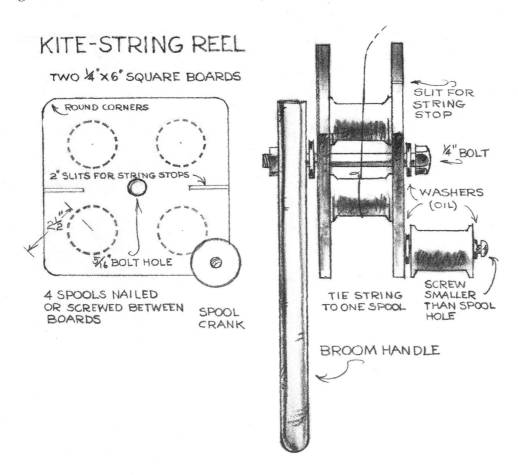

KITE-STRING REEL

TWO ¼"x6" SQUARE BOARDS

ROUND CORNERS

2" SLITS FOR STRING STOPS

2½"

5/16" BOLT HOLE

4 SPOOLS NAILED OR SCREWED BETWEEN BOARDS

SPOOL CRANK

SLIT FOR STRING STOP

¼" BOLT

WASHERS (OIL)

TIE STRING TO ONE SPOOL

SCREW SMALLER THAN SPOOL HOLE

BROOM HANDLE

SKEETER KITE

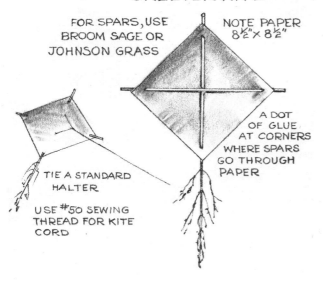

FOR SPARS, USE BROOM SAGE OR JOHNSON GRASS

NOTE PAPER 8½" × 8½"

A DOT OF GLUE AT CORNERS WHERE SPARS GO THROUGH PAPER

TIE A STANDARD HALTER

USE #50 SEWING THREAD FOR KITE CORD

Kite Fighting, Oklahoma Style

Monthly during the '30s dozens of "war-in-the-sky" pulp magazines were published. Drugstore racks bulged with these thick, illustrated 10-cent bundles of stories printed on cheap newsprint, displaying full-color action-packed covers. They brought to the reader glowing accounts, mostly fictional, of the men who fought in the air in World War I. Under the imprint of such provocative titles as "Sky Fighters," "Sky Devils," or "Death Angels," the formula plots of the stories followed the devil-may-care flying and fighting adventures of aces the likes of Georges Guynemer and René Fonck of France, Edward Mannock and Albert Ball of Great Britain, William A. Bishop of Canada, Edward Rickenbacker and Frank Luke of the U.S.A., and Manfred von Richthofen, the formidable Red Baron, the German pilot who was the greatest ace of them all.

WAR KITE

To the young kite flyer during hard times, the war kite was the epitome of kites. Easy to make, easy to repair, the war kite cost absolutely nothing to build. It was as free as the wind. Structurally, it was somewhat different from the run-of-the-mill two-spar pleasure kite: The war kite had a bowed cross spar (bowed approximately 2 inches), and the bridle was unusually long (about 6 feet). These two distinct variations gave it maneuverability a pleasure kite did not have. The lightweight, flexible spars, which were made from boxwood yardsticks (distributed free every spring and summer by most paint and hardware companies), endowed the kite with extra durability. War kites were covered with paper: newsprint, butcher paper, or sack paper. The Sunday funnies gave a kite cover a touch of class and a dash of color.

Bristling with its full armament of tin tail cutters and tin propellers, the war kite was as deadly as any fighter that ever took to the air. Asking a kid how he determined the proper tail components (length and weight) for this supreme flying toy was like asking Granny Porter how she concocted her delicious homemade jelly. The reply would be the same: "You just keep adding and subtracting stuff till you get it right." When the tail had the correct length and weight for prevailing wind conditions (the stronger the wind, the longer the tail had to be), and the cross spar was bowed just right, the war kite performed exactly as all excellent fighter kites should. It did not fly flat and stable as if it were glued to a cloud as store-bought pleasure kites would do. The war kite was a nervous flyer—jittery. Its menacing tail twitched. It wigwagged back and forth in the sky like a metronome. A tug on the string sent the kite speeding in the direction of the "wig" or the "wag." A sudden release of the string followed by a strong pull would put the war kite into a screaming dive a falcon couldn't duplicate.

Unarmed, with a short 36-inch bridle and with the cross spar unbowed, the war kite became a gentle, easy-to-control pleasure kite that would climb so high, given enough string, as to go right out of sight. In a stiff wind or gentle breeze it flew splendidly.

NOTE: *War kites were handled with extreme care since the tail cutters and propeller spinners were sharp. Children were cautioned to fly their kites in open areas away from crowds—and to stay away from power lines. Kids who were familiar with Ben Franklin's antics knew electricity could run down a string fast as lightning.*

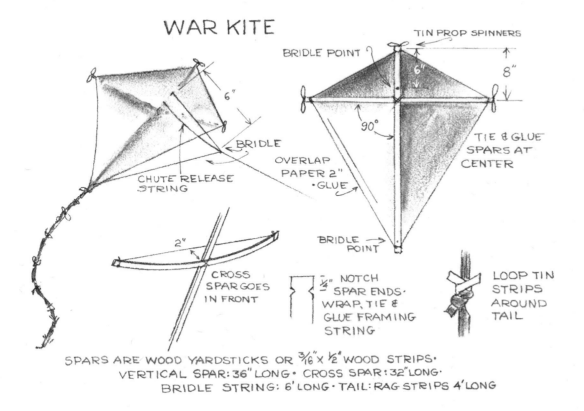

WAR KITE

BRIDLE POINT

TIN PROP SPINNERS

6"

8"

90°

TIE & GLUE SPARS AT CENTER

BRIDLE

6"

OVERLAP PAPER 2" ·GLUE

CHUTE RELEASE STRING

BRIDLE POINT

2"

CROSS SPAR GOES IN FRONT

¼" NOTCH SPAR ENDS· WRAP, TIE & GLUE FRAMING STRING

LOOP TIN STRIPS AROUND TAIL

SPARS ARE WOOD YARDSTICKS OR ³⁄₁₆" X ½" WOOD STRIPS·
VERTICAL SPAR: 36" LONG· CROSS SPAR: 32" LONG·
BRIDLE STRING: 6' LONG· TAIL: RAG STRIPS 4' LONG

TIN-PROPELLER SPINNERS (War Kite)

The tin propellers on a war kite not only simulated the engines of a fighter airplane, they were an important part of the kite's armament. These fast-spinning props made from strips of tin cut from tin cans were murder on an opponent's kite string and cover.

Some experimentation was required to bend the tin strips to the correct pitch of a propeller, but when just one had been accurately pitched to spin freely in the wind, it was retained as a model for others. The propellers were not mounted directly on the kite's spars. They were mounted on the ends of small strips of wood which were

Movies, too—*Wings, Dawn Patrol*—thrilled audiences, as daring young men in their Sopwith Camels, Spads, Nieuports, and Fokkers engaged in aerial combat, their long white silk scarves streaming, Vickers machine guns blazing. Such was the stuff Oklahoma kids integrated into their kite-fighting games.

We gave our war kites names and personalities and pretended they were real planes. They were built with loving care and armed with deadly weapons (tin propeller spinners and tin strips in the tail). And we felt they could fly rings around anything with feathers or wings. In our favorite air-war game, a German bomber kite and its escort of war kites endeavored to flour-bomb the allied headquarters (usually, cardboard boxes or old outhouses in an open pasture). The allied kites naturally tried to prevent this from happening by engaging in dogfights and blocking the bomber's flight path.

The six Air-war Rules were clear, concise, unbendable, and unbreakable:

1. A war kite couldn't be armed with razor blades or real knives.

2. A bomber kite couldn't drop flour bombs on people or animals.

3. A war kite couldn't try to shoot down a bomber kite (or a little kid's pleasure kite or balloon flying on a string).

4. A war kite couldn't get back into the battle after being shot down unless its pilot's chute had released and opened.

5. Ground observers (regardless of whom they were betting their marbles on) couldn't shoot at war kites or bomber kites with shingle darts, arrows, spears, slings, or slingshots during air wars.

6. A war-kite pilot couldn't, even if outnumbered, ask another person to hold his string while he ran home to use the privy.

Kite Fighting Around the World

Kite fighting originated in Asia.. And though the ancient sport is gaining in popularity in Europe and the Americas, Asia still remains its chief playground. There kite battles are fought from city roofs and rural fields daily. Combatants take to the air with highly maneuverable kites, their strings glazed with a mixture of glue and crushed glass. The fighters dart and slash; strings cross or overlap. Kites yaw, pitch, roll; the more skillful flyer manages to cut the other's string. To him belongs the spoils—if he can get to the downed kite first.

Fighter kites are armed various ways in different countries. Some use abrasive string: others have sharp knifelike cutters in the tail or elsewhere. Another type has an oversized, specially made fishhook attached to the bridle string. But, however armed, the toy provides sporting entertainment around the world.

INDIA

Kite fighting in India is as popular as baseball in America. Rich and poor alike participate or follow the sport religiously, and kite making is a dignified and profitable profession. Fighter kites of proven ability, priceless to their owners, are kept stored in dustproof, moistureproof, and mothproof containers. The basic Indian fighter kite, plain in appearance, is a delicately designed masterpiece of aeronautics, so well balanced it will fly in the slightest breeze and a scant six inches off the ground.

The kite is constructed by stretching brilliantly colored paper tightly over curved and tapered bamboo spars. The paper is scored with seashells to prevent its crinkling in flight. The kite's abrasive string, from 100 to 200 feet of it (the regular string is tied to this), is encrusted with ground colored glass, so sharp the handler must wear heavy gloves to protect his hands.

A kite fight in India is not always a scheduled event. Hundreds of fights take place daily where the opponents have never met or seen one another, and chances are they never will. When a fighter kite lifts into the air high above city rooftops, it is an open

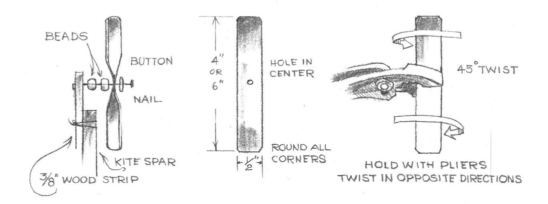

TIN PROPELLER SPINNER

BEADS

BUTTON

NAIL

KITE SPAR

3/8" WOOD STRIP

4" OR 6"

HOLE IN CENTER

ROUND ALL CORNERS

1/2"

45° TWIST

HOLD WITH PLIERS
TWIST IN OPPOSITE DIRECTIONS

PARACHUTE & RELEASE MECHANISM

TIE HERE

RELEASE STRING

RUBBER BAND

TAPE HOLE ON BOTH SIDES OF PAPER

CROSS SPAR

BRIDLE

IF BRIDLE BREAKS IN BATTLE
A TUG ON CONTROL STRING
WILL RELEASE CHUTE

KITE STRING TO OPERATOR

6" SQUARE LIGHT CLOTH

6"

METAL WASHER

AT KITE'S BALANCE POINT HOLD CLOTHESPIN TO SPAR
WITH RUBBER BAND · ADJUST TENSION TO BARELY HOLD WASHER
& CHUTE

then attached to the tips of the spars with string or rubber bands. A nail driven into a spar could weaken it. Glass beads served best for washers, although buttons would do too.

NOTE: *All toys cut from tin cans were handled with care, as tin edges are sharp.*

PARACHUTE AND RELEASE MECHANISM (War Kite)

If a war kite's bridle string was cut during a dogfight, a strong tug on the kite's flying string by the handler would release a parachute to float the imaginary pilot safely to the ground.

The parachutes were made of 6-inch-square pieces of cloth and 6-inch lengths of string—with a metal washer for weight. The release mechanism consisted of a clothespin mounted on the backside of a kite's vertical spar with rubber bands which had been tensioned to give the jaws just enough clamping power to hold the chute's washer firmly. One end of the release string was tied to the clothespin at the point shown in the illustration; the other end was run through a hole in the kite's cover and tied to the knot of the flying string and bridle. There had to be a small amount of slack in the release string when the bridle was pulled taut in flight. To ground test, the bridle string was pulled tight, the upper or lower string was then cut, and the flying string given a hard jerk. If the tension on the clothespin was correct, the chute would release. Also, the tension needed to be light enough to allow the chute to release when it was opened by a gust of wind—even though the bridle string had not been severed. Frequently, when a crippled war kite was fluttering earthward, the chute would fill with air and pull itself free from the clothespin release—thus saving the day for the young pilot.

BOMBER KITE

The bomber kite was a large open-end box kite capable of carrying one or more flour bombs aloft. The one illustrated was a super flyer; even in a moderate wind, it could transport as many as four 2-ounce flour bombs. Dried cane could be substituted for the ⅜-inch-square main spars. And yardsticks worked well for cross spars. Gluing and tying the cross spars together as the first step simplified construction. If the boxes were covered with fabric instead of paper, lightweight cloth such as flour sacking

challenge to fight. Soon another brightly colored kite rises to accept the challenge. The two kites engage in aerial combat until one manages to cut the string of the other. The defeated kite falls somewhere unknown within the city. The winner swings his kite into a victory salute and remains in the air to challenge another.

THAILAND

When Thailand was called Siam, King Mogkut of *Anna and the King of Siam* fame was credited with sponsoring the country's first official kite fight. Since then the sport of kite fighting in Thailand has attracted spectators by the thousands, who wager on the outcome of the fights much like horse racing fans bet on horses in other countries.

In an offical Thai kite fight there are two kites: *Chula*, the huge male kite, and *Pakpao*, the much smaller female. Both are constructed of paper and bamboo and armed with fishhook barbs, yet *Chula* is three times the size of *Pakpao* and carries three hooks to her one hook. The star-shaped male kite is roughly 7 feet across, and so strong it takes ten handlers to fly it. The petite, diamond-shaped female is only 34 inches long, with a short cotton-fabric tail, and is flown by one person.

The object of the contest, of course, is for one kite to hook or entangle the other, causing it to plunge to the ground. The *Chula* tries to accomplish this with its sheer weight, flying force, and multiple armament. The faster-flying *Pakpao* employs strategy to outmaneuver the male, either to hook it or make it entangle itself in its own strings. The betting odds are nearly always in favor of the heavier kite, sometimes as much as fifty to one—depending on the skill and reputation of the female kite's handler. If the underdog *Pakpao* wins, the jubilant fans lift both kite and handler to their shoulders and parade them through the streets.

JAPAN

Kite fighting in Japan reportedly began back in the 1570s when Portuguese sailors brought their fighter

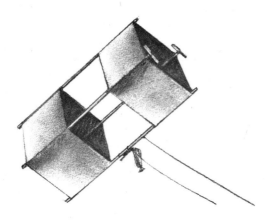

was satisfactory, but it was sewn onto the string frames, not glued. The design of the bomber kite eliminated the necessity of a bridle. The flying string was attached directly to the bottom spar slightly forward of the kite's balancing point. This position might vary, depending on the bomb load. The two tin propellers were for show only, not for aerial combat. War-kite flyers respected the fact that a bomber was somewhat difficult to build; therefore, no one ever deliberately tried to knock it out of the air. Usually just a threat to do so would suffice. Intimidated by a fierce war kite, the bomber kite would run like a scared rabbit.

NOTE: *In playing with bomber kites, rule number 2 of the six Air-war Rules was always followed.* (see page 125)

kites with them to the island of Kyushu. Farmland and rolling hills around the cities became the setting for the springtime sport. So many people attended the contests that once in 1781 the governor of Nagasaki banned kite fighting because the crops were being damaged by contestants and spectators trampling spring seedlings. The kite enthusiasts rebelled. Kite fighting persisted in Nagasaki; the unpopular governor did not.

Today, as in the past, the Japanese fighter kite is armed with abrasive string and knives strung together for the tail. The knives are pieces of bamboo slit lengthwise, with sharp blades inserted in the slits. The kites vary in shape and size, but all are made of bamboo and paper.

Unlike the Thai or Indian contests, where only two kites square off, the Japanese fights are usually armies against armies. It is not unusual for a hundred or more fighter kites to take to the air for a single battle. When a kite is struck down, it belongs to anyone who captures it. Japanese children carry long bamboo poles to the rallies to help retrieve the kites lodged in trees.

SOUTH AMERICA

In recent years, kite fighting has become very popular in Brazil, where kite enthusiasts pursue a type of aerial combat more violent than that in other countries, and much more dangerous to people on the

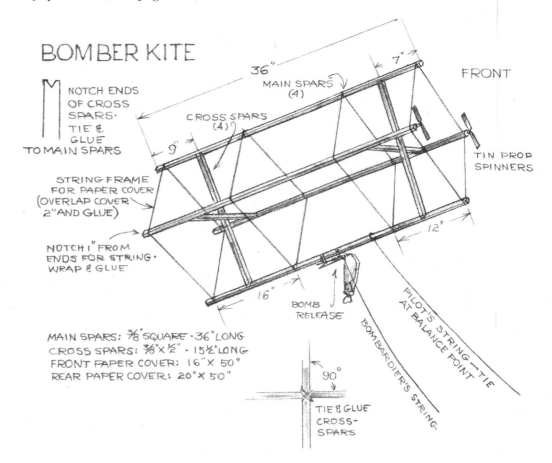

BOMBER KITE

NOTCH ENDS OF CROSS SPARS · TIE & GLUE TO MAIN SPARS

STRING FRAME FOR PAPER COVER (OVERLAP COVER 2" AND GLUE)

NOTCH 1" FROM ENDS FOR STRING · WRAP & GLUE

36"

MAIN SPARS (4)

CROSS SPARS (4)

FRONT

7"

9"

TIN PROP SPINNERS

12"

16"

BOMB RELEASE

PILOT'S STRING — TIE AT BALANCE POINT

BOMBARDIER'S STRING

90°

TIE & GLUE CROSS-SPARS

MAIN SPARS: 3/8" SQUARE · 36" LONG
CROSS SPARS: 3/8" X 1/2" · 15½" LONG
FRONT PAPER COVER: 16" X 50"
REAR PAPER COVER: 20" X 50"

BOMB AND RELEASE MECHANISM (Bomber Kite)

To the bottom spar of the bomber kite, just behind the kite's balance point, a clothespin was attached with rubber bands. The tension of the rubber bands needed to be adjusted to hold a flour bomb securely, but lightly, in the clothespin's jaws. The release string, to be handled by the bombardier on the ground, was tied to the lower jaw of the clothespin. A jerk on this string when the bomber was over the target would send the flour bomb screaming to earth.

Flour bombs consisted of paper bags or rolled pieces of newspaper containing a handful (about 5 tablespoons) of flour. Harmless, they were the greatest toy bombs ever invented. There was no disputing whether or not they dropped on target. On impact they burst into a cloud of flour.

The bomb-release mechanism on bomber kites was also used for carrying aloft and releasing parachutes, whirligigs, balloons, and paper airplanes.

ground. The public beaches of Brazil, where the fights are usually held, are often swarming with bathers, including small children. Nevertheless, the handlers stud the spar tips of their kites with razor blades and endeavor to slash opponents' kites to ribbons—which they often do.

Korea, Tibet, Arabia, and Malaysia are also lands of great kite fights and fighters. But in the United States kite fighting as a sport has yet to become popular. Outside of a few active clubs in Hawaii and some of the coastal states, it is relatively unknown. Every year, though, more and more American youngsters are discovering the wonders of fighter-kite making and flying. And these kids will tell you there's a lot more fun to flying a kite than just trying to keep it out of a tree.

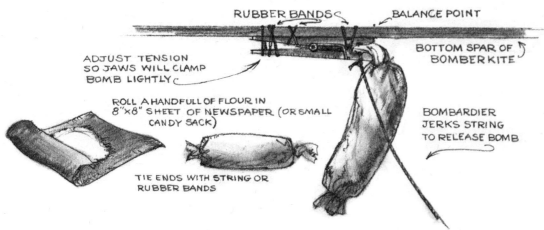

BOMB AND RELEASE MECHANISM

RUBBER BANDS — BALANCE POINT

ADJUST TENSION SO JAWS WILL CLAMP BOMB LIGHTLY

BOTTOM SPAR OF BOMBER KITE

ROLL A HANDFULL OF FLOUR IN 8"x8" SHEET OF NEWSPAPER (OR SMALL CANDY SACK)

BOMBARDIER JERKS STRING TO RELEASE BOMB

TIE ENDS WITH STRING OR RUBBER BANDS

7

Skill

Back during Paleolithic times—several thousand decades preceding the years known as the Great American Depression—grocery stores were few and far between. Talk about hard times! Before a cave-dwelling family could sit down to their favorite Sunday dinner of mastodon steaks and skunk cabbage, the food had to be hunted and gathered. The gathered portion of the meal was no big deal, unless cabbage was out of season, but putting meat on the spit was a whole new ball game. Mastodons, pachyderm-type beasts, were deliciously edible. But the smallest in the herd paralleled a locomotive in size and had the disposition of an irate bobcat. Hunters procured these huge, ill-tempered protein victuals with the aid of spears, darts, arrows, and all kinds of sharp-pointed implements that were blown, thrown, jabbed, or otherwise propelled through the air.

Most likely, youngsters were fascinated by the sharp-pointed tools their dads employed to bring home the big bacon and were always sneaking them outside to play games with. Sooner or later, most hunters got fed up with not being able to find their weapons when they needed to put food on the table or protect themselves from hostile neighbors. But there was a good, simple solution to the problem: Make the kids some toys that were blown, thrown, jabbed, or otherwise propelled through the air. Thus (hypothetically) the first toy weapons came into being.

The Great Labor Day Slingshot Shoot

The coming of September always signaled the end of something good and the beginning of something bad. Every kid in town could smell it in the air, and feel it inside like the start of a green-apple stomachache. Though we knew it was just around the corner, we tried to ignore it as the days grew shorter and an occasional refreshing coolness drifted off the river and chilled the evening breeze. Then, in the last week of August, portents of doom: the all-too-familiar signs went up in Mr. Boatwright's store window: BACK-TO-SCHOOL SALE!

The inevitable had arrived. Our freedom-loving feet, tanned and calloused, went painfully back into tight-fitting leather prisons. Soft, wash-faded clothes were replaced with scratchy new ones—starched board stiff and smelling of fresh factory dye. Yellow pencils, Big Chief tablets, and parental warnings of "behave yourself or else" accompanied us into autumn and back into the schoolhouse. But, dark time that it was, a bright glow pierced the gloom, for September also brought the annual Labor Day picnic and the Great Slingshot Shoot—the most exciting event of the year.

See-Thru, the town grapevine, brought us some astounding news on the Saturday before Labor Day. His sudden entrance into the Last Chance Saloon was so unexpected and dramatic that Frosty and I figured for sure Killer's cousin, the Black Stranger, was back in town.

"You never saw so many in your whole life!" he gasped, wild-eyed and breathing hard.

Knowing that our nine-year-old friend had a tendency to become overexcited, even about little things, like finding two prizes in a box of Cracker Jack, we ignored his histrionics and continued the business at hand. Frosty was trying to mark the backs of playing cards with pokeberry juice (in preparation for the afternoon poker game), while I, behind the bar, was filling the whisky bottle with red-eye left over from dinner.

"A whole half-gallon of 'em!" See-Thru yelled, jumping up and down as though standing on a fire-ant hill. "There must be a trillion!"

This got Frosty's attention. Being a mathematical genius, he found the mention of any large number most interesting, so he encouraged See-Thru to calm down and tell us what the shouting was all about.

"It's the grandest grand prize ever for the slingshot shoot!" See-Thru said. "Mr. Boatwright put it in the window just now!"

At this, my ears pricked up. However impressive the prize might be, it was as good as mine. All bragging aside, next to Slingshot Charley, I was the best slingshot shooter that ever plinked a can. In fact, I had won the grand prize two years in a row.

Frosty never entered the Labor Day Slingshot Shoot. More than that, it might be said he had shied away from slingshots altogether since that day two years ago when he accidentally put a rock through the fancy bottle-glass window in Granny Porter's front door. It was a traumatic experience for him, even though Granny had been most understanding. She talked it over with Mr. Youngblood, Frosty's dad, and they decided Frosty would pay for the damage by mowing her lawn every two weeks for free instead of for the nickel he usually charged her. After arduous arithmetical calculation, Frosty figured he had gotten off easy by not having any cash money deducted from his allowance. At a nickel a throw he would have the window paid for in no time—the summer of '49 when he was twenty-five years old.

"Jellybeans!" See-Thru croaked. "The grand prize is a half-gallon jar of jelly-beans!"

We scrambled for town fast. My mother was reluctant to let me go until I solemnly promised not to go inside any of the stores and to come straight home afterward. (Loitering inside business establishments was prohibited by most parents.)

In front of Boatwright's a bunch of kids had already gathered, pressing their faces against that portion of the display window usually reserved for ornamentally tooled saddles and boots. I scrouged in between Bluegill and Eskimo. Killer and Whetstone reluctantly made room for Frosty when he gave them his spine-tingling "move-or-get-scalped-right-on-the-spot" look.

Everybody was talking at once—ooh-ing and ah-ing and making a clamorous racket. I finally got the light just right, so I could see through the plate glass . . . and nearly fainted. There it was, shining like a big precious jewel: a half-gallon Mason jar filled to the brim with succulent jellybeans! They shimmered a rainbow of colors: orange, red, blue, purple, pink, yellow, green, and *black*. There were lots of black ones. Licorice-flavored black ones were my favorite jellybean of all. Trembling, I read the hand-lettered sign beside the jar:

FIRST PRIZE.

1934 LABOR DAY SLINGSHOT SHOOT.

AGES 8–12.

COURTESY BOATWRIGHT'S

"WHERE YOU SHOP FOR LESS."

It was mine! In two days the prize would be mine—

"Not this year, Hoppy," said Whetstone, reading my mind. "Your luck's run out." He grinned at Killer knowingly. "I made me a brand-new slingshot that can knock a squirrel's eye out at half a mile. Ain't that right, Killer?"

"You betcha," Killer answered, smirking and slapping his crony on the back. "Old Whetstone here could put Annie Oakley to shame. Come Monday, us Red River Renegades will be eatin' them jellybeans high on the hog!"

The other Renegades laughed and jeered. "Too bad, Hoppy . . . you want some jellybeans, go buy 'em . . . You'll never beat old dead-eye Whetstone. . . ."

I tore my eyes away from the jar and looked at the other prizes to be awarded without really seeing them: a case of oranges for horseshoe pitching; a box of five-cent cigars for arm wrestling, a huge three-dollar sack of groceries for croker-sack racing, etc.

Every year Mr. Boatwright donated expensive prizes from his store for the picnic. He was quite a philanthropist. Why, if you went in and bought as much as a pound of cheese, he'd throw in a nickel box of crackers for free. And if your mother sent you to the store for something expensive—say, a five-pound bag of sugar—he'd nearly always give you a jawbreaker or a licorice button. My folks said he did this so we wouldn't buy all our groceries in the big grocery stores over in Muskogee.

Turning around from the window and giving Whetstone my warmest Hopalong Cassidy smile, I patted "Jake Nailer" (my whistle slingshot), which was sticking out of my right rear pocket. Haughtily, I offered what I thought was a stinging remark befitting both the occasion and the prize to be awarded: "Oh yeah? Just like last year. It'll be like taking candy from a baby!"

Frosty was dying to know how many jellybeans were in the prize. It took him nearly all afternoon to come up with a reasonable facsimile: a half-gallon jar of dried beans. His mother only had about a pint of beans on hand, so he borrowed the rest. He got a couple of cups of pintos from my mother and about the same amount of navy beans from Grandmother Youngblood. Granny Porter offered the use of a whole bushel of butter beans if he would shell them for her first. Frosty thanked her politely but said they were too big and flat to give an accurate jellybean tally.

Afternoon business in the Last Chance Saloon was slow. Bluegill, Eskimo, Pete, and Kenneth, along with the Renegades, were out somewhere practicing with their slingshots. Bobby Ann, Norma, and the other girls were home, helping their mothers prepare food for the big picnic. Frosty had spread out an old tarpaulin and was sitting on the floor trying to count his half-gallon of beans. See-Thru, who had nothing to do, offered to help for the umpteenth time, causing Frosty to lose track. Declining this proposal of assistance, Frosty declared that See-Thru's esteemed generosity in volunteering aid was appreciated but deemed unnecessary. In other words, what he said was: "If you don't shut up so's I can count these beans, I'm gonna make you eat 'em!"

See-Thru retreated a little and, from a distance, asked Frosty why didn't he do the job faster by counting just one pint of beans, then multiplying that number by four, as there were four pints in a half-gallon. Frosty replied that he wasn't overly fond of multiplying. He found his pleasure in counting.

"You sure you're gonna beat old Whetstone again this year?" See-Thru asked me, coming over to the bar.

"Have you ever seen Jake Nailer miss?" I replied. Then, pulling out my slingshot and placing it reverently on the bar, I proceeded to tell See-Thru and Frosty again the story of how it got its famous name—even though neither they nor anybody else had ever asked to hear it.

"Back about three years ago, when I was even younger than you," I began, pouring myself a shot of red-eye—and one for See-Thru, on the house, "my Uncle Dan over in Fort Smith made it for me from the forked limb of a black-locust tree. The pouch here is made of real leather cut from the tongue of a Sears-Roebuck plow shoe—"

"A new shoe? A brand-new shoe?"

"Of course not. The leather in a brand-new shoe is too stiff to make a good slingshot pouch," I answered, surprised at See-Thru's enthusiasm. He never displayed such interest in my story before.

"Oh."

"Anyway," I continued, taking Jake Nailer in my hand, "Uncle Dan cut these rubber bands from a genuine Firestone tire inner tube that hardly had over a dozen flat patches on it."

"That's unbelievable," See-Thru said, astonished. He actually seemed amazed when I got to this part of the story.

"Truly it is," I explained. "But back in those days you could find real good inner tubes without patches on 'em lying around all over the place."

"Before hard times, huh?"

"TWO- HUNDRED- AND- THIRTY-SIX!" Frosty yelped, shattering our eardrums. "And I ain't even made a dent in 'em. Boy-oh-boy-oh-boy!"

Jubilantly, Frosty returned to his bean counting as I proceeded to enthrall See-Thru with the tale of Jake Nailer.

"The string that Uncle Dan tied the rubber bands to the stock and pouch with is real strong fishing line rubbed with beeswax so it won't slip."

"It sure does look strong. I wish I had a whole ball of kite string like that."

"Yeah, me too. Bet it would cost a hundred dollars though. Anyhow, after Uncle Dan got through making the whistle in the handle—which makes this the first slingshot in the world with a whistle in the handle—he looked it over real good and said . . . you know what he said?"

See-Thru beamed. "Yeah, your Uncle Dan said, 'That's a jake nailer if I ever saw one!'"

"Yep, that's what he said. Then he told me that if I go out wild turkey hunting and see a jake hiding behind a log—jakes is what wild turkey hunters call young boy turkeys—all I have to do is blow this whistle in the handle. Then, when that old jake turkey sticks his head up over the log to see what the whistling is all about . . . *kapowee!* I nail him good! And that's why I named my slingshot Jake Nailer."

See-Thru sighed. "That surely is a good story. It's almost as good as some Grandmother Youngblood tells. Can I shoot Jake Nailer a couple of times, if I promise to treat him like he was my very own?"

So that's why he listened so attentively to my story. He wanted to shoot my slingshot! Shocked, I reminded him sternly that there were three things a man would never let another man do: shoot his slingshot, ride his horse, or kiss his sweetheart.

"I didn't know you had a horse and a sweetheart!" See-Thru said. "Where do you keep your horse?"

Ignoring his questions, I went on to explain that a man never, *never* lets another man shoot his slingshot. His rubber gun, maybe—but never his slingshot. As no two men pull alike, it could stretch the rubber bands catawampus and throw the accuracy off. I told him he could blow the whistle in the handle, though, if it didn't interfere with Frosty's concentration.

"FIVE- HUNDRED- AND- TEN!" yelled Frosty. "And there's a mountain of 'em left to go! Whooee!"

That evening, while my family was eating supper, Frosty came over, haggard but exuberant. He returned the beans he had borrowed from my mother, explaining that they might not be the exact same ones she had lent him, but she wouldn't have to "look" them before cooking because he had picked out all the rocks and hulls while he was counting.

"You're not going to believe this, folks," he told us in a quavering voice. "But come Labor Day afternoon, Hoppy will be the rich owner of exactly *four- thousand- and- three* jellybeans!"

My head swam with the news. I asked him if he was certain he hadn't miscounted. His eyes mirrored a hurt, offended look—as if I had just called him a yellow coyote.

Right away, I apologized, assuring him he was the best mathematician in the world. I just never dreamed I would be the recipient of so *many* jellybeans.

"Seems to me you guys are counting your chickens way before they hatch," Dad cautioned.

"And if you think I'm going to turn you loose between meals with that much candy, you're crazy!" said Mother, pointing at my plate. "Eat your okra!"

"And I've got some news for you too," piped my sister, Beverly. "While we were setting up the picnic tables in the schoolyard this afternoon, your competition was practicing with his slingshot. That cute little Jones kid was popping snuff cans right and left. He didn't miss, not once. He even hit a couple that were thrown up in the air—"

"*In the air!* Oh, sweet sarsaparilla!" Frosty groaned. "I didn't know Whetstone was *that good!*"

I couldn't say a word. And when Mother pointed at the okra on my plate again, I thought I was going to gag.

Sunday afternoon, right after dinner, Frosty pumped us down to Grandmother Youngblood's house on the river. We left his bike in her yard and went out onto the gravel bar to gather ammunition for Jake Nailer. The stones had to be just so: round, smooth, and about the size of a sweet-gum ball. Within the Rules of the Big Shoot, contestants could use any size rocks, marbles, or "steelies" (ball bearings). I preferred rocks, mainly because I couldn't afford any steelies. And marbles, even chipped ones, were a commodity much too precious to use for ammunition.

We got sidetracked for a while, chasing crawdads, so it took us about an hour to collect a pocketful of suitable rocks before heading for Granny Porter's house. Going through her trash barrel, we found five one-ounce snuff cans (the size used for targets in the shoot) before we started up the hill to the school. As we rode off, Granny yelled at us through the screen door, "If you're so hungry you gotta raid garbage cans, you can have the old cornbread I was saving for the chickens!"

The area for the Big Shoot had been set up, as always, on the lower end of the school playground. A six-foot-high wall of hay bales served as the backstop. In front of this stood the sawhorse for the tin-can targets. Stakes, about 25 feet away from the sawhorse, marked the line where the contestants stood to shoot. The three official targets would consist of one large tomato can, one Prince Albert tobacco can, and one snuff can—set about 2 feet apart atop the sawhorse.

The rules for the annual Great Labor Day Slingshot Shoot were simple. Contestants took turns shooting according to numbers drawn from a hat. In the first round, shooters were eliminated if they failed to knock off all three cans with three shots. This usually cut the number of contestants down to half. In the second round, the big tomato-can target was not used, and each shooter had two shots to knock off the tobacco and snuff cans. This weeded out the has-beens and fly-by-nights and separated the men from the boys, so to speak. The second round continued until just two contestants (the two finalists) remained. During the third and last round, only the small snuff-can target was utilized. The first of the two finalists to miss it was the loser.

"And that's gonna be *you!*" Frosty said. "Unless you practice, practice, practice!"

The afternoon sky was blue and clear, but the fact that Whetstone had, unexpectedly, become an uncanny, expert marksman hung over us like a dark gray cloud. Fortunately, none of the Renegades were at the playground, and only a few other kids were around. They were engrossed in shooting marbles or spinning tops, so we went unobserved as Frosty set the snuff cans on the sawhorse.

I stepped up to the shooting line and loaded Jake Nailer. *Ready*. . . . I pulled until the pouch touched my right cheek. *Aim*. . . . Taking a deep breath and holding it, I brought the target can into the dead center of the forked stock. *Fire!* I released. *Clang!* The can went flying.

"Attaway to shoot!" Frosty yelled. "I can taste those jellybeans now!"

Loading up, I splattered the next can . . . and the next. Frosty jumped and whooped with glee. But then, on the following shot, I *missed*. I couldn't believe it. I shot again . . . and missed again!

I searched through the rocks in my pocket and found one that was absolutely perfect. "Round as a dollar," my Uncle Dan would say. Loading the pouch, I concentrated on my flawless shooting form and zeroed in on the target. I released. Missed it a mile!

"Well, there goes our danged jellybeans," said Frosty, jumping on his bike and riding off down the hill—without even a word of farewell.

The gray cloud hanging over my head had become utterly black. For me and Jake Nailer, it was a long, gloomy walk home.

I was convinced that See-Thru (or some other sneak) had been shooting my slingshot without my knowledge. Its accuracy was off something awful. Therefore, as soon as supper was over, I sat on the back porch and overhauled Jake Nailer with new rubber bands cut precisely the same width and length. They weren't cut from a genuine Firestone tube, but they would have to do.

"*Psst!*" Frosty, with his head stuck through Mrs. Smith's privet hedge, was motioning at me. "C'mon over to my house," he whispered loudly. "Got something important to show you. Bring Jake Nailer."

Morosely, I followed him over to his backyard. He pointed to a snuff can sitting on the stump at the corner of Mr. Youngblood's toolshed. "Think you can hit it from here?"

"Don't know. The light ain't too good. It's nearly dark."

Frosty ran over and stood behind the toolshed out of the line of fire. "Go ahead, shoot. I'll bet anybody in town fifty marbles you can hit it."

Nearly overcome by his renewed confidence in my marksmanship, I pulled a rock from my pocket, loaded up, and took careful aim. When I fired I knew it was a miss the moment the rock left the pouch. The rock went high and to the left. *Clang!* The can miraculously spun off the stump!

"Yahoo!" yelled Frosty. He ran out and put the can back on the stump. "Do it again. I'm betting a hundred marbles this time!" He scooted out of sight behind the shed.

Something very strange was going on. I knew for certain I had not hit that can, not even grazed it. But it *sounded* and *acted* as if it had been hit hard and true. "Whatcha waiting for?" Frosty asked, peeking at me from around the corner. "Show me your stuff!"

This time I just pretended to load Jake Nailer. I pulled back the empty pouch and fired. *Clang!* Like magic, the snuff can leaped mysteriously off the stump!

"Now just a danged minute! Frosty?" I knew he was responsible for the sorcery. But how?

He came rain-dancing out from behind the shed, beating on a pie pan with a spoon. *Clang! Clang! Clang!* He spun around in a circle, lifting his knees high, chanting: "Hi-yi-yi-yi, we-gonna-win-yi; Hi-yi-yi-yi . . ."

If I hadn't stopped him I guess he would have danced all night, and the Labor Day picnic would have been rained out for sure. Frosty often bragged he was a most effective rain dancer, as most Cherokee Indians are.

We sat on the grass and I listened mesmerized as Frosty explained how his fantastic plan would assure my walking away from the Big Shoot with enough jellybeans to last us a lifetime; how he would volunteer to set up the target cans as he did each year; how he would have the pie pan and spoon hidden behind the backstop of hay; how he would have the long piece of strong, black, practically invisible thread running from behind the hay along the grass out to the sawhorse; and how, during the final round when it was my turn to shoot, he would stick one end of the thread to the snuff can with a gob of chewing gum. . . .

". . . and I watch through a crack between the hay bales," Frosty whispered. "You draw back Jake Nailer and take aim . . . you fire! I hit the pan with the spoon and pull the other end of the thread to jerk the snuff can off at the exact same time. You'll win the jellybeans—hands down—from old Whetstone and become the greatest slingshot shooter in the whole world! I bet they'll even put your picture in the Muskogee *Times Democrat*."

I shivered with excitement. It was truly a marvelous, cleverly conceived, foolproof plan. And I told Frosty it was too.

Sleep was impossible. I tried counting jellybeans—black ones. Even that didn't help. Deep inside a little voice kept telling me that what Frosty and I were planning to do was blatantly dishonest, and if I went along with it I would never be able to look Jake Nailer or Uncle Dan in the face again. Just before falling asleep I decided I would tell Frosty, the first thing in the morning, that the plan was off. Win, lose, or draw—the plan was off.

Labor Day 1934 dawned a beautiful, sunshiny day. By noontime the picnickers had shed coats, ties, and sweaters. It was so hot the lemonade and penny drinks disappeared rapidly, and the ice-cream freezers and watermelons were moved into the shade.

The long planks that had been set across sawhorses for tables sagged under the weight of the food: fried chicken, baked hams and shoulders, potato salad, coleslaw, baked beans, pickle relish, and a dozen different kinds of pies and cakes.

Frosty and I pawed through platters of fried chicken until we found all the drumsticks my mother had brought. Her chicken was always crispy and salted just right. Earlier, I was quite surprised at how amiable Frosty had been when I told him, point blank, I refused to go along with the plan. He had smiled a truly understanding smile and said, "That's okay, Hoppy. I'll be willing to bet five hundred marbles you'll win anyway."

In the center of one picnic table Mr. Boatwright had prominently displayed all the wondrous prizes. The half-gallon jar of jellybeans was the focus of attention. If Frosty told me once, while we ate, he told me a thousand times: He had counted all the black beans that were visible, and there were exactly 87 of them. Whetstone was boasting that he would be eating them come sundown, as he went around showing everybody his new slingshot. The stock was coping-sawed out of yellow pine, and he had burned his initials into it with a heated nail. It certainly was an impressive-looking weapon. He had named it "Red Avenger" because it had red rubber bands.

After people had eaten their fill, county politicians made speeches, and the ten-piece high-school band played John Philip Sousa marches and a jazz-time rendition of "I'll Be Down to Get You in a Taxi, Honey." The grown-ups pitched horseshoes, played softball, or just sat around talking. Teenage couples strolled through the trees down along the river, while the smaller kids played games. The boys played marbles, rubber guns, or tag, and the girls had hoop races or played jack rocks and skip rope. Frosty and I watched the "professional" top spikers. But we gave them a wide berth—we had lost tops to them before.

At three in the afternoon the hour of truth arrived. Fifteen slingshot shooters drew numbers from Mr. Boatwright's hat, as he explained the rules (same as last year) for the Great Labor Day Slingshot Shoot. Naturally, all the Renegades had entered, along with all my sidekicks—except Frosty, of course. He wished me luck and ran to set up the target cans.

A large number of spectators gathered on the perimeter of the shooting area to watch the contest. Dad came over to shake my hand as though I had just enlisted in the Army. And I felt my face blush fiery red when both Norma and Bobby Ann blew me exaggerated kisses. The palms of my hands were sweating and the rocks in the right front pocket of my overalls seemed to be pulling my body down on that side.

The first round went as I—and most everybody—expected. Only six of us hit all three cans. Whetstone shot before me, and I crossed my fingers that he would miss. But he didn't. Neither did I. Jake Nailer knocked off the cans as if he had eyes of his own. Frosty, working like a machine, ran out from behind the backstop to set the cans back on the sawhorse each time.

The second round continued for a long, grueling period. Finally it narrowed down to Whetstone, Killer, Bluegill, and me. I was hoping against hope that Bluegill would stay in—but he didn't. And Killer suddenly got buck fever and missed the snuff can too. The competition was down to two: Jake Nailer versus the Red Avenger.

A murmured hush fell over the crowd as Whetstone stepped to the line for the third and final round. He took his own sweet time loading up with a brand-new steelie and making a big show about it. After what seemed a hundred years he aimed and fired. *Clang!* The snuff can flew high into the air.

The crowd roared.

Frosty had to set a fresh can up for me. Whetstone's steelie had turned the other one into a misshapen lump of tin. Meticulously, Frosty placed the target squarely on the top center of the sawhorse; then he scooted back behind the hay.

I loaded Jake Nailer. The crowd hushed again. Feeling confident—with cast-iron nerves—I drew the pouch back to my cheek; the rubber bands stretched to full capacity. *Ready.* . . . I took a deep breath. *Aim.* . . . The snuff can came into view in the V of the stock. I imagined the small target was the head of a wild turkey, a target Jake Nailer would never miss. . . . *Splat!* The broken rubber band stung my right wrist! *Clang!* Horrified, because I hadn't even shot, I watched the snuff can jerk sideways off the sawhorse—*as if it had an invisible black thread tied to it!*

The crowd booed.

Everything suddenly became a nightmare blur. I heard everyone booing and laughing, some of them hissing. I saw the broken rubber band on Jake Nailer dangling, the pouch in my hand still loaded. I caught a glimpse of Frosty peeking around the hay bales with a "how'd-it-go?" look on his face. Last, but not least, I saw my father approaching with fire in his eye. For me the Great 1934 Labor Day Slingshot Shoot and Picnic was over, dreadfully over.

"You've never seen so many black jellybeans in your whole life," Frosty reported, his head protruding through Mrs. Smith's privet hedge. "The Renegades are over in the Red-Horse Barn right now, gobbling 'em down like pigs."

"If you hadn't pulled that dumb trick, we'd be eating 'em," I said, still mad as a hornet at him. "I would have won—I was zinging 'em in there better than Slingshot Charley. You and your dumb tricks!"

"How'd I know you were gonna break a danged rubber band?" Frosty said. "I ain't no mind reader. Anyway, I was doing it all for you—because you're my best friend."

"Did your dad give you a lickin'?"

"Boy, did he ever!" Frosty moaned. "I think he broke his belt! You get a lickin'?"

"I'll say! My dad doesn't know it was all your fault. He put me on probation, too.

If I don't walk a mighty straight line, he said I couldn't even enter the Big Shoot next year."

"Gee, that's awful! See-Thru heard Mr. Boatwright saying he was gonna give away a Daisy BB gun for next year's prize. You know, the one he has hanging on the wall with the fishing rods—the one that's kinda rusty?"

"A Daisy!" I gasped. "Wow, that'd be the grandest grand prize ever! Lot of good it'll do me, though."

"Don't fret about it. I'm gonna go right now and tell your dad the whole truth. Sorry I didn't get to him before you got a lickin'."

"Really?" I said, my feelings softening toward my idol once again. "You'll really tell him it was all your fault? Cross your heart—hope to die?"

"Sure, that's what best friends are for. I'll tell him, and then he'll let you shoot next year for sure. And I'll bet a thousand marbles you'll win us that Daisy!"

"Yeah! I'll practice all winter long—"

"Ain't no need to do all that much practicing," Frosty said, giving me his famous "wait-till-I-tell-you-my-plan-for-next-year" look. "C'mon over to my house—got something important I want to show you. . . ."

BOW AND ARROW

It would be rare indeed to run across a boy growing up in the '30s who hadn't at one time or another made himself a toy bow and arrow: a tree limb for the bow, a straight stick for the arrow. A limb from most any tree will bend and "snap" back when green. But once it has dried, it will either break when bowed or become so stiff it can't be bent with a crowbar. It's the old tried-and-true standbys, hickory, ash, and Osage orange, that make bows unparalleled in strength and durability. And they retain their resiliency after seasoning.

The favorite hard-times Oklahoma toy bow was cut from Osage orange (also known as bowdarc, bois d'arc, bowdark, and bodock). Though bowdarcs thrived in abundance, they had no esthetic value and were not desirable for shade-tree sitting, as their thorny branches bore inedible, green, grapefruit-sized fruit—called hedge apples—which would drop like a bomb when a shade-sitter least expected it. A big bowdarc tree growing in a hog pen, however, was regarded as beneficial. Pigs—never finicky eaters—loved hedge apples more than slop, and they would stand looking up into a tree all day waiting for another green goody to fall.

A bowdarc limb about 1 inch in diameter and about 30 inches long made a sturdy, not-too-hard-to-pull bow. It was stripped of bark (bark was usually left on hickory bows) and whittled down, if necessary, to make it more or less uniform in diameter. Then, notched about 1 inch from each end, the bow was strung with a stout cord (waxed) or a thin rawhide thong (one end tied in a loop to make stringing and unstringing easy). In stringing, the limb was bowed to leave a distance of approximately 6 inches from the center mark of the string (the arrow's nocking point) to the center of the hand grip, which on fancy bows was wrapped with rawhide or colored string.

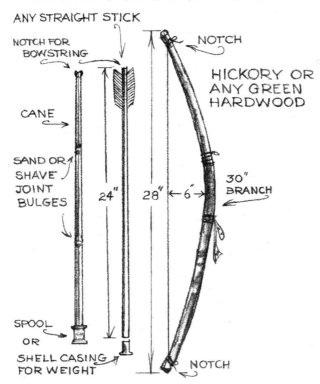

BOW AND ARROW

ANY STRAIGHT STICK

NOTCH FOR BOWSTRING

NOTCH

HICKORY OR ANY GREEN HARDWOOD

CANE

SAND OR SHAVE JOINT BULGES

24"

28"

6"

30" BRANCH

SPOOL OR SHELL CASING FOR WEIGHT

NOTCH

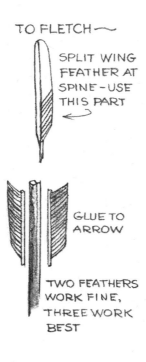

TO FLETCH ~

SPLIT WING FEATHER AT SPINE - USE THIS PART

GLUE TO ARROW

TWO FEATHERS WORK FINE, THREE WORK BEST

Wild-cane arrows about 24 inches long, fletched with turkey feathers, would fly straight and true. And spools on the front ends rendered safe, blunt arrowheads for knocking over yard targets such as water bags (paper sacks filled with water) or tin cans. For shooting small game when the hunting season rolled around, arrows were tipped with a nail, a carved fish-gig point, or a real Indian arrowhead (which young archaeologists collected). A dedicated bowman never stored his favorite homemade bow without unstringing it first. If left strung for a long period, a bow has a tendency to become permanently "bowed," which weakens it considerably.

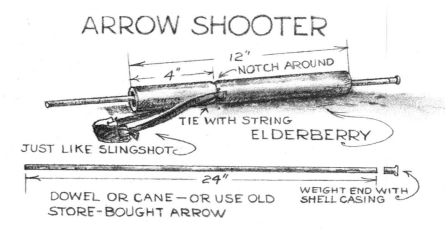

ARROW SHOOTER

12" NOTCH AROUND

4"

TIE WITH STRING

ELDERBERRY

JUST LIKE SLINGSHOT

24"

DOWEL OR CANE — OR USE OLD STORE-BOUGHT ARROW

WEIGHT END WITH SHELL CASING

ARROW SHOOTER

If a youngster did not possess the skilled archery eye of William Tell or Robin Hood but was reasonably accurate with a slingshot, he'd use his slingshot talent to improve his arrow-shooting skills. This was done through practice with a toy called an arrow

---

Toy Safety

Our parents always told us to be careful when playing with all toy weapons. Only responsible older children should play with them without adult supervision. All the toy shooting or throwing weapons in this section were used for target practice only. They were never used to play games of war or mock combat.

shooter. To construct an arrow shooter, a kid would run over to the nearest elderberry clump and whack off a limb about a foot long. Then he would tie the rubber bands and pouch from his slingshot to the elderberry branch with string. This resulted in a slingshot-type toy that would shoot a 24-inch unfletched arrow (dowel or cane) with plenty of zip and accuracy.

SPEAR THROWER

Sometimes a girl, who could not throw a spear any farther than she could chuck a brick, would infiltrate an all-male spear-throwing contest. The boys would, of course, razz her and offer such derisive comments as: "You couldn't throw a spear if you ate Wheaties for a hundred years!" or "Who do you think you are, Jack-*ie* Armstrong?"

Little did they know that this petite, unathletic-looking Diana, goddess of the hunt, compensated for what she lacked in brawn by employing intellect—and chicanery. As with all females, she wouldn't walk out of the house without at least one ace

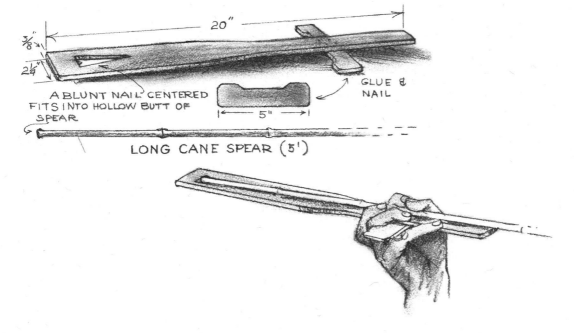

SPEAR THROWER

20"

⅜"

2½"

A BLUNT NAIL CENTERED FITS INTO HOLLOW BUTT OF SPEAR

5"

GLUE & NAIL

LONG CANE SPEAR (5')

The All-American Boy

The wise Tibetan monk looked sagely at the handsome young high-school athlete and said, "Tell the boys and girls of the United States this world is theirs. If they have hearts of gold, a glorious new golden age awaits them. If they are honest, riches shall be theirs. If they are kind, they shall save the whole world from malice and meanness. Will you take that message to the boys and girls of the United States, Jack Armstrong?"

"Yes," Jack replied solemnly. "I will."

And he did.

As an all-male chorus belted out the "Hudson High Fight Song," millions of kids tuned in to live through the latest radio adventure of the quick-witted, pure-as-the-driven-snow super-jock, Jack Armstrong, "The All-American Boy." Jack's missions in life were: to lead Hudson High to the top of athletic glory, to overcome the bad guys at every turn, and to sell a whole bunch of Wheaties (even though the old Tibetan monk had said nothing about breakfast cereal). Kids not only ate Wheaties, they gobbled up Jack's verbal servings of Mom, apple pie, and America. During the '30s Jack broke every athletic record in the book, beat up on scads of villains, and unloaded enough crispy flaked wheat cereal and box-top toys to sink a fleet of river barges. Every youngster on the block who could scrounge a couple of Wheaties box tops sported a Jack Armstrong whistle ring on his finger. Actually it wouldn't blow very loud, but it was a flashy ring with the look of pure gold, and it was accompanied by a swell secret code.

JACK ARMSTRONG'S SECRET WHISTLE CODE
Instructions
One whistle (short): "Attention."
Two whistles (short): "Be on guard for trouble."
Three whistles (one long, two short): "In danger, come at once!"
Four whistles (short): "We're being watched."
Two whistles (two long): "Important news—meet me at once."

up her sleeve. When it came her turn in the long-distance spear-throwing contest, Diana stepped demurely around to the side of the house (out of sight) where she had previously stashed her spear-thrower. Then she yelled, "Okay, you guys, here it comes!"

To the astonishment of the male contestants, the spear propelled by the home-made throwing-stick traveled twice the distance of the other spears thrown. After this happened, the stupefied boys usually moseyed on home without even bothering to collect their old spears.

This simple homemade toy was constructed of scrap wood, nails, and glue. Patterned after the *atlatl*, the Aztec Indian spear-thrower of ancient Mexico, it doubled the fun and distance of spear-throwing. And a five-foot length of cane, weighted with lead or an iron bolt in the head, constituted a spear equivalent to any javelin ever thrown—by the goddess Diana, by Jack Armstrong, or by anybody in a Tarzan movie.

SWORDS AND SHIELDS

Depression-era kids regularly pursued two space heroes in books, comics, or movies: Buck Rogers and Flash Gordon. The latter was the favorite as he got more media

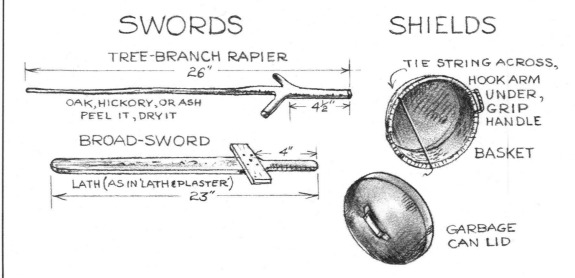

exposure. Flash's adventures on the planet Mongo depicted him using spear and sword rather than space weapons to defend himself and his girl friend, Dale Arden, against the evil forces of Emperor Ming.

When children squared off to pretend they were on Mongo fighting side by side with Flash against his adversaries, their awesome broadswords were fashioned from wooden lath strips. Their rapiers were hardwood tree branches about 2 feet long. An old discarded garbage-can lid or fruit basket employed as a shield would deflect the finest blade made. Eventually, of course, the shields would begin to show substantial wear and tear. And if they were not truly *old, discarded* lids or baskets, young swordsmen could find themselves in a lot of trouble when they returned to Earth. If, say, the bottom of Granny's sword-damaged egg-gathering basket should disintegrate while she was in the process of gathering eggs, a kid might even wish himself back on Mongo—for real!

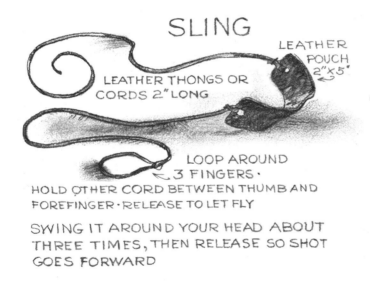

SLING

LEATHER POUCH 2"x5"

LEATHER THONGS OR CORDS 2" LONG

LOOP AROUND 3 FINGERS.
HOLD OTHER CORD BETWEEN THUMB AND FOREFINGER · RELEASE TO LET FLY

SWING IT AROUND YOUR HEAD ABOUT THREE TIMES, THEN RELEASE SO SHOT GOES FORWARD

SLING

If you think it is impossible for anyone to hit even a giant-sized target with a rock slung from this ancient toy, just try to check with the surviving descendants of Goliath. A sling could be contrived in a jiffy from an old shoe tongue and two pieces of strong cord or rawhide thongs about 2 feet long. The choice of ammunition reflected

Flash Gordon: Space Hero Number One

In 1934 when astronomers discovered that the planet Mongo was destined to collide with Earth, Flash Gordon and his beautiful girl friend, Dale Arden, were kidnapped aboard the rocket ship of mad scientist Hans Zarkov and transported to Mongo. With that for an opening grabber, artist-cartoonist Alex Raymond blasted off with the adventures of Flash Gordon, fearless forerunner of the space heroes of future generations.

Comics, Big Little Books, and films followed the harrowing, violence-laden escapades of the Yale-educated hero. For years the handsome blond Adonis battled with spear and sword the treacherous troops of Mongo, who were pitted against him by their yellow-skinned, slant-eyed ruler, Ming the Merciless. The ruthless Ming was a Fu Manchu-type villain bent on enslaving Earth . . . the whole universe . . . and the talented Raymond painted him as evil incarnate. Flash was incessantly the target for an unending string of carnal, curvaceous women and deadly cohorts of the wicked, wily Ming. Yet Flash never fell to the temptations of the flesh but remained faithful both to Dale and to his ideals of sportsmanship, fair play, and justice for all.

the imagination and enthusiasm with which children embraced toy making: sweet-gum balls, rocks, black walnuts, marbles, persimmons, hickory nuts. Rural kids always had great fun shooting pokeberries, blackberries, or mulberries too. They left a bright stain on impact, the colorful sign of a sure hit.

NOTE: *The juices of berries were also used for painting monograms on personal items and important messages on barn walls. But most farm children knew that pokeberries were poisonous and should never be ingested. They were kept out of reach of smaller Depression-era youngsters, who had a tendency to eat anything that wasn't nailed down.*

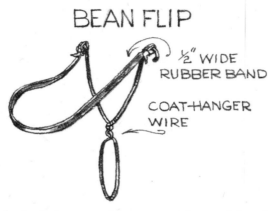

BEAN FLIP
½" WIDE RUBBER BAND
COAT-HANGER WIRE

BEAN FLIP

An old coat-hanger wire bent into a forked shape and strung with a rubber band about ½-inch wide created an effective flip that would put a bean in there! A leather pouch similar to a slingshot wasn't really needed on a bean flip, but some children preferred it. One never had to worry about running short of bean-flip ammunition. Dried beans were staple table fare during the Depression. And if a youngster wanted to shoot away part of his supper and end up with nothing but cornbread on his plate, that was his hard luck.

NOTE: *For safety, the bean-flip handle could be wrapped with tape. After all, a sweaty-palmed kid didn't want to lose his grip and let his flip slip.*

SHINGLE DART

A dart whittled from a wood shingle and weighted in the head with a chunk of lead would literally go out of sight when shot straight up into the air. When it reached the

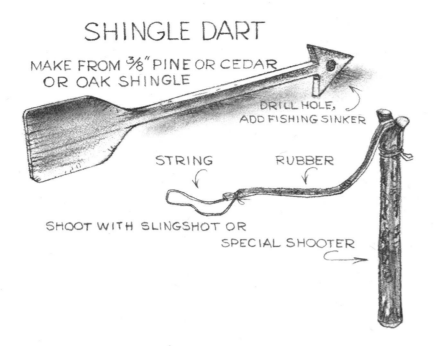

SHINGLE DART

MAKE FROM ⅜" PINE OR CEDAR
OR OAK SHINGLE

DRILL HOLE,
ADD FISHING SINKER

STRING

RUBBER

SHOOT WITH SLINGSHOT OR
SPECIAL SHOOTER

apex of its flight, the weighted head caused the dart to reverse direction in a split second and plummet to the earth—sometimes embedding itself a couple of inches on impact. It could be propelled by a special shooter (see illustration) or with a slingshot. The older boys used this toy in a game in which they shot at penny balloons (ten for a cent), that were released from a bomber kite way, way up in the sky. Windblown shingles were plentiful, and since a dart could be carved from one in no time at all, it didn't matter if a shingle dart occasionally was lost by falling in the next county.

NOTE: *Needless to say, shingle darts were extremely dangerous. They were never shot into the air over a crowd and were only played with in empty cow pastures or other isolated areas.*

SLINGSHOT

If you happened to notice a farm boy running around during the '30s without a slingshot sticking out of at least one pocket, you knew he was on his way either to school or to church. Or else the poor guy had fallen on hard times and had been

Slingshot Charley

On a cold November morning in 1928, "Pop" Adams, a show business promoter, was crappie fishing in one of the cypress-studded fingers of Reelfoot Lake in northwest Tennessee. Out of the gray overcast sky, a flock of mallards came in low for a landing, but something spooked them. As Adams and his guide watched the ducks swerve away, one of the drakes folded in midair and plummeted into the water as if it had been shot. But there had been no sound of gunfire.

When Adams turned to his Indian companion looking for an explanation, the guide said, "Charley Taylor," and pointed to a small boat in which a man was rowing out to retrieve the floating mallard. "We call him Slingshot Charley," he went on to say, making motions of shooting a slingshot. "Charley shoots ducks in the head!"

151

That chance meeting with Adams on Reelfoot Lake launched Charley Bell Taylor on a career that brought him fame and fortune during the hard times, earning him the title "The Greatest Slingshot Marksman in the World!"

Pop Adams became Charley's promoter. At first Charley performed his slingshot magic at carnivals and county fairs. But as his fame grew he got bigger and better bookings, sometimes making as much as $250 a week: state fairs, rodeos, and Wild West shows. Reaching the pinnacle of his popularity in the '30s, he appeared at the Chicago World's Fair, in Madison Square Garden, at the Los Angeles Coliseum, in the movies (short subjects), and on the Major Bowes Amateur Hour radio show, where he did duck calls. Charley was written up in *Life* magazine, Ripley's "Believe It or Not," and by some accounts even performed before Franklin D. Roosevelt, the President of the United States.

Growing up along the shores of Reelfoot Lake, Charley, like many Tennessee farm boys in those days, was using his slingshot by the time he was ten years old to help feed his family. The lake area, swarming with small game, was a hunter's paradise, and the young slingshot wizard's fame spread rapidly through the towns of Tiptonville and Union City, where he peddled his surplus squirrels, rabbits, and ducks. The carcasses had no visible marks on them; the flesh was not spoiled with rifle bullets or shotgun pellets. Young Charley shot for the head.

Married at the age of sixteen to his fourteen-year-old sweetheart, Charley quickly became established as a Reelfoot Lake hunting and fishing guide, amazing visiting sportsmen and tourists with his phenomenal slingshot skills. When Adams discovered him that day in 1928, Charley was thirty-eight years old.

At the height of his career, Charley was sometimes referred to as the "Slingshot Annie Oakley." Using ball bearings for ammunition, he accomplished feats with his homemade slingshot that Annie in her heyday couldn't manage with the finest rifle made. A typical

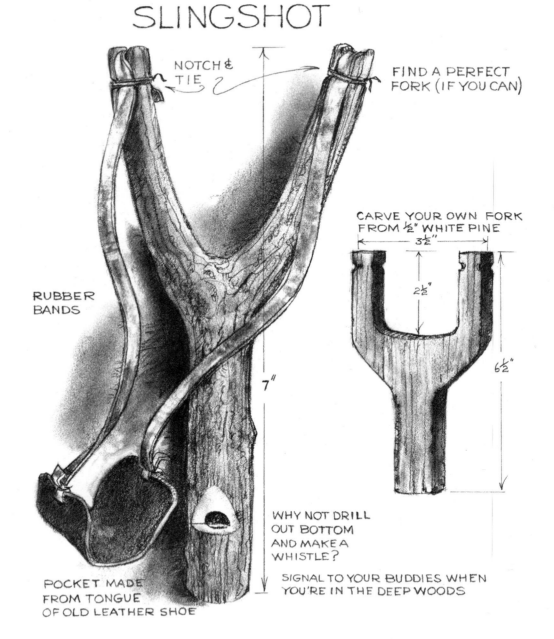

SLINGSHOT

NOTCH & TIE

FIND A PERFECT FORK (IF YOU CAN)

RUBBER BANDS

CARVE YOUR OWN FORK FROM ½" WHITE PINE

3½"

2½"

6½"

7"

WHY NOT DRILL OUT BOTTOM AND MAKE A WHISTLE?

POCKET MADE FROM TONGUE OF OLD LEATHER SHOE

SIGNAL TO YOUR BUDDIES WHEN YOU'RE IN THE DEEP WOODS

forced to swap it off for something critical to his survival, maybe a candy bar with only one bite missing.

Slingshot stocks came in two models. The one more highly favored, a perfectly forked limb cut from a hardwood tree, was 6 to 7 inches long overall. The other type of stock—none the less functional—was a U-shaped fork sawed from pine or other available lumber.

Two rubber bands, each about 12 inches long, were cut from old inner tubes, preferably from the same inner tube, and both were cut the same width. They were tied tightly with a string to the notched ends of the forks. A leather pouch cut from a shoe or boot tongue was tied to the other ends of the rubber bands via two slits cut in the leather. It was imperative that the two rubber bands be exactly equal in length (measure the same distance from fork to pouch after tying). If not, the slingshot would not shoot straight.

It was not uncommon for rural boys to become uncannily accurate with their slingshots. And until they reached an age to receive the responsibility of their first .22 rifle, the slingshot was used for plinking and harvesting small game for food. A rock, marble, or ball bearing fired from a well-made slingshot at full draw had the killing power at short range comparable to a .22-long cartridge; thus the slingshot could be a dangerous toy, and concerned adults made children aware of this.

WHISTLE SLINGSHOT

At the start of the summer there was only one whistle slingshot in the community of Fort Gibson. And it was mine. But before school had started in the fall, there were more whistle slingshots in town than you could begin to shake a stick at. What a bunch of copycats!

By adding a whistle in the handle, my Uncle Dan over in Fort Smith, Arkansas, transformed the superb new slingshot he had just made for me into the first of its kind in the whole world. He did this by boring deep into the handle of the stock with a ½-inch drill, cutting the whistle notch just so, and then inserting the half-round piece whittled to a precise fit into the forward air chamber. (See plain whistle on page 44.) It was outstanding for sending the Jack Armstrong secret whistle code to my best friend, Frosty. The sound it emitted was low and mellow, echoing like a hunting horn in the deep woods on a foggy morning.

thirty-minute performance by Slingshot Charley might include:
- Shooting the ash off a cigarette held in the mouth of a volunteer.
- Shattering glass marbles thrown into the air, one at a time.
- Popping twenty-four light bulbs swinging on the ends of strings.
- Hitting dimes, washers, and light bulbs thrown into the air by spectators.
- Knocking the bottoms out of pop bottles the hard way—through the neck—from 30 feet away.
- Cutting the string tied to a swinging rock from a distance of 30 feet.

For his grand finale, Slingshot Charley would stick a kitchen match into the ground, back off 40 feet, and with a single shot, strike the match into flame by grazing the head.

The Greatest Slingshot Marksman in the World retired from the glamour of show business in the early '40s and returned to live out his life as a guide on his beloved Reelfoot Lake. He died in 1961.

Probably nothing ever came closer to describing what Charley could do with a slingshot than the comment made by a Tulsa *World* newspaper reporter: "When folks talked about Charley's shooting, I said, 'I'll believe it when I see it.' Well, I've seen it, but I still don't believe it!"

8

Tops and Other Spinning Toys

The '30s was the decade of spinning toys. Toys that were spun with a string (tops, diablos, and yo-yos) came into their own in America as the country, trying to survive the worst depression in its history, was holding on by a thread.

While President Roosevelt was initiating his New Deal to create a million jobs, the Duncan Company was manufacturing a million or more yo-yos. As white-collar workers poured into WPA offices and common laborers marched off to CCC camps to build parks, dams, and bridges, children across the nation fell in love with a bright-colored wheel on a string and competed at "Rocking the Cradle" and "Walking the Dog." This most versatile toy, which had started many years earlier in the Philippines as a "spinning potato," had spun its way into the Great American Depression.

Bobby Ann's Banshee

In top-spinning circles they were known as the "Terrible Three." And their spiker tops had mean-sounding names: "War Hatchet," "Widow-maker," and "Green Cobra."

The ferocious and deadly Green Cobra, which belonged to thirteen-year-old Luther Spera, had bitten every top-spinning kid in town at least once. Some of them many times. Luther was the "top" top spiker in school and the leader of the Terrible Three. Charles Pratt and Dave Goldsmith were the other two.

My fifth-grade friends and I always tried to stay clear of the professional top spikers. But during top season this was virtually impossible. They just seemed to have a coon dog's nose for sniffing out a spinning game. No matter where you were playing—on the school grounds, inside the barn, or in your own backyard—sooner or later the Terrible Three would turn up, with a single evil purpose: to goad one of us amateurs into spiking tops with them. And if See-Thru was present, and had a top, he would jump right in. See-Thru, at just nine, was a hopeless "spikeoholic."

The three professional spikers were three years ahead of us in school, not to mention a step or two out of our social league. In church or not, they were always gussied up in store-bought clothes: white long-sleeved shirts and black pants with suspenders.

And the greasy, perfumed tonic which they used to slick down their hair smelled like a birthday cake. Since they had reached the responsible age of thirteen, their parents allowed them to stay out a whole hour after dark. And they enjoyed conspicuous behavior—like showing off by winking at girls and dipping Sen-Sen. Luther sometimes even carried a sack of Bull Durham around, with its yellow strings hanging out of his shirt pocket, so kids would think he smoked. All of them sauntered, swaggered, bragged, and bullied. The Terrible Three thought they were tougher than Tom Mix.

My friends and I thought so too.

It was a summer afternoon perfect for spinning tops—hot and dry. And the perfectly round top ring scratched into the hard, bare ground with a string-and-pencil compass was humming with activity. Under the shade of the massive black-walnut tree in my backyard, rowdy top enthusiasts from all over town had gathered to enjoy the games. My mother had already asked us once (very politely) to refrain—if possible—from expressing our enthusiasm quite so vocally. Sticking her head out the back door, she shouted, "Hey you kids, hold it down out there! You're making enough racket to wake the dead!" This probably meant she had a cake in the oven and didn't want it to fall.

Our clamorous game of Bump-Out, which Bluegill and Frosty had been winning all afternoon, was interrupted temporarily when Norma and Bobby Ann came over to show us Bobby Ann's new top. It was a beautiful bonus prize she had received for selling a whole bunch of *Grit* newspapers—even though Bobby Ann wasn't supposed to be selling the newspapers at all, according to *Grit*'s policy. A girl carrier needed to be eighteen years old. Now, don't think that Bobby Ann was dishonest, or a crook, or anything like that, because she wasn't. When she filled out her application, she just neglected to jot down her middle name, that's all. It certainly wasn't any fault of hers if *Grit* thought Bobby Smith was a twelve-year-old boy. Norma sold newspapers for a few months too. Somehow she inadvertently stuck an "n" onto the end of her first name.

Anyhow, Bobby Ann was really proud of her new *Grit* top, and well she should have been. It was truly a nice one. The light blue enamel was hard and shiny like paint on a car, and the spinning cord had a burnished metal ring—surely pure gold—attached to the end of it which looked like a wedding band. It was a splendid "rollie" (a top not converted to a spiker), and it spun like a champion. Frosty, See-Thru, Killer, Whetstone, Bluegill, and I had all tried to swap her out of it, offering untold treasures in exchange, but Bobby Ann had stood firm. No one could blame her. Why, a new rollie like that would cost at least a dime at Kress's. Bluegill wanted it in the worst way, saying he'd turn it into a spiker and name it the Blue Bandit too, the same as his war kite.

After Bobby Ann had let each of us spin her new top a couple of times, we resumed playing Bump-Out and were having a lot of fun when, without warning, through the gap in the privet hedge stepped the Terrible Three. Once again, they had sniffed out a top game. "Whatcha say, gang?" Luther said, sauntering over to watch the action. "Oh, playin' Bump-Out, huh? That's a baby game. Anybody wanna spike?"

I surely didn't, and I said so. I had learned my lesson the hard way a long time back. None of us had a chance against the Terrible Three. Killer said no also. He was a little bit afraid of Luther. Even a villain like Killer could sometimes be intimidated.

"Yeah, I wanna spike," piped See-Thru, accepting the challenge as he always did. "But I ain't got a top. I'll borrow one, though; then you're in real trouble. I can outspike you guys any time."

"You bet you can," Charles said, sugaring up See-Thru. "You're the best danged spiker I've ever seen."

"That's the truth," Dave intoned. "You just had an off day last time. Probably a touch of arthritis in your spiking arm."

"Yeah, that's what it was," See-Thru said. "Just wait, I'll borrow a top!"

Poor See-Thru was hooked again. Though he had lost more tops to the Terrible Three than he could count, he couldn't resist the compulsion to try spiking with them just one more time. I knew the feeling well. All of us did, I guess. And how marvelous it would be to win just once! . . . To carry around in your pocket the spoils of victory: Charles's Hatchet, or Dave's Widow-maker, or Luther's Green Cobra. What a joy! . . . To hear your friends say, "You won't believe this, but he outspiked the leader of the Terrible Three, and he's got the Green Cobra in his pocket to prove it!"

So now See-Thru, who had lost a brand new top to the professionals only a week earlier, wanted more than anything in the world to do it again. But his efforts to borrow a top proved unrewarding. No one wanted to see one of his spiker tops wind up in the hands of one of the Terrible Three via See-Thru. I not only told See-Thru no, I told him *danged no!* If Hoppy's Harpoon, my one-and-only spiker top, was to be thrown into the sacrificial fire, I'd be the one doing the throwing.

When the Terrible Three saw they couldn't find a sucker this trip they swaggered around, winking at Bobby Ann and Norma a couple of times to make them giggle. Luther remarked to me that if I weren't such a "sissy coward," I'd put my Harpoon into the ring against his Green Cobra. Frosty shut him up by saying, "And if you weren't such a sissy coward, you'd put your war kite back in the air again against Hoppy's Hawk!" Luther glared at me with his flinty blue eyes, remembering what Hawk had done to his famous Green Eagle on Wipe-out Wednesday.

While we boys bragged, bullied, and yarned, Norma and Bobby Ann started playing Spin-the-Longest. What happened shortly thereafter shocked the top world as nothing had ever shocked it before. And it spawned the making of the most indestructible and terrifying spiker top that man has ever known.

Norma and Bobby Ann had just spun their rollies into the ring for a new round of Spin-the-Longest. Both tops were spinning fast and smooth on the hard bare ground, and it appeared to be a close contest. But Norma's top veered into some loose gravel, went down sideways, and rolled out of the ring. Bobby Ann's top, still spinning hard, made her the winner.

"Girls can't spin worth a hoot," Luther said, removing the Green Cobra from his pocket to wind it. "Let a man show you how." Then, in his famous "over-the-head-and-down" delivery, Luther sent the deadly Green Cobra on its way. His awesome, battle-scarred spiker top struck like a lightning bolt.

The spectators gasped in dismay as Bobby Ann's beautiful blue rollie spun out of the ring to lie at her feet mortally wounded, a jagged chunk torn from its side. It looked like a beautiful blue pear with an ugly bite taken out of it. The Green Cobra continued to spin angrily, its sharp fang boring into the earth. All of us gasped in disbelief. An incredible, unforgivable, despicably vile deed had been committed. A defenseless rollie had been spiked, without cause or warning.

I've never believed Luther did it intentionally, because for just a moment his smile faded, a look of regret showed in his eyes, and he turned to Bobby Ann as if to apologize. But he must have remembered quickly that he had to protect his image as the leader of the Terrible Three. As we all stood immobilized, still stunned into silence, Luther picked up the two pieces of Bobby Ann's top. "Well," he boasted, "looks like the famous Cobra has added another beaut to his collection."

His sidekicks grinned sheepishly but said nothing. Norma, her green eyes flashing fire, tried to give Luther a piece of her mind, but she was too angry to talk. She could only stammer under her breath.

Bobby Ann, her big brown eyes glistening tears, looked at Luther as if he'd left her waiting at the church, then turned and walked slowly away. Luther caught up with her. "Hey, little bitty baby," he said in baby talk. "If you're gonna cry, take your old top back. Here, take it."

Without looking at him, Bobby Ann took her stricken rollie from his hand, threw the two pieces into my trash barrel, and walked on through the gap in the privet hedge.

"Everything okay?" my mother shouted from the back door. "It's quiet as a tomb out there!"

After supper Frosty got strapped with helping his dad plant late turnips, so I busied myself on the back-porch steps, trying to glue Bobby Ann's rollie back together. Even if the glue made it too heavy on the bad side, I reasoned, a carpet tack nailed into the opposite side might balance it so it would spin again. But I doubted it. Tops were mystifying creatures. The least little thing could cause one to become unbalanced and spin catawampus.

"*Psst!* Hey, Hoppy," came from the privet hedge. "Okay if I come over?" Bobby Ann came through the gap hesitantly, knowing if a ten-year-old boy was seen playing alone with a girl, he would be called a sissy before sundown, which would instigate a rubber-gun duel or, worse, a clod fight.

Before I gave her the okay signal to come on over, I shoved her top under the porch steps. No need to stir up unpleasant memories. But in fact Bobby Ann seemed to be completely recovered from the afternoon's traumatic experience. Losing a brand-new rollie to the Green Cobra would have put me in bed for a week! That's one thing you could say about Bobby Ann: She was a real trouper. As females went, I liked her a lot, nearly as much as I did my cousin Norma. And for an eleven-year-old girl, I guess you could say she was sort of pretty. She had my dog Nicky's eyes, big and honey brown, and her cotton-blond hair was naturally wavy, like a famous movie star's. In fact, all the grown-ups said she'd grow up someday to be the spittin' image of Jean Harlow.

Bobby Ann sat down on the steps with me—not too close—and asked if it was terribly difficult to learn how to spike tops. It was only fair to tell her that outside of diablo spinning, nothing equaled it in complexity. It took amazing skill, impeccable reflexes, an unerring eye, and nerves of carbon steel. Somehow, though, all this came out, "Naw, there ain't nothin' to it."

With this, Bobby Ann asked if I would do her a big favor, while keeping it a secret just between the two of us: teach her how to become a proficient top spiker like me. When I assured her I wasn't all that good, she flattered me with the truth: "If your folks didn't think it was wrong to gamble, you'd be the greatest top spiker in the whole world!"

Pumped up sky-high, I took my trusty Hoppy's Harpoon and under cover of twilight—and without bothering to ask her why she wanted to learn—gave Bobby Ann her first lesson in the intricate art of top spiking. Little did I dream that my student, this *girl* novice, who threw a top pathetically as if she were swatting a fly, would soon become a legend in her own time.

Every evening for more than a week I made excuses to Frosty, so Bobby Ann and I could rendezvous secretly underneath the black-walnut tree in my backyard. With a sense of pride and accomplishment I watched my student grow from an awkward apprentice into an uncanny, hard-throwing, true-eyed, poker-faced top spiker. Bobby Ann's crippled blue *Grit* rollie, which served valiantly as her target, became chipped away to a mere skeleton of its original self.

Then one evening that poignant moment came as it often does in a teacher-student relationship. The master realizes elatedly that he has taught all there is to teach. He gropes for the right words, then says, "By *danged*. You're almost as good as I am!"

Although I dared not admit it, not even to myself, I didn't want the lessons to end. I was sweet on Bobby Ann—and just knew she was sweet on me too. But as the last rays of the sun glowed faintly behind the Red-Horse Barn, Bobby Ann expressed her thanks, shook my hand like a war buddy, and then, without another word, slipped back through the privet hedge . . . and out of my life.

I didn't see Bobby Ann again until the following Friday after school.

The school playground was more crowded than usual with top spinners, diabloers, yo-yoers, jack rockers, and marble shooters, because my mother had declared my backyard off limits for the remainder of the day. This happened whenever the church Ladies' Auxiliary met at my house. On one of these occasions I had informed my mother that I had always thought the function of the church was to bring families closer together, and to kick a child out of his own yard hardly accomplished this. She clarified the church's position for me: "If I see your hide around here before suppertime, I'll nail it to the wall!"

Frosty and I got into a Hit-the-Bull's-eye game with Killer, Kong, Sticker, Bluegill, and See-Thru. See-Thru had a new yellow rollie, so recently purchased from Boatwright's he hadn't yet had time to replace the peg with a sharp nail and convert it to a spiker. As we played, Norma and Bobby Ann left a jack-rock game to come over and watch. Bobby Ann carried a King Edward cigar box that looked brand-new. I wondered where she had found it. Not at Boatwright's, surely. I had checked on the cigar-box situation there just that morning and found all the King Edward boxes were not even close to being empty. Just as I was preparing to try to swap her out of it, the Terrible Three swarmed down on our game like so many black locusts, sauntering, swaggering, and spitting Sen-Sen juice all over the place.

"Whatcha say, gang?" asked Luther amiably. "Anybody wanna spike?"

See-Thru opened his mouth to accept the challenge, but before he could, Bobby Ann said in a voice loud and clear, "Yes, I do."

The game stopped. All eyes turned to Bobby Ann. My stomach tied itself into a double zinger.

"Yes," she said again, smiling like Jean Harlow. "You bet I wanna spike with you!"

She said it again! *Oh, sweet sarsaparilla*! I felt like I was going to faint, knowing she would ask to borrow my Harpoon to spike with Luther. Deep down I must have known why she had wanted spiking lessons. Revenge! She wanted revenge for her *Grit* rollie. I had created a Frankenstein monster! I made myself invisible by stepping back to put Frosty between Bobby Ann and me. But just as I poofed into nothingness, I heard everyone *ohh*! in amazement.

Burning with curiosity, I took a furtive peek back into the circle through the crack between Frosty's hip and elbow. There, in front of my eyes, in Bobby Ann's hand, was the most elegant spiker top I had ever seen in my life!

The magnificent toy glistened like polished marble. The dark and light grain of its wood swirled and twisted in a design that looked like butter and molasses stirred together. Around the upper surface, a series of small holes of varying depths had been drilled into the varnished wood. With the cord that had come with her *Grit* rollie, Bobby Ann wound the majestic top. A faint smile played at the corners of her mouth. Slyly, she gave Luther a wide-eyed look of innocence, as she gingerly touched the end of her finger to the needle-pointed spike. The honed steel nail flashed in the sunlight, sharp as a dragon's tooth. The top, we discovered later, had been made for Bobby Ann by her uncle, who was a saddler over in Okmulgee. He'd turned it on a lathe from a burl of bowdarc, the same wood he used for saddle pommels and stirrups.

Luther grinned at Bobby Ann like a mule eating honey-locust briers. "Don't know where you got that purty top, little girl. But if you really wanna spike with it, it'll be mine before you can say Jack Robinson."

"If you say so, Luther," Bobby Ann replied sweetly. "I'll even let you spike first. Ready?"

With this, Bobby Ann spun her top into the ring, and I could feel myself fainting. Right on the spot. I knew I was, because there was an eerie, high-pitched, moaning sound ringing in my ears, wailing like a lost soul. Goose bumps broke out all over me. *EEEeeeOOheeeooheee*. . . . The moaning went on and on.

"It's her top!" See-Thru screamed. "It makes a noise like a banshee!"

He was right. It did! The small holes drilled in the top caused it to sound exactly as a banshee would sound if a banshee actually did make a sound. See-Thru became so excited he had to run to the privy.

The large group of kids that had gathered at the sound of Bobby Ann's "Banshee" watched in disbelief as Luther slammed his Green Cobra in for the kill. The Cobra's fang hit its target dead center and true. But when the Banshee skittered to a stop, not a mark was on it. Well, just one—a tiny pinprick that had barely penetrated the varnish. The Cobra's bite, for the first time in its life, had failed to kill.

Luther, shocked out of his suspenders, couldn't understand it. No one else could either. Why, if the Green Cobra had struck a brick wall, it would have inflicted more damage than it had to this wailing bowdarc top. If the Banshee's wood had not been so hard, the Cobra would have had a "spear-kill" for sure.

"Okay, Luther Spera," said Bobby Ann demurely, breaking the spell. "Put your Green Cobra in the ring . . . and kiss it bye-bye."

Sullenly, moving trancelike, Luther wound his top and spun it. Bobby Ann, turning first to blow me a kiss that made me blush down to my bare toes, spun her top with a throw that came to be known as the "Bobby Ann Blockbuster." The Banshee screamed and split the Green Cobra in two equal pieces. A blow from an ax couldn't have done it cleaner. Between the two halves of the Cobra, the Banshee continued to spin, wailing in wild, delirious satisfaction.

As the Cobra's past victims cheered Bobby Ann, she picked up the green remains and deposited them in her new cigar box. Then mimicking Luther, she asked sweetly, "Anybody wanna spike?"

Charles and Dave backed away as if Bobby Ann had the chicken pox. But Luther stood his ground, even though he was angry, humiliated—and sick to his stomach from swallowing a whole dip of Sen-Sen at one gulp. "Gimme your Hatchet,

Charles," he commanded. "Ain't nobody alive who can outspike me twice—much less a girl!"

Five minutes later, Charles's War Hatchet was laid to rest alongside the Green Cobra in Bobby Ann's new King Edward cigar box.

And at three-thirty, ditto for Dave Goldsmith's Widow-maker.

When the sun pointed at three thirty-two, the Terrible Three tucked their tails and slinked away. They did not saunter or swagger or say anything smart-alecky as they went. They just walked quietly, a little slump-shouldered, their heads down. Bobby Ann ran after Luther. "Hey, little bitty baby," she said to him. "If you're going to cry, take your old top back." And she dumped the contents of the cigar box at his feet.

The next day, Saturday, I received a blow that broke my ten-year-old heart. I thought at the moment that it would never, never heal—not even if I lived to be a hundred. After the Great Saturday Scootmobile Race, Frosty and I drifted up to the school to see what was going on. There we found Luther spiking tops with his cronies. He was showing off with the sensational new top Bobby Ann had given him. And to add salt to the wound, Bobby Ann was hanging on Luther's every word and rolling her adoring, rapture-filled eyes at him like a dying calf in a hailstorm.

Mortified, I told Frosty that in all fairness I, not old Luther, should have been the recipient of the Banshee, as it was I, not he, who had worked tired fingers to the bone night after night to teach Bobby Ann....

To my doleful tirade about how I did not understand girls, Frosty, instead of being sympathetic, quickly threw one of his old Cherokee aphorisms at me:

"Indian brave make squaw walk behind for good reason. If he can't see her, he doesn't have to try to figure out what she's doing."

STRING-AND-PENCIL COMPASS

The string-and-pencil compass was actually more of a tool than a toy. Children enjoyed playing with it, though, and it was indispensable for making yo-yos, diablos, and wheels. A slipknot in the string tied to the pencil provided a quick and simple

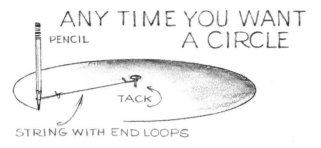

ANY TIME YOU WANT A CIRCLE

PENCIL

TACK

STRING WITH END LOOPS

Spinning Spuds

The yo-yo originated in the Philippines, where yo-yo means "come, come" (or return). It began there as a primitive hunting weapon, a stone attached to a rope. If a hunter missed the target, he could pull the stone back. Variations of the weapon/toy found their way to Europe in the nineteenth century, where they became popular under several names. In the United States they were introduced in the late 1920s when Donald F. Duncan spotted Philippine immigrant children playing with what resembled spinning potatoes, gadgets with spinning devices like tops. Manufacturing replicas of these playthings on a string, Duncan amassed a fortune while putting a toy in a kid's hand that would remain popular for decades to come.

method of adjusting the size of the circle drawn. For scratching a top or marble ring on the ground, nails were substituted for the thumbtack and pencil. For painting bull's-eye targets, a Crayola or paintbrush replaced the pencil. The string-and-pencil compass was so versatile that anyone who was brave and perhaps a bit of an acrobat could have used it to draw a circular target as large as a merry-go-round onto the side of a barn.

YO-YO

Sure, a small yo-yo could be purchased for a nickel or a dime, but a homemade one (small or large) didn't cost anything except a little time and effort. And it performed just as well as a store-bought model.

A yo-yo maker's first step was to search through a stack of cordwood to find a log as nearly round as possible and approximately 2½ or 3 inches in diameter. (It would invariably be at the very bottom of the stack underneath a hundred other logs weighing 50 pounds each.) A 3-inch-diameter log would render a finished toy about 2¼ inches in diameter. Size wasn't particularly important, though; neither was the type of wood. What *was* important was that the two wheels cut from the log be the same diameter and thickness—about ½ inch—and that the holes drilled in them for the dowel be in the exact center. The use of a string-and-pencil compass (see next illustration) made this a snap. After perfect circles were drawn, the wheels were cut out carefully with a coping saw. When the two wheels were sanded smooth, they were ready to be glued to the dowel, leaving a ⅛-inch space between them for the string. When the glue had set, the outer edges were rounded off and sanded to resemble a store-bought yo-yo.

The Yo-Yo Man

It was Saturday when the Yo-Yo Man came to town. When he parked his yellow '34 Ford coupé with the big red yo-yo painted on the doors, all the kids were already assembled to greet him in front of the corner drugstore. They knew he was coming because the show card had been in the window all week.

The Yo-Yo Man was wearing white pants, a straw sailor, and a candy-striped blazer with a yellow-and-red patch on the pocket that proclaimed him "Duncan Yo-Yo Champion." He greeted the children warmly and yelled, "Does everybody have a yo-yo?"

Most of them did, some of them homemade.

"Okay, the first thing we're going to do is learn a few tricks, and then we're going to have a contest to see who's the best yo-yoer in town. I'm going to give away a yo-yo to the six best. And to the grand champion, I'm going to give a blue-ribbon certificate, and this beauty. . . ." He held up a rainbow-colored imperial model that cost 25 cents in the store.

They gasped, and their eyes lit up like the rainbow in his hand.

From his pocket he pulled a bright-red yo-yo and went to work. The wheel on a string became a whirring blaze of color, magic in the hands of a wizard. The spinning disk skipped along the sidewalk like a dog on a leash. "Walking the Dog," the Yo-Yo Man said. The humming toy went out and back, around his head twice, and back to his hand. "Around the World," he explained.

1934 DESOTO AIRFLOW

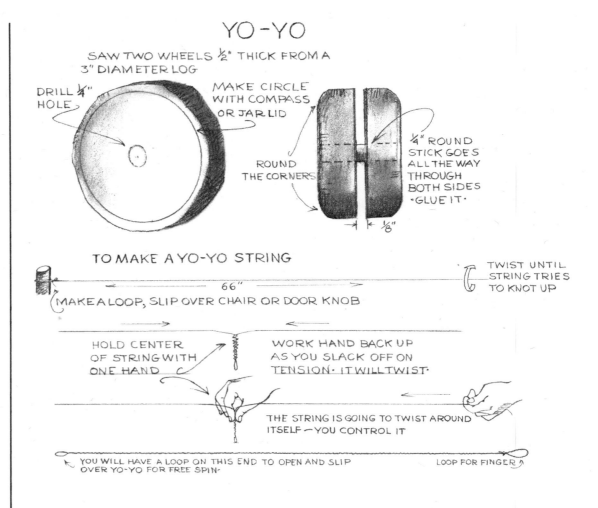

A yo-yo string was made as described in the illustration, but a piece of strong kite string or fishing line two to three feet long and waxed with tallow or beeswax worked well also. It was attached with a tight slipknot—or a loose loop knot if you wanted the yo-yo to be a free spinner. (A free spinner would spin at the end of the string until jerked back up.) A homemade yo-yo when painted or varnished was a toy that Donald Duncan himself would have been proud to call his own.

SPOOL YO-YO

The spool yo-yo was so simply constructed, it could be put together in ten minutes. And this little fellow performed beautifully—every bit as well as its big brother. The ends were sawed from a large spool and glued to a dowel (a round pencil was also just the right size). A 24-inch length of strong thread attached to the dowel turned out a pint-sized yo-yo that would spin mightily.

SPOOL YO-YO

SAW ENDS FROM SPOOL, REVERSE POSITION

SAWED SIDE

USE THREAD—24"

ROUND STICK THE SIZE OF HOLE IN SPOOL· GLUE IT IN

1/32"

SPOOL TOP

Tops have been around since ancient times. The earliest tops were spun with whips. A parent-to-child threat which survived the centuries was heard quite often by some children during the Great American Depression: "If you *ever* do that again, I'll spin you like a top!"

It was virtually impossible for a Depression-era kid to whittle from a raw chunk of wood an average-size top that would spin as well as a store-bought one turned to balanced perfection on a wood lathe. But baby tops could be whittled from spools and spun with thread. And making these was as easy as falling down the cellar steps. The little hummers spun excellently, too. A top of any size, shape, or description couldn't be purchased that would spin any better.

A large spool could be converted into twin tops by sawing it in half, whittling each piece to a cone shape, and cutting a groove around the upper portion to take the spinning thread (24 inches in length). A sharpened pencil stub made a satisfactory axis stick, but a sharpened dowel with a straight pin pushed into it worked best.

They were enthralled, captivated.

The Yo-Yo Man continued demonstrating.

He did the Three-Leaf Clover, Rock the Cradle, Loop the Loop, Skin the Cat, Sleeping Beauty, the Creeper, and a dozen more. He topped it off with the unbelievable Double Waterfall Into the Pocket!

And then it was the kids' turn.

They were nervous, excited; nothing went right. A string would tangle or break; the danged thing wouldn't freewheel. One kid tore the pocket of his good pants. Another split his lip doing Around the World. One yo-yo while Walking the Dog broke in two; one wheel went speeding down the sidewalk, the other crossed the street and rolled into the general store.

That's the way it was in front of the corner drugstore when the Yo-Yo Man came to town. And the kids who were there, winners and losers alike, would remember those days for the rest of their lives.

SPOOL TOP

3/4"

CUT GROOVE
FOR SPINNING
THREAD

KNOT

THREAD

MATCH STICK

SHARPENED PENCIL
OR DOWEL WITH
STRAIGHT PIN PEG

1/4"

Acting as a ball bearing, the head of the pin worked wonderfully as the peg, the pointy tip on which the top spun. The length of the axis stick was critical to the performance of all homemade tops. The stick was usually cut so it projected about ¾ inch from the top of the spool. Depending on the size of spool, this length could vary, but not much. When the axis stick was the correct length, the top would spin in a smooth, standup position. Spool tops were wound and spun by a 24-inch thread or by snapping the axis stick between thumb and middle finger.

SPOOL DIABLO (also known as "diabolo")

For kids who were hooked on diablo spinning, this "little devil" was a joy to make. *El diablo poco* was constructed from two spool tops. The two cone-shaped tops were whittled from a spool (same as the spool top), then glued onto a round pencil or dowel about 3 inches long, leaving approximately 1/16 inch of dowel exposed at the center. Before gluing in place permanently, however, the tops were moved back and forth on the dowel (the axis stick) until the toy would balance on the edge of a ruler. If the dowel protruded somewhat farther on one side than the other, it didn't matter, as long as the diablo was perfectly balanced.

The spinner consisted of a piece of strong thread, 18 inches or longer, which was tied to the end of each of two 12-inch sticks. To spin a spool diablo, the sticks were held as if they were drumsticks, one in each hand, far enough apart to cradle the diablo on the thread. Then, like beating a kettledrum, the sticks were moved up and down alternately (one up, the other down)—slowly at first—to start the diablo spinning on the thread. The faster the beat became, the faster the toy would spin. This basic procedure was used for spinning any diablo, store-bought or homemade.

Unlike the yo-yo, the diablo was not attached to the string, so it could get away from you before you knew what was happening. It was the goal of every would-be diabloer to toss it up in the air and catch it (still spinning) on the string. Of course, if a kid relished ostentatious behavior (enjoyed showing off), he might try doing a somersault or a back flip while the diablo was spinning skyward, as jesters in the royal courts of Europe did in ancient times. Court jesters were somewhat scarce in rural Oklahoma in the '30s, though, so diablo contests between children consisted mainly of seeing who could spin the toy the longest—or who could throw it up and catch it the most times without inflicting injury on anyone.

SPOOL DIABLO

ROUND PENCIL OR STICK 3" LONG • GLUE IT •

1/16"

1/2"

TRY DIABLO ON EDGE OF RULER TO TEST FOR BALANCE

18" THREAD

STICKS 12" LONG

DIABLO

SPINNER

GOURD-DISC DIABLO

Becoming adept at spinning any diablo required practice, but the gourd-disc diablo was the least difficult to master. Even an all-thumbs kid with the dexterity of a rag doll could make it hum like an expert. The 4-inch diameter discs (cut from the ends of a seasoned gourd and positioned on the axis stick, a slight 1/16-inch space apart) endowed the toy with stability on the spinner string that other diablos did not have. As long as the holes in the discs were drilled in the approximate center and the discs

Getting to Know the Diablo

This is one toy with a most appropriate name: *Diablo* in Spanish means "devil," and that's precisely what this toy is. Also known as a diabolo or Devil on a String, it is somewhat difficult to master. It provided the type of challenge, though, that Depression-era children loved, and they found great sport in learning to put the devil through its tricks.

The toy dates back to the fifteenth century. Court jesters and jugglers entertained royal courts of Europe with their spinning cones. Napoleon was a diablo fanatic and was said to be most proficient with the toy. From Mexico, where children could spin the devil by the time they lost their baby teeth, the toy came to the United States—where the American Indians found spinning the diablo more fun than counting coup. The infamous western outlaw William H. Bonney, better known as "Billy the Kid," was a diablo freak. He reportedly carried one around in his saddlebags and would demonstrate his spinning skills in New Mexico saloons for free drinks. Billy killed twenty-one men by the time he was the same age. Even so, can a kid who mastered the Devil on a String be all bad?

were glued to the axis stick to give the toy an overall balance (same as the spool diablo), it would spin impressively.

The spinner for this diablo was the same spinner used for the professional full-sized diablos. It consisted of a 30-inch piece of strong cord or twine tied to the ends of sticks each about 16 inches long.

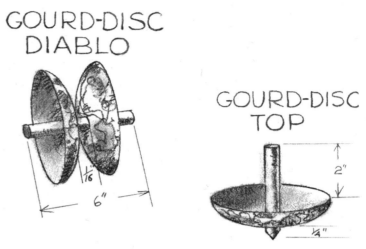

GOURD-DISC TOP

The gourd-disc top was the favorite of children who were too small to learn to spin tops with a string. It was spun by twirling the axis stick between the palms of both hands with a snapping motion. To construct this extraordinarily long-spinning top, a large disc like the ones used for the diablo was cut from a gourd. The disc was then fitted with an axis stick (sharpened dowel or pencil) approximately 3 inches long through a hole drilled in the exact center of the disc. About ¼ inch of the axis stick projected through the disc at the peg end.

DIABLO

The regulation-sized professional-type diablo was danged hard to make, and harder than Hades to spin. But this is where the dedicated diablo buff could really show off his skill at toy making. The diablo was whittled from a pine or other softwood log

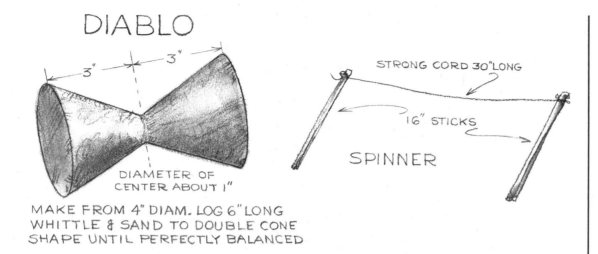

DIABLO

3" · 3"

DIAMETER OF
CENTER ABOUT 1"

MAKE FROM 4" DIAM. LOG 6" LONG
WHITTLE & SAND TO DOUBLE CONE
SHAPE UNTIL PERFECTLY BALANCED

STRONG CORD 30" LONG

16" STICKS

SPINNER

about 6 inches long and 4 inches in diameter, and carved into its double-cone shape down to a diameter of about 1 inch at the exact center. It was then carefully shaved and sandpapered until it would balance on the edge of a ruler or a knife without a waver. A well-carved diablo was a cherished toy that ranked high on the list in swappin' value . . . unless, of course, you were trying to swap it off to some new kid in town who didn't even know what a diablo was, much less how to spin the devilish thing.

SPIKER TOP

In the strictest sense of the word, the spiker top was not a homemade toy. It was a store-bought "rollie" (a wood top with a ball-shaped peg) that had been modified for playing the greatest top-spinning game of all times, Top Spiking. Without a doubt, this was the favorite game of top spinners during the Great American Depression. To convert a rollie to a spiker, the ball-shaped peg of the top was removed and replaced with a spike, a sharpened nail. "Anybody wanna spike?"

Top Spiking

During hard times when an ordinary unpainted wooden top with a spinning cord cost a nickel—one twentieth of the working man's average daily wage—top spiking

Learning to Spin the Devil

Learning to spin a diablo might be compared to trying to milk a cow for the first time. It feels unnatural, somehow, and downright scary. But after you get the hang of it, you'll go moving along just as pretty as you please. Before long, milk from the cow will start hitting the pail in long steady streams, and the old diablo all of a sudden is spinning away a mile a minute.

For the moment let's put cow milking aside and concentrate on diablo spinning. Okay, get down on your knees in the kitchen (the floor needs to be smooth like linoleum), and place the diablo in front of you with the spinner string underneath—no, turn it around the other way with a round end facing you.

Now, grasp the spinner sticks firmly in each hand as if they were flyswatters, and lift one up until the string contacts the center of the diablo enough to make it roll. When it starts rolling, bring the other stick up to roll it back the other way. There you go! Roll it back and forth on the floor by raising one stick while lowering the other. Good. Now do it faster; gradually lift the diablo off the floor. Let it spin on the string. There—keep it going. Back and forth; move the stick up and down. Faster . . . that's great! Get to your feet now; keep it spinning. Sensational! You've got it spinning good. . . . You're gonna throw it up in the air? Like the experts do? Well, I dunno. Maybe you should wait until you . . . *watch it!* Where'd it go? I think it hit the ceiling and ricocheted off the icebox. . . .

Lord have mercy! It's in the soup pot! Get it out quick! I know it's hot; use a spoon—use *two* spoons. If Granny finds out, we're dead! No, you dummy, it'll never pass as a soupbone. Who ever saw a soupbone shaped like a diablo. . . . Good, put it in the sink to cool. Yeah, it did turn a pretty red. I've never seen a tomato-colored diablo before. Grab that thing and let's get out of here. Let's go out to the barn, and I'll teach you how to milk a cow. The first thing you do to milk a cow is situate the stool so when the cow swishes her tail, it doesn't hit you in the back of the neck. . . .

Old-Time Top-Spinning Games

BUMP-OUT

Two or more players spin their tops into the ring simultaneously. If a top spins out of the ring or is bumped out of the ring, it is eliminated from the game. The players spin again. The game continues until only one top is left spinning in the ring. This is the winner.

JAR-LID GOLF

Nine jar lids varying in size are placed around the yard. They are numbered from 1 to 9 to represent a nine-hole golf course. The player who throws his top to spin inside all nine lids with the least number of throws wins the match.

SPIN-THE-LONGEST

Two or more players spin their tops simultaneously. The top that spins the longest wins.

HIT-THE-BULL'S-EYE

A series of three inner rings are drawn inside the main ring to represent a bull's-eye target. The bull's-eye is about the size of a quarter. The space inside each ring is worth a given number of points: 10, 25, 50, and 100 for the bull's-eye. The players spin spiker tops at the target. The one who chalks up 150 points first is the winner.

(or top busting, as it was sometimes called) was the most exciting and expensive game in town.

For the kid who was faint at heart, or had only one top to his name, top spiking was definitely not recommended. He was probably better off, financially at least, sticking to Bump Out or some other top-spinning game in which the loser merely lost face—not his one-and-only extremely valuable top.

Top spiking, like trading in commodity futures or playing roulette, was a high-risk game. It required skill, bravery, and a tremendous amount of derring-do. The pain of defeat was excruciating, the thrill of victory brought fame, glory, and remuneration (winner takes all).

A top-spiking contest involved a "spiker" and a "target." When a top-spiking challenge was accepted, the two adversaries drew straws or flipped a coin to determine which one would be the first to offer his top as a target. The target top, when thrown, had to land and spin inside the ring, a large circle scratched into the bare earth, and continue spinning for at least ten seconds (to the count of ten). Within this period of time the spiker, keeping both feet outside the ring, had one shot at spiking the target by throwing his spinning top at it. He could throw it overhanded, under-

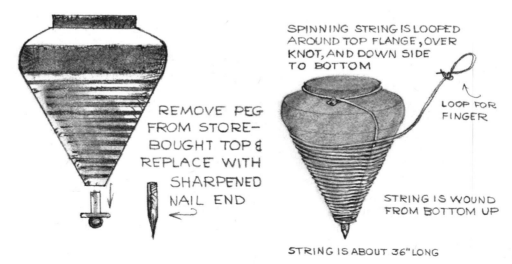

SPIKER TOP

REMOVE PEG FROM STORE-BOUGHT TOP & REPLACE WITH SHARPENED NAIL END

SPINNING STRING IS LOOPED AROUND TOP FLANGE, OVER KNOT, AND DOWN SIDE TO BOTTOM

LOOP FOR FINGER

STRING IS WOUND FROM BOTTOM UP

STRING IS ABOUT 36" LONG

handed, sideways, or whatever, as long as he stayed outside the ring. If his throw damaged the target top sufficiently (knocked off a chunk at least as large as a pinto bean), the wounded target top became his property. But if his throw missed, the roles of target and spiker were reversed. Sometimes the spike of a spiker top would stick into the target top like a nail driven into a board. This was called a "spear kill" and constituted an immediate uncontested victory for the spiker.

A top-spiking contest was terminated at nightfall, by a draw, or else when one lucky high roller walked away with another top to add to his priceless collection . . . a damaged top, true, but one he just knew could be repaired to spin good as ever.

NOTE: *During a top-spiking contest, spectators stood back away from the ring. A spiker top could spike a toe as well as another top.*

9

Animals and Dolls

Little kids are people too. And they enjoy toys just as much as anybody. During the Depression years the small fry (too old for diapers, too young for rubber guns) had more fascinating homemade toys than they could stuff in a croker sack. And they played with them too, whenever they weren't diverted by the attractions of the wide and wonderful world outdoors, where there were more delights than there were minutes in a day. These entrancing outside activities might include flipping over a log or a flat rock to discover if any creepy things lived underneath, or perhaps following behind Pa's plow to search for pretty pebbles, arrowheads, night crawlers, or whatever treasures a freshly turned furrow could reveal. Another captivating pastime provided by Mother Nature for young children was catching insects—ladybugs, doodlebugs, or chicken chokers.

Whenever a five-year-old kid was spotted crawling around the yard on all fours with one eye close to the ground, chances were, if he wasn't searching for a lost penny or a four-leaf clover, he was looking for a chicken choker or doodlebug home.

A chicken choker, an immature tiger beetle, was a harmless, white, brown-headed worm, with hooklike appendages protruding from a body so mean-looking only a small boy could appreciate it. Old-timers maintained that if a chicken swallowed one of these creatures, the hooks would catch in its throat and the chicken would die. The worm's home was a neat little round hole in the ground, and being a fastidious housekeeper, it did not like anyone poking a broomstraw into its living room. And that's just what kids would do. First, they'd drop a straw into the chicken choker's house, and then they'd wait until the critter attempted to remove the intrusive object by grasping and wiggling it. When this happened, the straw was quickly jerked from the hole, along with the surprised chicken choker. The object of the game was to see who could catch one first. Some kids spit on the straws for luck, others applied a mud paste.

Many youngsters would call any interesting or funny-looking insect—even a ladybug or a chicken choker—a doodlebug. Actually, though, the larva of the ant lion was the true doodlebug. Like the chicken choker, it lived in a little hole in the ground, and it was equally as gullible—and even more forbidding in appearance (the less said about this creepy crawler's looks, the better). Techniques for catching doodlebugs varied depending on the locale. In some areas a magical incantation was frequently intoned, such as: "Doodlebug, doodlebug, come up and get a grain *of corn—your house is on fire." This chant supposedly would bring them from their tunnels every time.*

After catching a few doodlebugs (or chicken chokers), young entomologists held the specimens awhile for clinical observation. Reflexes were tested to see if one would roll itself into a ball when touched (some Oklahoma doodlebugs would). And they were compared for size and aggressiveness to see if a couple of them would fight each other (sometimes they did). Afterward, the temporarily evicted tenants usually were allowed to amble back home to be caught again another day.

Ladybugs, small, friendly, gaily colored beetles, were the favorite insects of little girls. The Ladybug Game, very popular with five-year-olds, involved not only magic but witchcraft as well. A ladybug was placed in the palm of the hand, fingers extended, and the little witch would chant, "Ladybug, ladybug, fly away." At this, the ladybug would walk from the palm out onto the end of a finger. "Fly away, ladybug, I can't play." Here, the ladybug would stand on the very tip of the finger and peer over the edge. "Fly away, ladybug, your house is on fire!" That did it! The ladybug would take off.

Now, this may not sound much like witchcraft, but if the magic words were not spoken ("fire" was always included in magic words), the dumb bug would just crawl around in the palm of your hand all day.

The Legend of Reelfoot

Every fall in our town, when the nights first turned cold, we had what we called a riverbank cookout down at Grandmother Youngblood's house. Invariably, it was an evening of fun for young and old alike. We'd cook over a driftwood fire, play games of skill, sing songs, and, if there was no school the next day, tell stories until the wee hours (nine-thirty or ten o'clock). To youngsters, any kind of a cookout was a special treat, but a riverbank cookout at night was almost as much fun as Christmas.

The star of this festive get-together was Grandmother Youngblood, the favorite person of every child in town. No one knew her age for sure. But we figured she must be very, very old—maybe even a hundred. Widowed when her husband was killed during the Spanish-American War, she had never remarried. And after her two children were grown, she lived alone in her small house by the river.

Whatever her age, it didn't show all that much. True, her face was etched with time, crisscrossed by a million tiny roads, all leading in the direction of a big smile, but she was spry, active, walked erect without a cane, and her steady hands were free of arthritis. Her hair hung down in two long, heavy, granite-gray braids. And the look in her eyes was pure sunshine, her voice as melodious as a bubbling stream. Grandmother Youngblood had a soft, clear way of speaking that would give you goose bumps when she was telling a story. Without a doubt, she was the greatest storyteller in the whole world.

Every one of us loved her dearly and thought of her as our real honest-to-goodness grandmother, and she treated us as if she were, too. Sometimes this made Frosty a little jealous, and he would remind us in no uncertain terms that he, Frosty Youngblood, was her only by-kin bona fide grandchild. He'd pursue the subject even further by pointing out that it was genetically impossible for Caucasian youngsters to be the legitimate grandchildren of a full-blood Cherokee Indian woman. His actual words were, "She's not your grandmother! She's mine! You paleface kids have no danged right going around claiming she's yours!"

We paid no attention whatever to Frosty's fits of jealousy because we knew that he knew that he was the apple of his grandmother's eye. When we were playing at her house, she always gave him the biggest piece of cake, the longest joint of sugarcane, the lightest of her tongue-lashings, and the best of her homemade toys.

It wasn't easy to say which of Grandmother Youngblood's toys were the best. We cherished them all. From the many odd-shaped gourds that grew around her house, she fashioned dozens of toys, including cup and balls, stick and rings, stick and balls, and tops. And the diablos she whittled from small pine logs were balanced so perfectly, just about anyone could learn to spin one in hardly any time at all.

She delighted the younger kids with gifts of corn-shuck dolls, corncob dolls, doll dishes, furniture, and funny little pine-cone animals. For the grown-ups she made corncob pipes, gourd dippers, bowls, birdhouses, and even toad huts for gardens. Grandmother Youngblood might give you one of her splendid homemade toys just about any time you saw her. But mostly she saved them for special occasions, like birthdays, or gave them as prizes at the annual cookout.

For our 1934 riverbank cookout, Grandmother Youngblood predicted the night would be clear and cold with a heavy frost. Now, when she said the weather would be this or that, you could bet your bottom dollar she would hit the nail right on the head. Back in early summer on the day of the big tornado she had warned it would storm before sundown. Maybe a bit of an understatement, but nevertheless her forecasts were a lot more accurate than old run-of-the-mill standbys like "If it thunders before seven, it will rain before eleven" or "No dew in the morning is a rainy day warning." She was nearly as good at weather forecasting as the professional weatherman in the newspaper.

On that October Friday afternoon, Frosty and I, like all other kids, rushed straight home after school to change our clothes before heading for the river. But, as luck would have it, our mothers wouldn't let us go until we ran down to Boatwright's to fetch some groceries.

We could have finished the errand in twenty minutes, but Frosty lingered, admiring the BB gun at Boatwright's that he was willing to bet at least a million marbles I would win in the Great Labor Day Slingshot Shoot next year. When he bragged to Mr. Boatwright that the gun was as good as mine, Mr. Boatwright grunted and gave me a jaundiced eye. On top of this, he didn't even throw in a free jawbreaker with our orders, which were sizable, totaling 57 cents: a can of baking powder, 1 pound of coffee, a box of crackers, two loaves of bread, a box of salt, and four spools of thread. Mr. Boatwright did say, though, he would see us at the cookout when he closed the store at eight, and that he would bring lots and lots of marshmallows.

By the time Frosty and I finally got down to the Grand River, nearly half the kids in town were already there. Some were scurrying about on the sand and gravel beach, which was practically in Grandmother Youngblood's front yard, gathering driftwood for the cook fire that was burning brightly. Others were setting up the bales of wheat straw which Mr. Buford had hauled over in his wagon. Most of the bales were being placed at a safe distance around the fire pit—a large circle of flat stones—so the old folks wouldn't have to sit on the ground. A few bales were being stacked into a backstop for the archery and spear-throwing contest (which Frosty always won). Killer and the other Renegades were working amiably, just as nice as you please, alongside Eskimo, Kenneth, Pete, and See-Thru. That was another thing about Grandmother Youngblood: She had a talent for bringing out the good—if there was any—in everybody, even Killer.

Bluegill, shirking work as always, was fishing; two of his sardine-can fishing boats were sailing around out in Skull-Head Cove.

Grandmother Youngblood gave us a friendly wave. She was watching over the activities from where she sat on the rock steps which had been cut into the bank leading up to her small three-room house on the bluff. Some of the younger kids couldn't understand why she didn't live in a tepee as storybook Indians do. When they'd ask her why she didn't have a house like Hiawatha's, she'd reply, "Lord, a body could freeze to death in one of those drafty things!" Once, when See-Thru suggested that a few scalps hanging on the walls would brighten up the living room and add authenticity to her heritage, she shut him up quickly by saying, "Don't tempt me, young man!"

By the time the setting sun had painted the river silver and gold, all the kids had arrived, and Frosty had already won the archery shoot. But not the spear-throwing contest this year. Killer beat him out the last throw. I came in second in the cup-and-ball game. Bobby Ann got lucky and walked away with first prize: the cup and ball. Kong took top honors in stick and ball, and good old Laughing Pete laughed his way victoriously through the stick-and-rings contest. Grandmother Youngblood barred Frosty from these contests, because he was so proficient with anything on a string no one else could win. When she passed out the prizes and gifts to everybody, I got a diablo. Just my luck. I couldn't spin one of the danged things for a million dollars. Slingshots were my game.

It was pitch dark before most of the grown-ups arrived and we could eat. Over the fire-pit coals we cooked sausage balls and apple slices skewered on long sticks. Grandmother Youngblood passed around her drop biscuits, big as saucers, dripping with butter and molasses. We washed it all down with hot cocoa or with steaming cups of coffee from Uncle Frank's gallon-size enamelware pot that bubbled on a hot rock.

Mr. Boatwright and my father came at eight-thirty, bringing what all the kids had eagerly been awaiting: marshmallows, enough to feed a CCC camp! To us, these puffy balls of sweetness were the greatest treats ever invented, especially when toasted. Old fat Kong, who could gulp down marshmallows faster than a goose eats corn, didn't bother to toast his; he ate them raw. As expected, Norma let her first marshmallow catch on fire because she was a terrible cook. And See-Thru, who couldn't wait for the molten lump to cool, burned his tongue. Fanning his mouth with both hands, he whooped and hollered, "Owwweee. Ain't nothing hotter than a hot marshmallow!"

When, stuffed to the gills, we finally finished eating, more driftwood was fed to the flames. As blackness closed in, the rushing river, a stone's throw away, echoed scary splashing sounds. The kids sat as close to the fire as possible, pretending the weather was colder than it really was. Frosty and I let Killer squeeze in between us. We knew he was afraid of the dark. Several of the teenagers—also Bobby Ann and Luther—sat back out of the firelight, so they could hold hands or make goo-goo eyes at each other. Grandmother Youngblood sat on the ground, Indian-style, like the youngsters.

After we sang all our favorite old songs, including "The Ballad of Floyd Collins" and "Tiptoe Through the Tulips," Mr. Buford told us a funny story about his old coonhound, Rosemary.

"This roaring fire here reminds me of the time our house burned down when we lived over in Warner. Rosemary weren't more than a pup then. But smart? Smartest dog you ever seen! Anyhow, our house caught fire in the middle of the night, and Rosemary run from bed to bed, barking and snapping at our toes, until she got us all outside. When we was all safe, she counted heads and run back into that raging inferno. We just knew she was done for, 'cause she was in there for quite a spell. But when the rafters started falling in, she come running back out, pretty as you please. Not hide nor hair was scorched—and she was a-totin' the fire-insurance policy wrapped in a wet towel!"

When everybody (except Laughing Pete) finally stopped laughing at funny old Mr. Buford, we started shouting our requests to Grandmother Youngblood. It was story time. Each child had a favorite of all the stories she told, but I always preferred the one about Reelfoot. I could relate to that, because of my bout with polio. Reelfoot had a bad leg like mine—and Hopalong Cassidy's.

Grandmother Youngblood's stories were Indian legends, beautiful, magical fantasies that had been told and retold by generations of her people. And as it always is with folktales, these narratives about the mysteries of God, man, and nature are told in many different versions, not one of them any less fascinating than the others. They were exciting, mystical tales about why the seasons change, why animals are named the way they are, why there are droughts and floods, why smoke rises and snow falls, and why there are "blackberry winters" and "strawberry springs."

After a lot of good-natured haggling, we finally voted unanimously for Grandmother Youngblood to tell us again the legend of Reelfoot. She nodded in agreement and gave me a special smile. I knew it was her favorite story too. She and her husband, when they were first married, had lived near Reelfoot Lake, where they'd spent many happy years.

Reelfoot Lake was formed by an earthquake in 1811. The tremor had been felt across an area of 40,000 square miles. Forests were uprooted, and some places the elevation of the land changed as much as 15 feet. The Mississippi River temporarily changed its course to flow backward and created the 15,000-acre lake in northwest Tennessee. In the New Madrid, Missouri, area where damage was most severe, only a single death was verified. The lack of casualties was attributed to the fact that most of the houses in the sparsely settled region were log cabins. Their flexible construction made them virtually earthquake-proof. But on the Tennessee side of the river, the Chickasaw Indians said they lost many lives, among them, a young chief called Reelfoot and his bride of a few hours. Thus the Indian legends were born.

As we waited breathlessly for Grandmother Youngblood to begin her story, the fire crackled and popped. The flames danced and changed colors from orange to red, blue to green—the colors of jellybeans. Sparks flew upward like tiny skyrockets, and the driftwood smoke smelled like incense from exotic, faraway places. Grandmother Youngblood filled her corncob pipe and lit it with a glowing taper. And while we watched her weathered face grow solemn in thought, the firelight flickering in her eyes, I felt that everyone there wondered just for a moment if this might be the last time we would hear her tell us a story. She was very, very old. . . .

"More than a hundred years ago, a Chickasaw tribe of My People lived on the bank of the Great River," Grandmother Youngblood began in her soft, lyrical voice. "Their village lay at the base of bluffs which rose hundreds of feet above the water, providing shelter from the angry, twisting winds that Man-Above sometimes sent roaring out of the southwest.

"My People were peaceful and happy. The Great River furnished them an abundance of fish and mussels, also water for the maize fields during summer drought. The woods were alive with white-tailed deer and small game. My People were never hungry, and at the rising of each moon they thanked Man-Above for this. Their grateful words were carried up to Him by the smoke from the evening cook fires. But sometimes the smoke would not rise. When it hovered low and filled the shelters, they knew Man-Above was not listening. He was occupied with more important things.

"Spotted Hawk, chief of My People, was a wise and gentle ruler. He had sired three daughters but not a son. His heart was heavy because he longed for a son to whom to pass his stately robes. His shoulders grew stooped, and his teeth broke with age. In his sixty-fourth year, Man-Above answered his prayers and delivered to him a son. My People rejoiced, and the feasting and dancing lasted for many days.

"The infant grew healthy and strong, but in his fourth summer, he was struck on the left foot by the deadly Snake-That-Rattles. He lived through the racking fever, but the poison rotted the flesh. When his foot healed, it was turned inward and the ankle was twisted. Thereafter, he walked and ran with a rolling motion, so at the age of ten—the age of name-giving—he was called Reelfoot. This was by no means a name of ridicule, as My People loved him deeply. And names were never given to cast mockery. If not called after animals, children were given names describing special things about the way they looked or acted. By custom, at a later age Reelfoot could take another name of his own choosing. But he did not.

"At the age of eighteen Reelfoot was strong and handsome, highly respected, and, of course, he was Spotted Hawk's pride and joy. The lad was a skillful hunter, a master horseman, and a stiff competitor at games. A better bowman never lived, and he could throw a spear hard and true. He was the best of all at stick and rings. His eye was sharp, like the red-tailed hawk. But he was unhappy because his youthful blood stirred thoughts of romance, and even though he was the son of a chief, the young maidens found his crooked foot unattractive. By the time he was twenty-one, Reelfoot was still unmarried and very lonely.

"Time and again, he watched with an aching heart as one of his companions would deliver a pony to the father of a maiden that he himself had longed for. Then the maiden would be led in front of the assembled council. Slowly, she would approach her betrothed, extending her hands and offering herself to him. As always, Reelfoot would heartily congratulate the groom and slap him on the back, but in his heart he was sad and bitter with envy.

"Early one spring when Reelfoot was twenty-three, he journeyed with his father far down the Great River, as the Chickasaws went to pay respects to Neshoba, the great chief of another tribe of My People called the Choctaws. Their canoes held gifts of dried fish and leather pouches filled with mussel pearls. In return the Choctaws, whose land lay inland to the east, would give them woven cane baskets and tobacco.

"The journey took many days because the aged Spotted Hawk tired easily. The canoes would beach for long periods to let him rest. When they arrived at the Choctaw village, they were greeted warmly. Spotted Hawk and Reelfoot were ushered to

Neshoba's council. The old friend of Spotted Hawk made them welcome and offered them smoking pipes and food. He then proudly introduced them to his many grandchildren, one of whom was the most beautiful maiden Reelfoot had ever seen. Her name was Laughing Eyes, and she was seventeen. Nervously, Reelfoot approached her, trying not to limp, and offered her a black pearl from his pouch. She accepted it and, raising her eyes to his, pressed it to her lips. It was a sign that she deeply appreciated such a rare gift and would cherish it forever.

" 'Misfortune befell your journey?' she asked. 'I see that your foot is injured.'

" 'No, our journey was safe,' Reelfoot replied. 'I have been this way all my life. I am called Reelfoot.' Laughing Eyes took his hand in hers and smilingly said, 'I am so happy to know you are not injured.'

"In the days to follow, Reelfoot and Laughing Eyes felt their hearts beating as one. But it was a hopeless romance, for they could not marry. In those days it was forbidden to mix the blood of one tribe of My People with another. Spotted Hawk, seeing his only son suffering, was willing to break this custom, but Neshoba and the Choctaws were not. They would fight to preserve the ancient ways. So Reelfoot returned home. But before he left his beloved Laughing Eyes, he had whispered to her, 'I'll come for you at the first snow.'

" 'Where the Great River bends,' she had whispered back. 'I'll meet you there, my heart.'

"The long summer passed slowly for Reelfoot. When finally the frosted leaves of the chestnut trees turned to red and gold, he confided in his father and asked his advice. Spotted Hawk, who was preparing for the Last Journey, told Reelfoot from his deathbed, 'Since the beginning, Man-Above has made many changes to better His plan for all things. He will forever change the course of the river, reshape the mountain, and grow the mighty oak where it has never grown before. Man will make changes also. Forever and ever man will replace the old customs with new, some for better, some for worse. And man will always know in his heart which of these do or do not please Man-Above.'

" 'Will Man-Above be angered when I take Laughing Eyes for my wife?' Reelfoot asked his father.

" 'For the marriage, no, for that is not Man-Above's law you break,' the old chief replied. 'But if you bring war to My People you do a very bad thing. Many will die. Man-Above will judge whether the love of two, or the deaths of many, fit the better His plan for all things.'

"When the cold north wind swept down the Great River, Spotted Hawk departed on the Last Journey, and Reelfoot became chief. He called My People together and told them he was going to marry Laughing Eyes. And, if war threatened after he did so, he and Laughing Eyes would go to a far-off land and live in exile in order to prevent bloodshed. My People would not agree to this. They would not have their chief run and hide like the weasel, even if it meant war with the Choctaws.

"Soon, the first flakes of snow fell, and while Reelfoot kept his rendezvous with Laughing Eyes, My People crushed berries into war paint and readied their weapons.

"When the lovers returned they were married immediately, and there was rejoicing and feasting by My People. But the festivities ended when scouts brought word that Neshoba approached with many Choctaw warriors. The Great River floated their war canoes, more numerous than leaves, and the air thundered with their war drums.

"On opposite banks of the Great River the two armies gathered. The waxing winter moon reflected on polished weapons that on the next sunrise would surely turn the sparkling snowdrifts red with blood. Hand in hand, Reelfoot and Laughing Eyes knelt before the cook fire and spoke as one into the smoke to Man-Above: 'Must My People die because of our love for one another? Are You not love itself? Can You, in Your plan for all things, arrange for us to be together without spilling the blood of our brothers? We ask this, for our love is strong—for each other, for My People, and for You.'

"The smoke ascended straight up into the cloudless starry night, and Man-Above heard, and He listened. He thought quickly about His plan for all things—and then He stomped the earth once with one mighty foot.

"Just where the lovers were kneeling, the ground trembled, shook, and crumbled inward. The towering hills spread aside and the giant forests were uprooted. My people backed away in terror as a deep, wide hole larger than many villages was Formed in the earth. Then the Great River, backing on its course, flowed into this sunken land carrying Reelfoot and Laughing Eyes to eternity. The river rushed inward—with such force that the thundering sound was heard in the far reaches of the land—until a large lake was made full. Then there was stillness as the Great River went on its way again.

"From that day until now, the Chickasaws and Choctaws of My People have lived together in friendship and peace. One winter years later, at the first snow, an eagle came to the lake. From the tops of the towering cypress trees, he scanned the blue-green depths of the waters with his piercing eyes and saw that the spirits of Reelfoot and Laughing Eyes were also at peace—together.

"My People say the eagle took this message up to Man-Above. And He was greatly pleased."

Grandmother Youngblood finished telling her story, and the riverbank cookout of 1934 came to a close. The fire was banked, toys collected, and relatives, friends, and neighbors departed homeward. As we walked up the river road, Frosty and I listened to the grown-ups as they discussed President Roosevelt's New Deal, the PWA, the CCC, and in general the hard times—would they ever end?

The night had turned much cooler and our breaths, making steamy vapors in the icy air, signaled that winter was close at hand. Grandmother Youngblood had predicted it would be the worst one since 1930. But Frosty and I were not worried about the harsh season to come, or the hard times. We only knew how wonderful the summer had been.

And what a joy the next one would be. . . .

WAGON AND WAGON TRAIN

Besides playing with bugs, there's nothing small children like better than being pulled or pushed around in a wagon. One made from scrap boards and old lopsided wheels usually pleased them as much as a store-bought model costing $2.50 or more. If a kid came from an affluent family—one that had as many as eight dilapidated

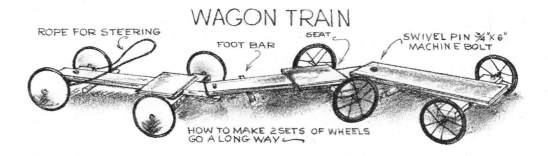

WAGON TRAIN

ROPE FOR STEERING

FOOT BAR

SEAT

SWIVEL PIN ¾"x 6" MACHINE BOLT

HOW TO MAKE 2 SETS OF WHEELS GO A LONG WAY

wheels lying around not doing anything—the toy maker of the clan would often come up with a wagon train. This toy served two purposes. It entertained three or four troublemakers for hours, and it kept them corralled in a bunch almost as effectively as stringing them together with a rope.

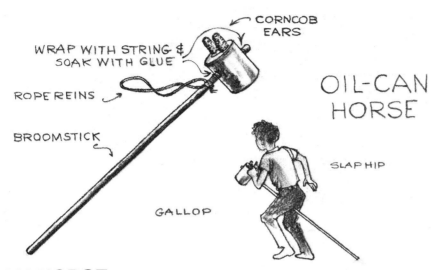

CORNCOB EARS

WRAP WITH STRING & SOAK WITH GLUE

ROPE REINS

BROOMSTICK

OIL-CAN HORSE

SLAP HIP

GALLOP

OIL-CAN HORSE

A quart oil can and a broomstick could put a six-year-old cowpuncher astride a cayuse that was the envy of the bunkhouse. A little paint dabbed here and there, corncob ears, bottle-cap eyes, and a piece of rope would lasso the finest roan, buckskin, piebald, pinto, or Appaloosa that ever was foaled. It was a stick horse that had spirit and endless stamina, one that whinnied constantly and could gallop louder than a stampeding herd of buffaloes. It was a stick horse that prompted any mother, trapped inside the ranch house with a young cowpoke on a rainy day, to declare wearily, "If I ever catch that toy critter when he's not on it, I'll burn it!"

PINE-CONE ANIMALS

Little kids love small toy animals more than rabbits love salt. And pine trees furnished rural children with an abundance of raw materials that could easily be con-

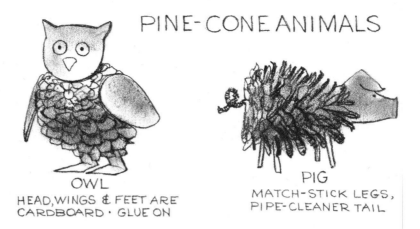

PINE-CONE ANIMALS

OWL
HEAD, WINGS & FEET ARE
CARDBOARD · GLUE ON

PIG
MATCH-STICK LEGS,
PIPE-CLEANER TAIL

verted into wondrous wee creatures. With the help of twigs, pipe cleaners, horsehairs, scraps of cardboard or cloth, and pictures cut from magazines, pine cones became a menagerie, limited in species only to the child's imagination.

When Pilgrim children came to America they found a new breed of dolls. And their stuffy old English ones soon wound up in a box under the bed, for their Indian friends showed them simple homemade dolls made from tree branches, corncobs, and shucks that were much more intriguing. They were colorful, charming, and bubbling with personality, and one could be created in less time than it took to dress a wild turkey.

The young colonists took these quaint dolls to their hearts. And as the years rolled by, their English way of doll making blended with the designs of the Indians, resulting in a doll-making art that would survive the centuries. The cornhusk doll became so popular it was found in the richest New England homes on the shelf alongside exquisite London "fashion dolls," which are considered some of the most elegant ever made.

Fashion dolls were three-dimensional, full-colored advertisements distributed by the leading fashion houses of the world. Instead of magazines and catalogs, which were practically nonexistent in the early 1700s, London garment merchants advertised their fashions by sending these tantalizing dolls across the Atlantic twice a year to the wealthy colonist women. The fashion-conscious lady of the New World eagerly awaited the next ship scheduled to arrive from London with the newest fashion dolls. These beautifully detailed toys, of papier-mâché, pasteboard, or wax, were about 14 inches high, bewigged, slippered, and dressed in exact replicas of the latest mode, undergarments included. The enchanting little mannequins were carefully boxed and shipped abroad so that the aristocratic lady, even in the remotest part of the world, would know the proper cut of neckline and the proper length of hem.

Whether or not the lady ordered gowns from London, she could still wind up with a stylish new wardrobe—for the fashion doll became the center of attention in the sewing room. After the seamstress had carefully dissected the doll's clothing, a tiny seam at a time, to make patterns for her mistress, the doll garments were re-sewed. Once the doll was reclothed, it was put up for grabs. Undoubtedly, if the household contained more than one "little mistress," the squabble that sometimes ensued could make an Indian raid seem as tame as a Quaker social.

TREE-BRANCH DOLL

During the '30s, half the fun of making a tree-branch doll was searching for an appropriate branch. The idea was to find one that contained four twigs proportioned

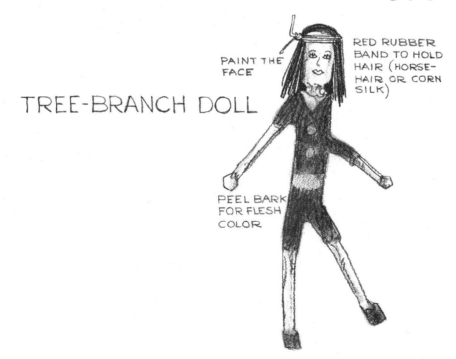

TREE-BRANCH DOLL

PAINT THE FACE

RED RUBBER BAND TO HOLD HAIR (HORSE-HAIR OR CORN SILK)

PEEL BARK FOR FLESH COLOR

The Golden Age of Shirley

In 1934 at the age of five, a golden-haired moppet named Shirley Temple sang and danced her way through the movie *Stand Up and Cheer*, to capture the affection of a nation caught in the throes of a major depression.

Americans by the millions forgot their cares and woes when Shirley as Little Miss Marker or the Littlest Rebel made them laugh or cry. From 1935 to 1938 she was Hollywood's top box-office draw, grossing five million dollars annually for Fox Studios. Beauty shop businesses also boomed during Shirley's years of popularity; they were swamped by rich little girls who wanted a hairdo exactly like Shirley's.

The average of four movies a year brought Miss Temple an annual salary of $300,000, which was boosted notably by royalties from a flood of Shirley Temple-endorsed dolls and accessories. The dream of every girl-child in America was to own a Shirley doll, which cost from $3 to $30 and came in a box bearing the little star's very own signature. Clothes for Shirley dolls ran from sportswear to costumes to formal—and oftentimes the outfits cost more than clothes for real children. And the doll's super deluxe doll carriage of cloth and brass, with rubber-tired wheels, was considered the Rolls-Royce of doll transportation.

to resemble arms and legs. Although it was rare to discover such a branch, many would display twig arms and legs which could readily be whittled into cartoon-type characters. A tree-branch search might uncover a fat doll running, a skinny doll dancing, and so forth. The possibilities were unlimited. Most tree-branch dolls were left dressed in nature's latest fashions of bark. The face, of course, was peeled away and painted on in bright colors. Most times the doll's hair came from a generous horse or cow which made a "donation" from its tail, but if the doll maker wasn't personally acquainted with any mild-mannered barnyard animals, it was better to confiscate a few hairs from a shaggy dog of one's acquaintance.

CORNCOB DOLL

On many American farms, tucked away in a corner of the barn protected from weather, there stood a barrel, and the winding path leading from the house to this barrel was generally as worn as the straight path pointing the way to the privy. For

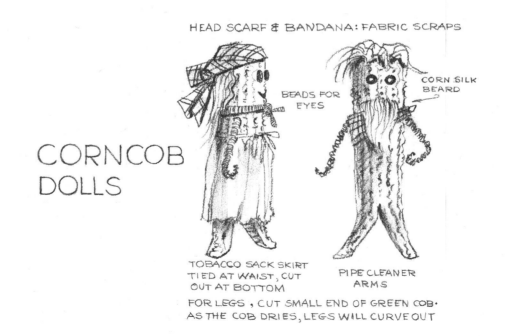

HEAD SCARF & BANDANA: FABRIC SCRAPS

BEADS FOR EYES

CORN SILK BEARD

CORNCOB DOLLS

TOBACCO SACK SKIRT TIED AT WAIST, CUT OUT AT BOTTOM

PIPE CLEANER ARMS

FOR LEGS, CUT SMALL END OF GREEN COB. AS THE COB DRIES, LEGS WILL CURVE OUT this container in the barn held a commodity—a cheap-as-air agricultural by-product used by every member of the family.

When Father needed a stopper for the coal-oil can or for his jug of cider, he went to the barrel. Mother took kindling for the kitchen range from the barrel, and mulch for her flower beds. Grandpa poked around in the barrel when he or Granny needed a new tobacco pipe, or when he wanted to plug the knotholes in the smokehouse. Son rummaged through the barrel to replace the recently lost toy whirligig. And Daughter looked tearfully into the barrel to find the makings of another doll, one that in time would be just as dear to her as Little Susan, the doll she'd accidentally dropped into the cistern.

No, the barrel didn't contain a sorcerer's talisman, and it hadn't secret powers of any sort. It was a plain oak barrel full of corncobs.

When Daughter finally found the cob she was looking for, one from an ear of field corn picked, husked, and dekerneled just that morning, she took it to Granny. Granny made a cut about three inches long in the pointed end of the green cob with a knife. This cut would allow that portion of the cob to separate, forming the doll's legs as it dried.

After the cob had dried in the sun, Granny sewed button eyes onto the large end, by punching holes through the cob and tying the thread behind. Then she glued on hair made of corn silk from a fresh ear of corn and secured it in place with a kerchief fashioned from a scrap of bright material, or a ribbon. In a few days the doll's hair would start changing color as the corn silk aged—from light blond to dark red or brown.

The doll's lips and rosy cheeks were painted on with pokeberry juice. The crimson liquid made an adequate dye. Birds loved the berries, but children were cautioned never to put pokeberries in their mouths, for they were toxic to humans. Only the leaves and tender shoots of the plant were edible; Granny gathered them in the early spring before the berries started forming and boiled them seasoned with fatback. This treat was called "poke sallet." From the pokeweed roots she concocted a home remedy good for arthritis—and a purgative good for what ailed you.

After Granny completed the corncob doll by adding pipe-cleaner arms and dressing it in a tobacco-sack skirt, she handed the little beauty to her delighted granddaughter along with a bit of sage advice: "See if you can keep this one out of the cistern. The water tastes like croton oil as it is!"

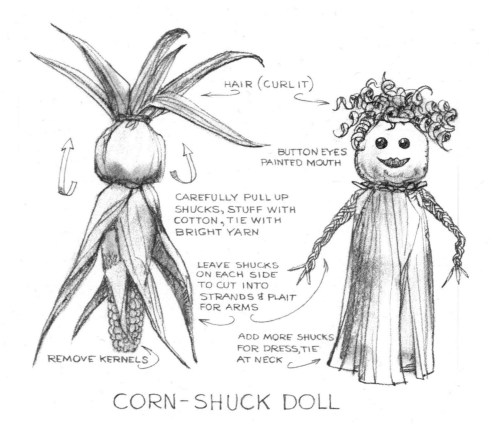

HAIR (CURL IT)

BUTTON EYES
PAINTED MOUTH

CAREFULLY PULL UP
SHUCKS, STUFF WITH
COTTON, TIE WITH
BRIGHT YARN

LEAVE SHUCKS
ON EACH SIDE
TO CUT INTO
STRANDS & PLAIT
FOR ARMS

REMOVE KERNELS

ADD MORE SHUCKS
FOR DRESS, TIE
AT NECK

CORN-SHUCK DOLL

CORN-SHUCK DOLL

Homemade corn-shuck dolls, like store-bought dolls, came in a variety of styles, shapes, and sizes. The doll favored by small girls growing up during the '30s in rural Oklahoma was not a true corn-shuck doll, since the cob was used too. However, keeping the cob simplified construction and gave the doll a wear-and-tear durability that dolls made entirely from shucks did not possess.

First, the shucks of a dried ear of field corn were carefully pulled up and away so the corn could be shelled from the cob. Before constructing the doll, the shucks were dampened by soaking in water, as they were brittle and unmanageable when dry. The head was formed by gluing and tying the shucks around a wad of batting (cotton used in making quilts), leaving enough shucks above for hair. A shuck on each side was cut into strands and plaited for the doll's arms and hands. Shucks from another ear, tied at the neck and glued together around the cob, dressed the doll in a stylish gown. The eyes and mouth were painted directly onto the husks, or else button eyes were sewed on through the husk and into the cotton batting. A doll might have either curled, braided, or straight hair. To make curls that looked like Shirley Temple's, the wet strands of husks were rolled up on a drinking straw or pencil, clamped with bobby pins, and left to dry thoroughly. When dry, the curls were arranged in the coiffure desired. As with all elaborate hairdos, though, it was not weatherproof.

DOLL FURNITURE

Sure, the Shirley Temple doll, the rage of the '30s, had an expensive wardrobe and a doll carriage that would knock your eye out. But the poor little rich doll didn't have any decent furniture to her name. This was not the case, however, with a homemade doll, who moved around in a cardboard-box dollhouse surrounded with luxurious furnishings fit for a queen.

The typical rural dollhouse style during the Depression was the popular "rambling ranch," in architectural vernacular, which meant a large cardboard box with the lid and one end removed. The interior was furnished with homemade furniture

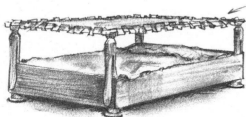

USE BOX TOP FOR CANOPY·ADD PAPER TRIM

CLOTHESPIN POSTS

HALF SPOOLS FOR LEGS

CIGAR-BOX BED

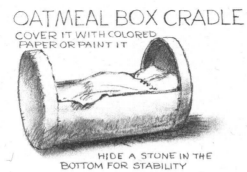

OATMEAL BOX CRADLE

COVER IT WITH COLORED PAPER OR PAINT IT

HIDE A STONE IN THE BOTTOM FOR STABILITY

A Garden of Toys

From the bounty of preformed materials nature provides for young toy makers, the lowly gourd, prolific distant cousin of the pumpkin, emerges supreme. In addition to the many different toys made from gourds, their varied sizes and shapes also inspired early craftsmen to turn them into dippers, ladles, forks, spoons, bowls, dishes, mugs, vases, jugs, buttons, bracelets, rings, birdhouses, fishnet floats, wheels, and musical instruments, to list just a sampling.

The texture of a dried gourd closely resembles medium hardwood, so gourds can be sawed, sanded, whittled, and drilled. A gourd also takes wax, stain, varnish, shellac, or paint as well as, or better than, most woods.

Some gourds come shaped like balls, others like pears, cucumbers, bottles, melons, and eggs. Old folks called the egg-shaped gourds "sim'lars," which meant they were so similar to eggs a hen couldn't tell them

193

from the real thing. As any farm kid knows, a hen will not lay in a nest from which her eggs are continuously removed. Instead, she'll start a new nest out in the grass and weeds where no one can find it. Therefore, when a child gathered eggs from the hen house each night, a solitary "egg" was left in every nest to fool the gullible birds. Gourds were valued as nest eggs, since they were unbreakable, would not spoil or hatch, and were safe from chicken snakes and egg-sucking dogs.

Some gourds have handles, short or long. A few varieties have rough skins, but most are smooth. Many are naturally colored and banded, striped or mottled in various shades of green and yellow; these were highly prized by young Depression-era toy makers.

Rural children in our area thought of the trellises of gourd vines shading the porch as their "garden of toys." In early March the seeds were started in pots. They were transplanted outdoors on Good Friday, the day the vegetable gardens were usually planted. The young gourd vines were kept watered and fertilized with manure throughout the growing season. When the yellow- or white-flowered blossoms began to form tiny fruit, the children protected their immature toys on the vine from harmful insects by picking off those pests they could see and by transporting all the ladybugs they found elsewhere to a new home on the gourd-vine trellis. Ladybugs would devour many of the unwanted insects.

When the fruit was full grown in the fall, it was left to mature and harden on the vine. If there was an early frost warning, though, the gourds were harvested, handled with the utmost care, and allowed to dry and cure indoors. Stems about 1 inch long were left on the fruit as it was cut from the vine. When the stems were dry and shriveled and the gourds felt hard as a rock, the kids knew they were ready. They grabbed their toy-making tools and went to work.

"Hey, wouldya look at this beauty! A nice big cup for a cup and ball!"

"Lotta good it'll do you. You couldn't catch the ball if you had a cup as big as a dishpan!"

194

GOURD CRADLE

CUT GOURD IN HALF, FILL WITH COTTON

GOURD CHAIR

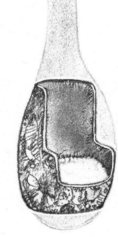

CUT FROM GOURD, USE A WAD OF COTTON FOR SEAT

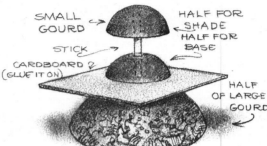

SMALL GOURD

HALF FOR SHADE

HALF FOR BASE

STICK

CARDBOARD (GLUE IT ON)

HALF OF LARGE GOURD

GOURD TABLE AND LAMP

ACORN DOLL DISHES

SLICE OFF TOP, REMOVE MEAT

GRAPEVINE

CUP

ADD SPOUT, REPLACE TOP AND YOU HAVE A TEAPOT

GLUE ON HANDLES & SPOUT

SAUCER (BASE OF VERY LARGE ACORN)

constructed from colorful cigar boxes, cereal boxes, matchboxes, scraps of paper, and, of course, gourds—the most desirable furniture-making material around.

The cigar-box bed was the ultimate in bedroom fashion and comfort. Sturdy half-spool legs and clothespin posts gave this four-poster stylish beauty and ample strength to support even an overweight doll—one that had been overfed on mud pies. And during story time or before drifting off to sleep, the doll could look up and admire King Edward's portrait or a likeness of Robert Burns on the frilly canopy.

Each dollhouse contained at least one cigar-box bed, an oatmeal box cradle, a gourd cradle, and many chairs, tables, and lamps also made from gourds.

Draperies, rugs, and tablecloths were fashioned from fabric scraps, and the dining-room table was set for a tea party with the finest Spode china: acorn cups and saucers imported from the big oak tree in the backyard.

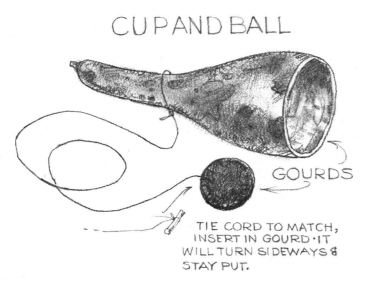

CUP AND BALL

GOURDS

TIE CORD TO MATCH, INSERT IN GOURD · IT WILL TURN SIDEWAYS & STAY PUT.

CUP AND BALL

American Indian boys did not possess a built-in knowledge of tracking animals and moving through the forest quiet as ghosts, nor did they have inherent talent for shooting a bow and arrow with deadeye accuracy—though back in the '30s my Cherokee friend Frosty Youngblood often boasted that they did. These skills were acquired through learning, by putting the old nose to the grindstone, so to speak.

Story Time

Listening to grown-ups tell stories was an integral part of growing up in the '30s. For many rural children it was the prime source of entertainment. True, some farm families had battery-operated radios, and there were books, lots of magazines, and an occasional movie. But none of these had the impact, the drama, or the down-to-earth captivating qualities of the tales and yarns told word-of-mouth: "You're not going to believe this, but it really happened, so help me. . . . "

Some storytellers were much better at their trade than others. But this mattered little. Story-hungry kids did not mind if the narrator wasn't especially articulate or animated—the story was the thing! Whether it was funny, scary, exciting, believable, or incredible meant not a whit. For at the telling, youngsters listened to the words, supplied their own pictures, and lived every minute of the tale from beginning to end—and then begged to hear it again. Later they would reflect on the wonder of it, talking about it for days as they pondered the many fascinating and mysterious facets of heaven and earth, man and beast, life and death.

Any time of day was fine for story time, but late evening set the best stage. During the summer after the supper dishes were put away, the family moved to the cool of the front porch. Rocking chairs and porch swings creaked in slow rhythm as dusk deepened. Grandpa fired up his pipe, and Grandma fell to her crocheting. The heat of the day mellowed, the mosquitoes began their nightly search, and the lightning bugs came out to be caught—a Mason jar turned into a glowing lantern of cold, pulsating fire.

Along the river road, twin lights brighter than fireflies flickered through the trees. "Company's coming," someone would say. "Wonder who it can be?"

"Sounds like Vernon Brown's old Chevy."

"I heard he got on with the WPA over in Kentucky."

The children stopped their play, anxious to welcome their visitors.

Therefore, when we were kids growing up in Oklahoma, I could challenge Frosty to a bow-and-arrow shoot any time with expectations of a 50-50 chance of winning.

But if I happened to get into a game of cup and ball with him, I had to be prepared to lose my pants. In fact, the same humiliating consequences held true when we competed in stick and ball or stick and rings. For some reason, Frosty always seemed to excel in any game which encompassed a toy tied on a string. He took to these games of skill like a squirrel to a nut tree. And his typical comment after victory was, "Only an Indian can do such things."

It would have been absurd for us to buy a wooden cup and ball at the store when one could be made from two gourds in five minutes. The hard part was that first we had to locate a round gourd, to serve as the ball, that would satisfactorily fit the cup made from a larger gourd. To operate this toy, the cup was held by the handle in one hand with the ball dangling free at the end of a string about 14 inches long (which was tied to the handle). Putting the ball into a swinging motion the player then swung the ball up into the air to catch it in the cup. Or, more accurately, to *try* to catch it in the cup.

STICK AND BALL

The mechanics of playing with the stick and ball were precisely the same as those used in mastering the cup and ball. But there was one major difference: A person might swing the ball up in the air from now till doomsday and never impale the danged thing on the stick when it came down. Even enlarging the hole in the ball to twice its normal size didn't seem to help the score appreciably. The kid who could spear the ball, say one time out of every ten tries, was indeed an admirable stick-and-ball virtuoso.

STICK AND RINGS

To the uninitiated, it might seem that the guy who came up with this hardest-thing-I-ever-tried-to-do-in-my-life toy must be locked away in some institution, passing the time by banging his head against a padded wall.

True, it was a difficult toy to master—but more fun to play with than a litter of six-week-old puppies. The aim of the stick-and-rings game was to swing the rings up

STICK AND BALL

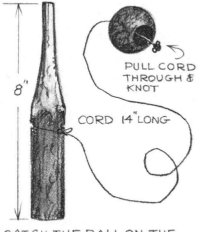

8"

PULL CORD
THROUGH &
KNOT

CORD 14" LONG

CATCH THE BALL ON THE
STICK

STICK AND RINGS

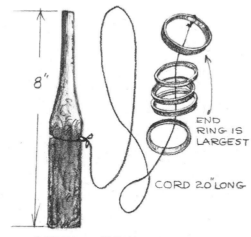

8"

END
RING IS
LARGEST

CORD 20" LONG

CATCH THE RINGS ON THE STICK

in the air and catch as many rings as possible on the stick as the rings came down. The rings cut from gourds could vary in diameter, as long as the end ring tied to the string was the largest; this prevented the other rings from slipping off the string when they were swung into the air.

Where this toy originated, or how long ago, nobody knows for certain. But since its beginning, if there has ever been a kid who has successfully ringed all five rings on the stick in a solitary throw, he deserves the coveted, undisputed title of "The Stick-and-Ring Champion of the World."

"Why, it's Beckie and Jim and the young'uns! Haven't seen you in a month of Sundays. . . ."

Room was made on the porch, more chairs were brought from the kitchen, and rags were lit to smolder in a tin can to repel the insects. The children resumed playing hide and seek or Annie Over. The men discussed crops and weather, while the women swapped recipes and chatted about babies, quilting, and Mrs. Wilson's new washing machine powered by a gasoline engine.

As the first stars came out, a bat swooped across the yard, prompting the kids to seek the safety of porch steps and protective laps. Night deepened to black velvet as conversation turned to the way it was "back in the good old days." Then the awaited moment came. Drowsy young eyelids opened wide as the best storyteller in the group would say, "I recollect the day back in '89 just like it was yesterday when a one-armed man they called Bowie Knife Bill rode into town. . . ."

Epilogue

We hope you enjoyed spending the summer of 1934 with us. The Great American Depression is history now. Those hard times departed long ago . . . slipped away like five-cent candy bars, ten-cent movies, and childhood innocence. Gone are the days of whittling homemade toys, listening to stories while sitting on shady porches bathed in sun-rippled shadows, delighting in the sound of raindrops on rusty tin roofs, and exalting in that special peace of mind mirrored only in the young.

Were the good old days really good? I think so, although in memory they are, perhaps, somewhat romanticized. I went back to the old hometown recently just to have a look.

The Red-Horse Barn and Standpipe Hill are gone. The pastures where they stood are modern subdivisions. Sudden Canyon is now a bustling parking lot.

On the manicured front lawn of one house, where some children were playing on a gym set underneath a large sweet-gum tree, a carpet of red and gold leaves shimmered in the October sun. Could this be our tree? Do sweet gums live so long?

For a brief moment I imagined the wind off the river was carrying the smoky scent of an Indian cook fire, the soft voice of a beloved old woman, the peal of children's laughter from long ago. The big tree sighed in the wind as more leaves fluttered, detached themselves from the gnarled limbs, and swirled to the ground. Like colorful, discarded pages of an ancient calendar, they would decompose and vanish into eternity.

What a beautiful Saturday afternoon it was for children to play outdoors. But where were their toys?

I strained my ears for the sounds I knew I wouldn't hear: clacking scootmobiles, rattling tin cans, the slap of rubber guns and slingshots, piercing homemade whistles, a spinning top wailing like a banshee. I heard another sound, though—familiar, but alien to my nostalgic reverie.

They came roaring up the river road from town, the boy about eleven, the girl a little younger. Their motorbikes were shiny, magnificent. They wore helmets to match. Her colors were white and robin's-egg blue; his were maroon and black. They waved at me and tooted their horns in friendly greeting. What marvelous machines. And what fun they must be! I would have gladly *died* for one back in 1934.

Surely the children today live in a most wondrous age, with the promise of even brighter tomorrows. But as I watched the boy and girl round the curve and ride out of sight just about where Frosty's house once stood, I felt a little sad for them. They would probably never make a simple toy, find a honey tree, or play in a deserted, ramshackle barn. They would never experience the thrill of hearing that old barn door squeal on rusty hinges. It was a sound so loud that folks could hear it all the way over in Muskogee.